No longer a wandering spirit

Family and kin reclaiming the memory of Minang woman Bessy Flowers

First published in 2023 by
UWA Publishing
Crawley, Western Australia 6009
www.uwap.uwa.edu.au
UWAP is an imprint of UWA Publishing,
a division of The University of Western Australia.

This book is copyright. Apart from any fair dealing for the purpose of private study, research, criticism or review, as permitted under the Copyright Act 1968, no part may be reproduced by any process without written permission. Enquiries should be made to the publisher.

Copyright Ezzard Flowers and Sharon Huebner © 2023
All photographs are copyright © Sharon Huebner unless stated otherwise.
Illustrations by Beth-Emily Gregory, 2012.
The moral right of the author has been asserted.

Readers are advised that this book contains images and names of people who have passed away.

ISBN: 978-1-76080-222-6
Design by Upside Creative
Printed by Lightning Source

Kia Kia, Noogiting Wirren,
Minang Yorga, Minang Boodja

We acknowledge the sleeping
spirit, the Minang woman, from
Minang country

Foreword

I must declare a conflict of interest: I was once mentioned in the same sentence as Bessy Flower(s).[1] The sentence framed her as the 'most "literary" Indigenous reader and writer of the 19th century'[2] and I was thrilled to stand in her disarmingly modest shadow. I greatly admire Bessy Flower(s).

The sentence in question was part of an insightful study of the entanglement of Australian Aboriginal oral traditions and print – *Writing Never Arrives Naked: Early Aboriginal Cultures of Writing in Australia*.[3] As demonstrated there and elsewhere, Noongar people have always had a propensity for literature. Nineteenth-century New Norcia mission documents show Noongar children learning the alphabet in a matter of minutes, and list other examples of the prodigious intelligence their culture provided.[4]

But talent and literacy do not guarantee safety or justice and, as you will read in this book, brutish and nasty colonial imperatives entangled and hurt the Minang woman Bessy Flower(s). I wish I could sing to you of her strength, her love and bad luck, her resilience and talent. This book has similar aspirations.

But there's more to declare: the Bessy Flower(s) letters have long charmed me, for example the voice in phrases like:

> the second officer came to us and was talking about Albany. He said they considered it a great banishment to be sent there, that nothing grew but rocks and stones and I said that added to the beauty of the place. He laughed so, and said a good deal more…I did not answer rudely though, dear Missie.[5]

I tried to let that voice flavour a novel of mine (if I may):

> Oh imagine sailing on one of those very fine days on the ocean. Clear sky, sun and bright air, foam and bubbles at bow and wake, and taut, swelling sails…[6]

Because you see Bessy was sent away, was both stolen and stole away; Bessy sailed away from Albany and…she may even have wanted to help; after all, she played the harmonium in the church, taught in the school, had a strong relationship with her dear Missie. Tasting salt on her lips, she sailed further, deeper into that freezing, heated, sometimes stormy emotional infrastructure, the lashing racism and sexism and various cob-webbed, creaking hierarchies of colonial Australia.

I've also quoted Bessy in a Miles Franklin Literary Award oration[7]:

> I had to fight so hard…I will not say much on his style of calling us niggers…I know the way niggers have been treated in America…(we will) go on our way, trying what is in our power to bring up our children…[8]
>
> it comes hard…wandering about without a home, & I feel it the more as I had a good home when I was young, & then to be tossed about in old age.[9]

FOREWORD

Politically astute, emotionally intelligent, talented, *enchanting*...believe it or not, Bessy's *Indigenous Cosmopolitanism* was not so unusual in nineteenth-century Noongar country: Major Lockyer, stepping onto the sandy edge of what became my south coast hometown, was startled by a Noongar shaking his hand and opening the conversation in French.[10] Some decades later, Henry Lawson listened to a booka-clad Noongar who also spoke French. There is at least one example of a Noongar at the very beginning of British colonisation of Western Australia taking up pen and paper in order to extend their repertoire of communication.

So much promise and humanity has been betrayed, extinguished, and is all part and parcel of what comes courtesy of colonial imperatives. Ezzard says, 'She probably wouldn't have asked why, and do a tantrum and say: "Why can't somebody else go?"' There is great tragedy in *No Longer a Wandering Spirit.*

Bessy Flower(s) is a hero of mine, and I'm very glad she's at the centre of a book that features her images and writing, along with the remarkable journey to situate her in family and Country. Images and words link us to people of the past and of the here and now, and in this book they lead back to the sphere of countless ancestors, and to the very earth they trod and to the very same air, more or less, that they breathed and that is refreshed, we hope, by us, forever.

There's even more conflict of interest to be declared: I count Ezzard Flowers as family and friend and am proud to know him.

I met Sharon Huebner courtesy of Ezzard, and the work they've done and the love they've given helps make Bessy family again, and so too the Flowers and the Bryants and the Camerons and the many other people you'll meet as you read. Go with Sharon and Ezzard as they bring families together across the continent and, guiding us through a hostile history, follow the spirit of Bessy Flower(s).

Kim Scott

In memory of
Melva Flowers, Dolores (La La) and Donald Flowers,
Russell Nelly, Rita Hood, Betty Hood, Sedeena Flowers,
Cynthia Flowers and Lynthia Flowers

Dedicated to
Bessy, Ada, Nora, Rhoda, Emily
and their families

Contents

Foreword vii
Preface xiii
Family Spokespeople xxv
Notes xxx

Chapter 1: Bessy 35
Chapter 2: The Bryant family 779
Chapter 3: The Flowers family 115
Chapter 4: Two families united 143
Chapter 5: Never forget – who we are and why we're here 179
Chapter 6: The certainty of love 209
Chapter 7: Where our spirits go 251
Chapter 8: A lost grave and a pressed flower 279

Afterword 291
Appendix A: Children of Bessy and Donald Cameron 297
Appendix B: Parliamentary report by Anne Camfield, 1871 . .300
Appendix C: Letters (1867–1894) 310
Notes 344
Bibliography 353

Preface

I came to know of Bessy Flowers while searching historical records specific to Nora White.[11] The letters, reports and colonial correspondence I found revealed the lives of these two women who were raised in the benevolent care of Anne and Henry Camfield at Annesfield, an institution for Aboriginal children set up in the early 1850s in Western Australia's southwest. The records also told of the departure from Annesfield in June 1867 of five young women: Bessy Flowers, Nora White, Ada Flowers,[12] Rhoda Tanaton (or Toby)[13] and Emily Peters.[14] As a group of young women, they were sent to the eastern colonies and to an Aboriginal mission named Ramahyuck situated near Murla, Lake Wellington, in Victoria. They never returned to Western Australia.

Understanding why these Aboriginal women were moved from their home in the 1860s relied upon historical records in the archives. The records detailed many aspects of their journey and their naming was useful for retracing family connections and life experience spanning multiple family generations. Enriching the documents were the personal accounts and everyday insights shared through letters that were written by Bessy to the Camfields and to others who were living at this time within colonial settler society.

***

In 2002, the Koori family of Nora White began the search for heritage material with the resolve to identify the birth country of their Aboriginal ancestor, whom they knew came from Western Australia. The family longed to find links in this history to relations of Nora living in Western Australia. At our first meeting, the Thorpe family explained that the search for Nora's cultural kin was on behalf of an elderly family member, Matilda Thorpe. The Thorpes are Gunai-Kurnai people from the East Gippsland region of eastern Victoria. They're a family connected to a place known as Bung Yarnda, the Lake Tyers Aboriginal Trust, which has been Koori-managed land since a state government hand back in the early 1970s.[15] It's a place culturally saturated with ancestor histories, and is regarded as a significant site of Koori family memories, stories and legacies.

The initial search for Nora's history took place at the Melbourne Archives Centre and the National Archives of Australia. Collectively, both institutions hold collections relating to the management of Victorian Aboriginal missions, reserves and stations between the years 1869 and 1957. The records comprise correspondence by the Board for the Protection of Aborigines, which was granted statutory authority by the Victorian *Aborigines Protection Act 1869*.[16] The Act increased the Board's powers to regulate the lives of Aboriginal people. The information gathered by the Board included the distribution of family rations, allocation of clothing and blankets, passes to leave the mission, and paper documentation of births, deaths and marriages.

Such records detailed how the young Aboriginal women from Western Australia spent much of their lives, struggling against the control of the Board, the authority of missionaries and other colonial officials with law-enforcement powers. Over many years, personal letters described very tired, oppressed and emotionally broken women fighting against the system to care for their families. The women wrote letters telling authority figures regulating their lives about their concerns, such as the need to create a home and desire to secure income to provide food, clothes and safety for their families. Their requests were rarely responded to; if answered, the reply was often notably barren of positive or beneficial action. The administrators did, however, record the details of their missionary interactions and everyday observations of the women. This included noting in reports the sufferance and untimely death of some of the women's children and even the particulars of their passing.

The request by the Thorpe family happened while working at the Koorie Family History Service (KFHS),[17] situated at the Koorie Heritage Trust Cultural Centre in Melbourne (known as The Trust).[18] The KFHS was set up to support Koori people in their search for family connections. As a team, we assisted senior Kooris who, as children, had been taken from family without the permission of their parents or the consent of other family members in whose care they resided. In 2001, the state government's Aboriginal Victoria body funded the service at The Trust, as a response to the Commonwealth Government's national inquiry findings reported in 'Bringing Them Home'.[19] This report, which was tabled in federal Parliament on 26 May 1997, informed government and community as a whole about the strength and the struggles of Aboriginal and Torres Strait Islander children who had been forcibly removed from their families. The testimonies shared by many thousands of Stolen Generations, as they became known, revealed deep emotional loss, multitudes of hardship and long-lasting trauma. Their heartfelt testimonies continue to be a tribute to, and legacy of, all the children who never returned home.

Understanding Koori histories from the perspectives of Koori people was a critical part of my teachings from Koori colleagues and Elders representing the Victorian Aboriginal community. This education enabled a research practice to be developed that consolidated heritage records with that of Koori lived experiences. It required listening to stories that depicted traumatic events and revealed conflicted feelings about being in the world, resulting from painful and internalised memories. It also meant learning to memorise family relationships that involved mapping in my mind Koori networks of family and kin. Over time, I learnt how Koori identity is defined by knowledge about who you are and where you come from or, for Stolen Generations, how wayfinding steps might help one to find family and to reconnect with ancestral homelands.

Bessy's letters, written between 1867 and 1894, together with those letters by the secretary of the Victorian Board for the Protection of Aborigines and overseeing missionaries, are a revealing record of events, people and places from the past. The letters grant insight into the belief systems, emotions, values and attitudes that continue to resonate within the stories told by past and present generations of Koori people. Grief and loss, tenacity and survival are evident in historical Aboriginal letters, and often amplify for readers the depth and breadth of emotions attached to remembering the breakdown and loss of family networks. There are social and political nuances that arise in the stories shared, and understanding these distinctions reveals something about why Koori and other Aboriginal people throughout Australia fiercely protested the disruption to their families and fought against any harmful changes being inflicted upon the ecologies of their cultural livelihoods, that being their cultural ways of knowing animated by the visceral symbiosis between country and kin.

Extensive family history research and support from record-holding agencies greatly assisted the process of linking ancestors and kin from the past to their present-day descendant families. The creation of a family tree was a proactive and appropriate method for identifying the connections binding one family member to another across the generations. Though this pictorial reconstruction of family was mostly a positive undertaking, there were times when gaps appeared within family knowledge and challenged an individual's quest to establish a position of self within a network of family.

Finding an answer to the Thorpe family's question of where Nora belonged in terms of her cultural identity was unachievable in research terms. The historical record left no tangible evidence emplacing Nora within ancestral country in Western Australia or in context to her relations from this place. For the descendant families and kin of Bessy Flowers, however, the results fashioned from similarly enacted research presented a different pathway to a story of memory reclamation. The research yielding inconclusive results when used to explore Nora's kin connections did in Bessy's case reveal productive historical detail that warranted further investigation. Branching out with a more expansive viewpoint, I decided to engage with another kind of material media that, by its nature, encouraged a more imaginative and deepened inquiry – historical photos.

In the archives there existed historical photos picturing the people who were mentioned by name within Bessy's letters and the correspondence of the Board. These same names helped to create a timeline of events and to also construct networks of kin characteristic to a family tree. Family time spent on photos helped to alter the social navigation through time and space of Bessy's past. The agency of meaning granted to the photos became an intimate and insightful gateway for eliciting novel perspectives of individuals and families not detailed within the historical record.

Using cultural principles in the work of building bridges between temporal-based histories and gaps in oral knowledge guided Bessy's movement from a place in history and to the energised social dynamism of her family. Photos engaged individuals and families in practices to remember their ancestor and to restore from the public spaces of the archive a meaningful position for her within the cultural sphere and wide reach of family. Photos also kindled recuperative practices that sought to reaffirm and restore cultural identities that could be built from knowledge of relational networks and responsibilities of knowing rightful connections to kin and to country, the ecologies of living cultural heritage that are always vital for resourcing and sustaining Aboriginal futures.

I first came across Bessy's portrait in *Aborigines of the Albany Region 1821–1898: The Bicentennial Dictionary of Western Australians* (vol. VI, 1989), compiled expertly by Neville Green, a noted historian of Australian history.[20] The dictionary has been created from hours of labour-intensive research and lists by name Aboriginal people from the Albany region. Each entry has assembled biographical information relating to each individual taken from private journals and letters between the years 1821 and 1898. In the dictionary, Neville Green has inserted historical photos of some of the Aboriginal people who are named. One photo of interest sourced from the JS Battye Library of West Australian History, at the State Library of Western Australia in Perth, pictures Bessy as a child when living at Annesfield in the care of Anne and Henry Camfield.

Bessy wrote of Annesfield many times and in these writings she showcased regularly an ability to perform the expected manners and behaviours that she had been dutifully taught. She undoubtedly adored the Camfields, addressing them in her letters by pet names, 'Missie' and 'Martie'. In those early years, the mood of Bessy's letters is one of hope and exuberance. She's excited about the move to Ramahyuck in 1867, an anticipation that was shared by the other Annesfield women who travelled with her, including her younger sister, Ada. In the years to follow, her changed fortune, together with the pressures of missionary expectations, systematically shifted the nature, mood and the tonal quality of her written word.

As much as Bessy's letters provided a site for her living descendant families and kin to engage with key events of her life, the social activity of speaking back to the past and reclaiming her memory began with the historical photo of Bessy as a child in the 1860s. This photo, as well as other photos from the same period of time, invited independent and collective imaginings by her descendants that engaged who (as part of a family) she was in the world. They were imaginings used as the social vigour for stepping earnestly into both known and unknown understandings of what it means to belong.

In the years 2009 and 2010 I began first talks with Bessy's descendants, the Bryant families from the East Gippsland region in Victoria, followed soon after by her western kin, the Flowers family with connections to the Great Southern of Western Australia. The Bryant family spokesperson in the early meetings was Phyllis Andy (née Bryant). In later years I met her sisters and other senior members of the Bryant family and their families. Ezzard Flowers was the nominated spokesperson for the Flowers family in Western Australia.

The practice of seeking family permission to carry out research before engaging with the correspondence made by government officials, including members of the Victorian Board for the Protection of Aborigines, as well as the materials by missionaries, informed the ethics of my collaboration with the

PREFACE

Bryant and Flowers families. When working at The Trust, gaining consent was a prerequisite to accessing personal and family information, even if such records were considered by the archive or the record-keeping institution to be publicly accessible and useable.

The concerted effort to create a meeting place to understand Bessy on cultural terms and through the perspectives of her descendant Bryant families and Flowers kin became central to our collaboration. Our work together was about family reclamation of Bessy's memory from the colonial archive, it was also about how researchers of other ancestries gained trust and appropriate permissions to become involved with personal and community practices expressing cultural heritage identities.

As can often be the situation with Aboriginal histories fixed within archives and archival systems, the families connected to Bessy had never seen photos of their ancestor, nor had they read her letters. The reproduction of Bessy's childhood photo (from a digital file) and printed hard copies of the letters allowed the Bryant and Flowers families to respond, as part of our conversations, to both the cultural heritage materials and to each other. It was an interactive dialogue initiated by the cultural act of emplacing her image within the multilayered and familial contexts of everyday social living. This meaningful dynamic of remembering lived pasts within the present led to further interactions that unearthed the many and varied complexities of memory reclamation and ancestral restoration within story. Social family responses to the past were often shaped by the performances of existing memory and the known physical connections to people and to country.

In this particular family story, acknowledging Bessy's absence from the memories of her living descendant families and kin drew attention to the strong hold of past colonial ideals and values. Colonial social systems had effectually worked to obscure, over time, Bessy's identity as a Minang woman. The generation of meaningful spaces for renewing ancestral memories was crucial to discovering social relatedness through photos and understanding the intrinsic bodily language of identity.

Numerous Australian historians, such as Phillip Pepper with Tess De Araugo (1985), Bain Attwood (1986) and Neville Green (1989), have considered the social and political dynamics of Bessy's identity as it was framed by the past.[21] However, they accomplished this exploration by relying on the historical record, and not as a practice of engagement involving consultation with her living descendants and extended kin. It was not common practice at this time for historians to undertake such pathways in their work, or to consider where Aboriginal ancestor histories might be best placed and for what purpose. They were not governed by cultural protocols requiring permissions be granted by senior family members or Elders for access to archives, nor were they initiators of inclusive and participatory research. Families were not given rights of joint authorship or rights of reply to the historical representations of themselves or their ancestors.

To restore Bessy's lost memory, photos became a key tool for negotiating an alternate family history. Photos supported the social actions needed to conceptually shift the historical narrative depicted in her letters and those of the colonisers. They facilitated family knowledge exchange and memory-making processes that channelled present-day beliefs, values and emotions into an ancestor's past. The powerful social language of photos meant also that there was merit in learning more about the photographer responsible for capturing in time Bessy as a child.

Alfred Hawes Stone was an English colonist and amateur photographer. He took Bessy's photo sometime in the early 1860s. Arriving in the Swan River Colony from England on 12 October 1829 at 28 years of age, Alfred was reportedly a good shot with a rifle, very adventurous and also an eager and flamboyant storyteller. He had accepted the land grant of 5,000 acres (2,000 hectares) being offered to colonial settlers. For Alfred, a solicitor in his hometown of Tunbridge Wells, this was an opportunity to live on the land, a lifestyle he had imagined for many years but never completely fulfilled. As it happened, Alfred would relinquish his land title to serve in the colony as a high constable, justice of the peace and, in later years, as a Crown solicitor and registrar-clerk of the Civil Court.[22]

Bessy's portrait is one of two black-and-white photos that were taken by

PREFACE

Alfred after living for more than 30 years in the colony. His amateur photos reside within the pages of two separate albums – the 'Hampton Album' held in the collections of the JS Battye Library and the second album held privately by his great-granddaughter in Perth (and now also as a digital album at the JS Battye Library).[23] The second photo, depicting Bessy in the company of Anne Camfield, is held in the collections of the Royal Western Australian Historical Society in Perth and names Anne and Bessy on its reverse side. If not for this detail, Bessy's studio portrait may have become an age-old orphaned photo.

Finding Alfred's photos of Bessy inspired searches of other collections that visually portrayed the events of her childhood and of her adult life. Of most interest to the Bryants were those photos that confirmed a familial connection, such as Bessy pictured with her husband, Donald Cameron.[24] This photo activated a deep sense of family curiosity followed by hearty discussions about Donald's ties to the Ebenezer Aboriginal Mission situated in northwest Victoria on Wergaia/Wotjobaluk country, near the Wimmera River.

Equal to this interest was a series of photos taken at Ramahyuck during the early 1900s. One of the photos shows Bessy and Donald's daughter Mena, while another photo shows the Ramahyuck Cemetery as it appeared in the 1970s. In this cemetery photo, a Koori boy is pictured standing among wooden crosses marking the burial of adults and children from the Ramahyuck mission community. Today, the cemetery is empty of all historical grave markers except for a single headstone memorialising Nathaniel Pepper, a Koori man who features extensively within Victorian historical records detailing mission life.

Upon her death in January 1895 and burial at the Bairnsdale Cemetery, Bessy faded into the shadows of history, a realm unfixed by family stories that were usually passed with intent between generations to preserve memories of loved ones. In this unsettled and dull place she might have stayed, if not for the Thorpe family's courage in approaching the KFHS for help in finding the birthplace of their ancestor Nora and her ancestral homeland. Their quest for answers awakened other questions, or if not more questions, at least a distinct kind of cultural social engagement and reckoning.

In conversations with the Bryants, they often lamented how not knowing the whereabouts of Bessy's grave was an issue. Respecting right ways of acknowledging the dead and measuring up to community expectations of cultural remembrance and memorialising seeded how Bessy's family decided to perceive and interact with their ancestor's past. Cultural action with purposeful intent became about bringing a physical presence to the sites that symbolised her life and those representing her death. Locating Bessy's final resting place proved to be more difficult than first supposed, with only several published newspaper death notices, a formal death certificate, and a burial registration system complicated by muddled record-keeping practices.

In order to heal gaps identified within a family history, and to craft anew family connections geographically distanced, Ezzard Flowers made his way in 2011 to East Gippsland with the intention of meeting Bessy's great-granddaughters as well as other members representing the Bryant families. This first meeting was supported by Noongar Elder and lawman from Western Australia, the late Russell Nelly.

The families gathered at the Lake Tyers Aboriginal Trust and then at the Bairnsdale Cemetery where Bessy was buried, but without access to information about the exact location of her grave due, in most part, to lost cemetery burial records. The official records noted that Bessy's passing was on 14 January 1895, with her burial taking place in the days that followed. A place in which to grieve departed loved ones, the cemetery presented itself as an appropriate site for mourning lost and misplaced family memories of Bessy. This happened in the same fashion the Bryant and Flowers families would normally farewell and respect recently deceased kin. In the end, they would humbly confront the challenge of not being able to locate the exact whereabouts of their ancestor's grave.

Bessy's story crosses the continent from Minang country in the Great Southern of Western Australia to Gunai-Kurnai country in the East Gippsland region of Victoria. It's a history in the colonial archive holding meaning and value, and through the emotive stories told by Bessy's family in this book, it's also a history with modern cultural vivacity. How the Bryant and Flowers families chose to act on Bessy's photos and letters symbolises the heartfelt tensions in which family networks are made and kept intact.

The Bryant and Flowers families have made deep tracks in their efforts to recuperate the history of their ancestor as part of their own story. The trail they have made is traceable through the stories that are shared herein and which express grief and shame, but also courage, love and determination. Through their ancestor's letters, together with other historical colonial letters, photos and recorded oral histories, all the families involved in this story emphatically prompt the archive into an energetic process of giving up its memories of Bessy. Such liberal acts of making space for an ancestor within prudent minds and opened hearts affectively secures for both the Bryant and Flowers families an experience of healing and of hope.

The unfinished cultural business of returning Bessy *in spirit* to her rightful resting place in the country of her Minang Noongar ancestors unified her living descendants and kin as one family. Kin with cultural authority told the stories granted to them by their Elders, and amenably expressed the meaning of reconciling personal and family questions existing at the heart of identity and belonging. Gathered at the base of a significant mountain and in view of thickly laden clouds, the bonds needed for cultural cohesion between family members, and between people and country, were put right. The sincerity of these richly laden emotions have restored the powerful attributes of family and kin that now permit future generations to commemorate, honour and celebrate the legacy of a cherished and much loved ancestor – Elizabeth *Bessy* Flowers.

Acknowledgements

Thank you to the Bryant families and the Flowers families for guiding the research of this book with deepest knowledge, cultural insight and powerful storytelling.

Special thanks to the five Bryant family women who travelled open-heartedly and with courage to the traditional country of their ancestor for the first time in 2013 – Phyllis Andy, Regina Wilkinson, Flo Hood, Amy Hood and Betty Hood.

Ezzard Flowers embraced with care the spiritual return of Bessy to ancestral country. To the Elders of both the Flowers and Bryant families – thank you for sharing your knowledge grown from the unity of family created across borders and from which the form of making new memories with cultural consciousness and humility was to emerge.

Special thanks in Melbourne to Reg Thorpe and members of the Thorpe family for making time to share cultural knowledge about their ancestor Nora White. Also for support and advice along the way, a very sincere thank you to the Coyne family in Albany, including Lester and Harley Coyne and their families.

Elder leadership by Jim Berg with his soul mate Kylie (Sarah) Berg created new ground for bridging gaps in cross-cultural relations. The years spent with The Trust family in the 2000s were foundational to lessons learnt about cultural survival, resilience, and practices supporting family reconnections. Thank you to the founding team members of the Koorie Family History Service (at The Trust) and to an expert within the field of Koori ancestries and return of heritage, Kooramyee Cooper.

With deep gratitude, thank you to Robert and Vickie Reynolds for their generosity that supported the trips made to Albany. The gifting by Robert of local heritage knowledge and introductions to Noongar Elders and senior family members has been immeasurable.

Finally, thank you to the support of the Monash Indigenous Studies Centre (MISC) at Monash University, the State Library Victoria Creative Fellowship program, the City of Melbourne Arts Grants and the Creative Victoria Arts Grants programs. I also acknowledge the support of the Australian Research Council for a Discovery Early Career Researcher Award (DE220101048).

Family Spokespeople

Flowers families

Ezzard Flowers

Ezzard Flowers is a Goreng–Wirlomin man with connections to Minang country in Western Australia's Great Southern region. He was born on the United Aborigines Mission Gnowangerup on 10 September 1958. Ancestral country for the Flowers family is Goreng and Minang country. Ezzard's connection to Bessy Flowers is through his grandfather Clifford Flowers. Ezzard's identity is deeply rooted in stories shared by his community Elders, which reflect family beliefs and values that acknowledge Goreng–Wirlomin and Minang legacies of cultural resilience, care of family, and respect for heritage practices upholding connections to country and kin.

Figure 1

Bryant families

Betty Hood (née Bryant)

Betty was born 2 July 1947 in East Gippsland, Victoria, to parents Margaret Bryant and William Johnson Lewis Hood. Margaret Bryant was the third eldest daughter of Keith and Esther Bryant (née Marks). Betty grew up at the Lake Tyers Aboriginal Mission and was often cared for by her grandparents Keith (Pop) and Esther (Nan). Betty was also granddaughter to Julian (Dingo) and Gertrude Amy Hood (née Wandin). Her siblings included Glenis, William, Keith (Georgie), Kevin, Flo, Marjory, Norman, Mary and Colin. She passed away on 16 January 2017 at 69 years of age. She was buried at the Bruthen Cemetery on the great Alpine Road in East Gippsland.

Betty was the eldest niece to Bryant and Hood family members Roma (†) and Alan Rowe, Joan (†) and Percy Saunders, Phyllis and Robert Andy (†), Regina and Les Wilkinson, Julia and Frank Hood, Joseph (†), Mickey (†), Rita and Kevin Hood (both †), John and Lucy Bryant (both †), Bessie, Frank (†), Ivan (†), Gladys (†), Bindie (†), Johnny (†), Emma and Billy Murray (both †), Henry (†), Cleave (†), Myrtle and Gertrude (twins, †), Eva and Mona (twins, †), Maise and Cappy Mobourne (both †), Stevie and Nancy Hood (both †), Jimmy and Ivy Hood (both †), Stella and Benny Everett (both †), Barry (†), Florance (†), Minna (†), Martha (†) and Albert (†).

Figure 2

FAMILY SPOKESPEOPLE

Phyllis Andy (née Bryant)
Phyllis (pictured bottom left) was born 23 August 1951. She married Robert Andy.

Regina Wilkinson (née Bryant)
Regina (pictured bottom right) was born 4 July 1953 at Orbost, Victoria. She married (1) Joe Wandin and (2) Les Wilkinson.

Phyllis and Regina are the daughters of Keith Flowers Bryant and Esther Bryant (née Marks). Keith Bryant was born in 1908 in East Gippsland, Victoria. His parents were Annie Magdalene (Maggie) and Thomas Bryant. Keith was 10 years of age when his father died. His siblings were Elizabeth, Thomas, Muriel and William. Thomas and Magdalene (as she was often referred to) married at the Ramahyuck Mission Church on 25 December 1890. Thomas was aged 23 and was a labourer from Braidwood in New South Wales. Thomas's parents were William Bryant and Margaret Chapman. Magdalene was 21 years old when she married Thomas. She was Bessy and Donald Cameron's eldest daughter.

Donald's family was connected to Ebenezer, a mission in northwest Victoria and ancestral country of the Wotjobaluk peoples. Bessy belonged to Minang people in the Great Southern of Western Australia.

Bessy and Donald's great-grandchildren Phyllis and Regina belong to a large family of Bryant children. Their siblings are Myrtle (†), Gertrude (†), Margaret (†), Joe (†), Gladys (†), Emma (†), Rita (†), Phillip (Mickey) (†), Frank (†), Henry (†), Emma (†), Joan, Cleve (†) and Julia.

Figure 3

Figure 4

Flo (Marion) Hood

Flo was born in 1971 in Bairnsdale, Victoria. Her mother was Margaret Bryant, the third-eldest daughter of Keith Flowers Bryant and Esther Bryant (née Marks). Margaret was born at Lake Tyers Aboriginal Mission in the early 1930s. She married William (Jock) Hood, the son of Julian (Dingo) Hood and Gertrude Amy Wandin. Flo lives in East Gippsland.

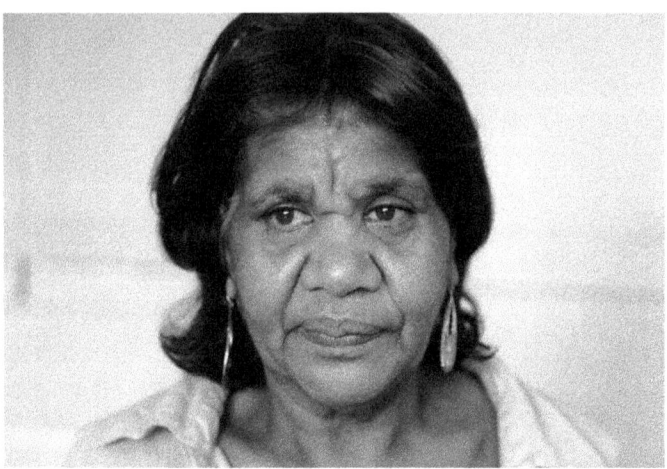

Figure 5

Amy Hood

Amy is the daughter of Rita (née Bryant) and Kevin Hood, son of Julian (Dingo) Hood and Gertrude Amy Wandin. Rita's parents were Keith Flowers Bryant and Esther Bryant (née Marks). She was sister to Phyllis and Regina. Rita was born on 3 November 1938 at the Lake Tyers Aboriginal Mission.

In 2013, Amy travelled to Albany with the consent of her elderly mother, Rita, and on behalf of her siblings Madge, Wayne, Joe and Pam. Amy is a creative writer and a poet and she continues living on the country of her ancestors at the Lake Tyers Aboriginal Trust. Amy's great-great-grandparents were Bessy and Donald Cameron.

Her mother Rita passed away in 2014. She is buried at the Lake Tyers Trust Cemetery.

FAMILY SPOKESPEOPLE

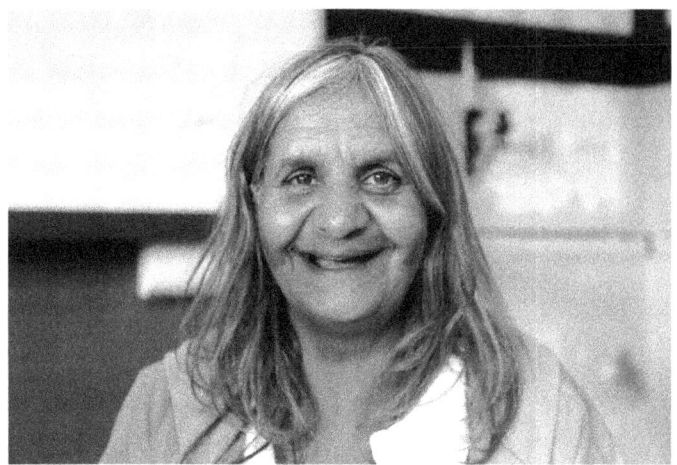

Figure 6

Figure 7

Notes

On language

'Koori' identifies Aboriginal people from Victoria and the southern region of New South Wales. The term describes different and varied languages, cultures and social family groups belonging to this region. In records from the 1800s onwards, different spellings include Koori, Koorie, Kuri and Coori.

An ever-changing group identity, Koorie ending with 'e' is used by the Koorie Heritage Trust Culture Centre founded by Gunditjmara Elder Jim Berg. Jim has said that Koorie (with an 'e') means 'we are one' and respects Elders and senior knowledge holders from the Framlingham Aboriginal Mission in western Victoria. The Bryant families prefer Koori (without the 'e') as an acknowledgement to families from the Lake Tyers Aboriginal Trust.

'Noongar' identifies Aboriginal people from the southwest of Western Australia and describes related languages spoken by Aboriginal families who are connected to country south of Geraldton and in the South West and Great Southern regions. There are different spellings of Noongar, including Nyungar, Nyoongar and Nyungah.

Letters

The original letters of Bessy Flowers are privately held in Western Australia. The custodian of the letters has not been named within the collection registers of state or national record-holding institutions. The letters appearing in this book are copies of copies from the State Library Victoria. The copied letters were transcribed in 1869 and often omit the names of settlers, missionaries, church officials and other non-Aboriginal people. Redaction of these names has been by the original donor and not the state collector. Locating the original letters is very important for expanding what the families know about Bessy and knowledge about the other women who were moved from Western Australia to Victoria in the 1800s. Any

NOTES

information about the original letters, or other letters that reveal more about Bessy's life, would be most welcomed.

Included in this book are transcriptions of Bessy's letters, which can be found in Appendix C. The excerpts used in the chapters are taken from these transcriptions.

Interviews

Also included in this book are selected interviews and personal conversations with Bryant and Flowers family members made between 2009 and 2014.

Bessy's name

The spelling of Bessy's name changes throughout the historical record. On the marriage certificates of Bessy and Donald's daughters dated 1890, 1894 and 1911, the spelling used is Bessy or Bessie. The surname on these same certificates is Flowers, though her surname is also written as Flower. Elizabeth Flowers is the name used in genealogies of Lake Tyers families compiled by ethnologist Norman Barnett Tindale in 1939. In signing off her letters to the Camfields and others, she has written 'Bessy'.

Photographs

The historical photos in this book are reproduced with permission from different archival collections throughout Australia. Also featured are portraits and photos of family taken by Sharon Huebner over the years of the research collaboration, which document the heartening and experiential journey of the Bryant and Flowers families as they reclaimed for themselves and their families the memory of their ancestor Bessy.

The flower

Thelymitra corninicina, Lilac Sun Orchid, is indigenous to the southwest of Western Australia from Perth to Albany. A unique and rare flower noted for its long slender stem and striking blue flowers, it has been used on the front cover of this book to symbolise Bessy Flowers and her connection to Minang country.

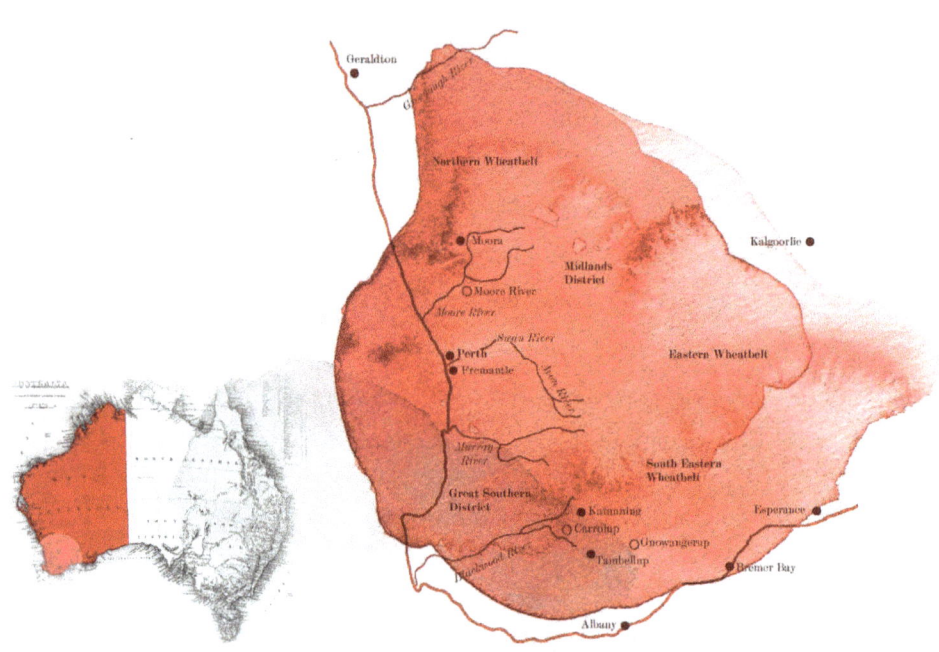

Map 1. This map shows traditional Noongar country and the sites of former Aboriginal missions, stations and reserves in the southwest of Western Australia.

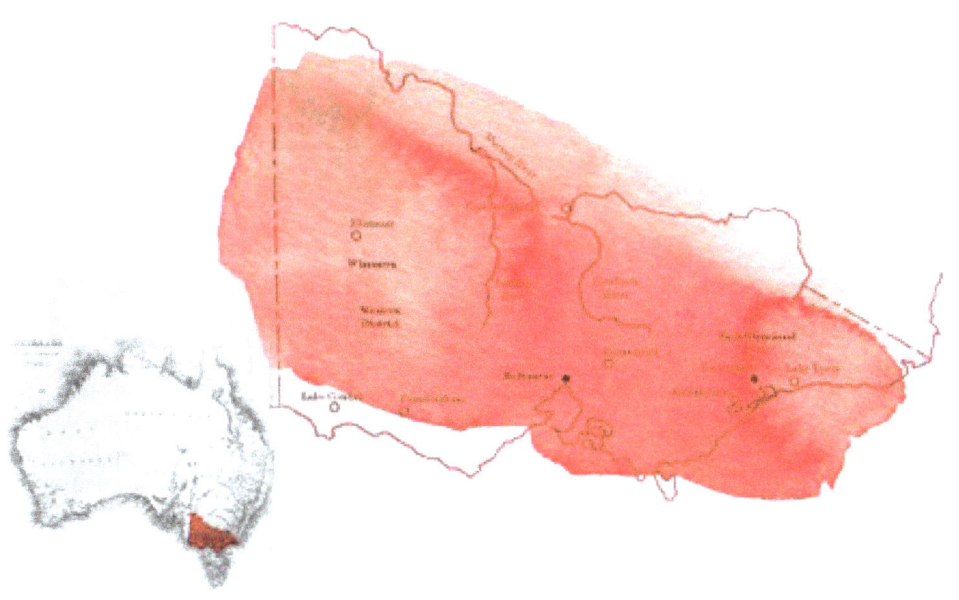

Map 2. This map shows traditional Koori country and the sites of former Aboriginal missions, stations and reserves across Victoria.

Figure 8 Elizabeth Bessy Flowers, c.1860s © Alfred Hawes Stone. Collection: JS Battye Library, State Library of Western Australia.

Chapter 1:
Bessy

Sometime in the early 1860s in a simple studio, a Minang girl belonging to families from the southwest region of Western Australia was photographed by a colonial settler, Alfred Hawes Stone. She appears in a European style dress and sits demurely with her feet resting upon a cushioned stool. The child holds in one hand a hat adorned with a thick ribbon, and this hat appears bold against the studio backdrop of a plain piece of cloth. Looking away from the camera, she appears disinterested, or perhaps shy and awkward about having her photo taken.

This Minang girl is Elizabeth (Bessy) Flowers or, as she would sign many of her letters in later years, *Bessy*.

Bessy's family connection to the Great Southern is a network of inter-relationships between people and between people and country that reflects a dynamic of knowledge culturally maintained and safeguarded by generations of Minang Elders, senior knowledge holders, and their communities of family and kin. The viscosity of family relationships plays an important role throughout this book, particularly in the process of unifying family groups from different geographic communities and the generation of events supporting memory discoveries, cultural enactments of reclamation, and the spiritual return of an ancestor.

Bessy's presence within record repositories throughout Australia is the result of standard archival acquisitions, arrangements and descriptions of historically collected materials. Many aspects of her life have been documented by authority figures granted statutory powers to administer the Victorian Aborigines Protection Act 1869. During the nineteenth century (and until the abolishment of the Act in 1957), its provisions influenced the day-to-day lives of Aboriginal families forced to make a home on missions, stations and reserves.

Reference to Bessy appears in the writings of overseeing missionaries who featured prominently in her life. She was well acquainted with these people and regarded them with fondness and admiration. The missionaries' letters frequently described how Bessy was perceived in the context of her institutional care as a child, and then as an adult deeply embedded within the structures of everyday mission living. Valuable are the letters that Bessy herself wrote between the years 1867 and 1894. Her writing portrays many key events that took place throughout her life, particularly the social interaction she was to have with Christian ministers placed in charge of the missions, the authorities representing the Board for the Protection of Aborigines, and colonial settlers working fixatedly to grow the social and economic wealth of the colonising community.

For more than a century, Bessy's history has been told through official reports, journals and letters, rather than as a meaningful story culturally animated by the social lives of her descendant families and fellow Minang kin. Bessy was born in 1849 or 1850. Within archival records there is mention of her parents being John Bunger and Mary Flower. Mary's Aboriginal name appears in the records as Kuibbalan. Other details about John and Mary are sparse as Bessy was raised not by her parents, but rather under the guardianship of Anne and Henry Camfield at Annesfield.

In the *Perth Inquirer and Commercial News* in 1858, a report was published about 'the asylum for the children of Aboriginal natives'.[25] The article reviews the operations of Annesfield, an institution for Aboriginal children located in Albany, Western Australia, with guardianship rights for 18 children: 13 girls and five boys.

CHAPTER 1: BESSY

The six older girls were aged 10 to 15, the younger girls aged eight to 18 months, and the boys aged seven months to eight years. Anne Camfield was the English colonist educator and carer of the children. The journalist introduced Anne to its readership as the wife of the Government Resident Henry Camfield, and wrote of Anne's motherly and Christian role as being a special quality and a duty made possible through her simple yet devoted love of God.

The article describes the live-in school. It's comfortable, considered dry and airy, and also clean and homely. Other particulars for the reader included where the children slept and how their days were spent under the care of the governess, Anne. Further details described the children sleeping on iron bedsteads or stretchers and their home as a dormitory at the school or the alternate boarding at the government resident's house, which was situated next door to Annesfield.

Anne Camfield taught the girls in her care domestic skills that were considered essential for survival within colonist society. Ironing, cooking, baking, scrubbing floors, butter making, and caring for the young within the nursery were all part of suitable skilfulness for adult lives outside Annesfield. Anne was also the children's tutor, teaching them reading, spelling, literacy and basic numeracy.

In the newspaper article, Bessy was singled out from the group of children in care. She was portrayed as a bright-eyed and intelligent child, about eight years of age, who was observed reciting fervently the gospel each Sunday, as well as being adept with a needle and a thread. She was described as gentle and loving, and endearing when close to Anne, often placing her hand into that of Anne's. Aged about four years, Bessy's younger sister Ada also appeared in the article. She was promising in regard to a settler lifestyle and demonstrated well-trained obedience. Such compliance was credited to the successful social and Christian integration of her older sister Bessy.

Enthusiastic encouragement from Rev. John Ramsden Wollaston, together with a limited allocation of funds from the government, allowed the married English colonists, Anne and Henry Camfield, to set up Annesfield as a 'native' institution. In June 1852 they took into their care Matilda, her Aboriginal name spelt differently in the official records of the time – Kojunupat or Kojonotpat. The *Perth Inquirer* suggested that the Camfields obtained the consent of Kojunupat's mother and reasoned that she was a child harshly treated. The journalist offered no evidence for this claim of child mistreatment and, without more detail, this statement from the past risks being read in the present as the historical truth.

Also exhibited in the newspaper article was an inquiry into settler judgements and attitudes about Noongar culture and family. The journalist praised Anne for her determination to 'ameliorate the condition of the wretched aborigines, whom the Europeans had deprived of their all, without making them the slightest compensation'.[26] Considering that the betterment of Aboriginal people was an important colonial ambition, the Camfields' work was considered to be genuine advocacy for improving the livelihoods of Minang people and other Aboriginal people who had been moved to the southwest region. Part of this betterment was the act of taking children away from families and into care, effectually endorsing beliefs in Christian values and human salvation that aimed to 'save' children from their culture.

The children at Annesfield were obliging participants in practices of the Anglican St John's Church, in particular the rite of baptism, which was performed to attain both grace and forgiveness, while also symbolising Jesus Christ's burial and resurrection. Birth names were replaced with Christian names during this religious process and only a record of the newly acquired Christian name was captured on baptismal records, not the birth name identifying a child's ancestral lineage to family, kin. The Camfields were influential figures in the lives of the Flowers children and the other children who are identified within the colonial record by the names that were given to them by the Camfields from the early 1850s through to the 1860s.

Anne Camfield (née Breeze) was born in England. She was a child orphan and her relatives in England are unknown. Anne came to Fremantle on the western coast of Australia in 1838, travelling as governess to an English missionary's family, the Mitchells. From England, the Anglican Church Missionary Societies provided

CHAPTER 1: BESSY

sponsorship to Rev. William Mitchell and his second wife, Frances, to set up a school in Fremantle for Christian education. The archive provides detail about the school and its intake of Noongar children from the Swan River Colony as well as any other children relocated, likely against their will, to the colony from other parts of Western Australia.

Anne provided practical tuition that aimed to prepare the children for domestic lives beyond the school and as participants of the growing colonial settler community seeking to expand its workforce. Along with daily duties of cooking and house cleaning, Anne also took care of the animals that were kept for food – chickens, geese and the like. She continued in this role for at least two years, and until her marriage to Henry Camfield in 1840.[27]

Henry arrived in Fremantle in 1829. It was a long journey from Kent in England aboard the *Caroline*, a ship that had been commissioned for travel by the wealthy Henty family. Coincidentally, also aboard the same ship was Alfred Hawes Stone, the colonial settler photographer who would take Bessy's photo decades later. Henry was born in 1800. In letters by Stone and others, he was portrayed as being adventurous and ambitious, a man of social substance who acted with integrity. The letters Henry wrote to his family in England and to officials in the colony reveal him to be modest when describing his personal and work life and as being sympathetic to Noongar people.[28]

As a newly arrived colonial settler migrant, Henry's goal was to purchase land within the colony and to improve his income opportunities. He planned to recuperate money lost to him in England during a time of economic downfall. Henry's education and determination helped him progress his quest for success. He became financially secure and took up work in the colony, including positions as postmaster and justice of the peace. In his forties Henry married Anne, and accepted an appointment as government resident in the southwest region of the colony. It was a role that required Henry to report back to the government in Perth about local affairs, including governance issues and settler community needs.

In Albany, situated between the hills of Mount Melville and Mount Clarence, and looking down towards the Princess Royal Harbour, Henry and Anne followed the advice of Rev. John Wollaston to set up a 'native' institution. Henry named this place 'Annesfield' after his English wife.

Rev. Wollaston had journeyed from England to Fremantle in 1841. He was an Anglican minister who appeared energised by the challenges that the isolation of the Swan River Colony presented, being a place with a community need for greater Christian spiritual guidance. Rev. Wollaston worked tirelessly on his godly duties, even building a church with his sons in Picton near Bunbury as a response to collapsed settler community Christian values and beliefs.

In 1848 Augustus Short, who was the first Anglican bishop of Adelaide in South Australia, appointed Rev. Wollaston as archdeacon. He became very familiar with the southern regions of Western Australia and those areas beyond Bunbury, travelling on horseback to many of the developing settlements. In his years as archdeacon, Rev. Wollaston kept a diary. Many of the entries detail paternalistic observations of vast stretches of land and settler attempts to build cohesive communities. He also responded to observations made of Noongar people, who he witnessed struggling against the influx of convicts and settlers who numbered in the tens of thousands by the 1850s. It's not surprising that Rev. Wollaston crossed paths with the Camfields and that they chose to align their efforts with that of his own to encourage Christian social obedience.

In a diary entry dated Monday 21 February 1853, Rev. Wollaston reflected upon the Camfields' establishment of Annesfield, and the placement of Noongar children within an institution away from family and community. He believed that, 'Children must be trained from infancy in habits of civilisation and industry, or they'll never be fixed anywhere'.[29] Rev. Wollaston made these comments while reflecting upon an elderly Aboriginal man – 'old native' – who he had watched wearing to church a scarlet uniform provided to him by the Commissariat Department, or in plain terms, the police force of the day.

To Rev. Wollaston, the uniform was a sign that the old man had accepted settler 'civilisation' and had given up his cultural beliefs and practices. However, as Rev. Wollaston reflected in his journal, when the old man knew that his life was nearing an end, he elected to meet his death out in the bush and clothed in kangaroo skin, not the uniform. Rev. Wollaston resolved from this experience that there was a strong need to consciously dispense with, and dismiss, cultural connections in the early years of childhood in order to successfully Christianise Aboriginal people.[30]

The efforts of the Camfields to carry on this work started at Annesfield on 21 June 1852 when Bessy's older sister Kojunupat was taken into care and renamed Matilda. Her younger siblings identified in the historical record would be given the names Bessy, Ada and Harry. Matilda died in 1858 after only three years at Annesfield. She had been baptised by Rev. Wollaston, who was the minister at the St John's Anglican Church on Albany's main street during Annesfield's early years, and it was there that he also baptised other Annesfield children.

In Anne's words, the purpose of Annesfield was '[t]o wean them [Aboriginal people] from their wild habits' and 'give them a little insight into the comforts of civilisation, together with teaching them some of the simplest but most important Truths of the Gospel'.[31] Anne's ambition for Annesfield echoed Rev. Wollaston's strong views about setting up institutions for the purpose of assimilating Aboriginal children, as noted in a letter that he wrote to the Colonial Secretary on August 16 1852:

> I take the liberty of adding a few words respecting consignment of the Children to our care; which indeed will prove the most difficult point of all. Experience proves that it would be in vain to attempt a school unless the Children were formally surrendered for a stated time under the guarantee of Government protection.
>
> The age Mrs Camfield stipulates for, in which I entirely agree, is between two and five years, and the period of their consignment to the School not less than 10.

> [...] I think the most hopeful way of getting the Sound natives to fall in with the plan would be to commence, if possible, with Children from another district. Such a step would, I have little doubt, have the effect of stimulating the natives here, whether from a feeling of emulation or jealousy, to get as many of their Children as they could enrolled amongst the rest.[32]

Anne and Henry set up Annesfield next door to their own residence in Albany. Annesfield first consisted of a room for teaching children in their care, followed by the addition of a kitchen and a shared sleeping dormitory, amenities considered adequate for the children. In 1850 Henry wrote to his sister Bessy in England about Anne's interest in the colony's Aboriginal people or, as he referred to them, the 'sable race'. He remarked how Annesfield would be a place in which to 'cultivate' what he termed to be their 'presently dark minds'.[33] Henry's attitude towards Aboriginal people was widely held by government administrators, officials and Christian missionaries, all colonial contributors to the social and political development of the colony.

Anne's missionary experience was certainly influenced by her earlier work at the Fremantle 'native' school with Rev. Mitchell as well as by Rev. Wollaston, who had spent more than a decade in the colony with the intent of spreading the word of God. Rev. Wollaston's desire was to strengthen what he believed to be weakened beliefs and spiritual faith throughout a colony showing signs of poor religious practice. Wanting to solve this issue, he sourced the funds needed to purchase land for a chapel. In diary entries and in letters to organisations such as the London-based Society for the Propagation of the Gospel in Foreign Parts, Rev. Wollaston relayed how the future of the colony depended on dedicated Christian instruction. He believed this would counter the immorality of white settlers and the reach of their corruptness into the lives of Noongar people. Rev. Wollaston perceived Noongar adults to be wanderers. He claimed that, 'No kindness will ever wean them from their bush habits and wild licence',[34] and for this reason, training children from a young age justified his multifarious proposition to set up institutions for the young. They were words that Anne would later repeat with sureness when compiling a report about Annesfield to the Western Australian government in the early 1870s.

Rev. Wollaston believed that Aboriginal children taken into the care of an institution from young ages was the most effective method for providing Christian training and education. He also believed that the provision of religious and domestic training would enable the children, grown up at the institution, to be locally employed as domestics, married or hired as labourers for nearby farms and growing settlements. Gaining funds and permission to set up a 'native' institution, Wollaston recruited the support of the Camfields, taking advantage of Henry's position as government resident in Albany. The establishment of Annesfield was of great interest to the Western Australian government, missionaries, and those involved in the official reporting on the colony's public affairs.

As more children were recruited, Anne became the housemother and teacher. In a report on the establishment of Annesfield to the Western Australian Parliament in 1871 (see Appendix B), she says: 'The natives of Australia are capable of great improvement, but it will be in some generations hence that much good will be visible'.[35] She goes on to explain that Annesfield began privately with one child, before more funds were secured in order to support the care of another six children.

Anne informed the parliament of the early death of Kojunupat (Matilda) from 'inflammation of the lungs'. She also reported how Annesfield's 16-year operation had seen the 'poor children of the wilderness' being brought up in a 'more refined way'.[36] All the children in care at Annesfield, she wrote, received 'civilised training, so as to make them useful members of society'. To demonstrate this success, Anne mentioned Bessy in the report, telling of her musical skill and keen interest in, and passion for, reading. She highlighted what she believed to be the positive attributes of taking children into care:

> Bessy who is now a teacher in Gippsland was never without a book in her pocket by day or under her pillow by night. Her love of reading often brought her into scrapes, from reading at inconvenient times, but not withstanding, it was very improving to her, as (though she liked as well as any girl to read stories, yet) she is much interested in History, and Travels, and more serious works…Her memory is so very good that she retains what she reads.
>
> This girl alone is sufficient proof of the intelligence of the Aborigines, for she was not chosen by us to receive greater advantages of education than the rest from anything superior in her. She was selected simply because she was the sister of the first child we took, and who died after being in the school three years, and also because she was the daughter of a very faithful old native servant, who died believing in Jesus Christ (as far as I cannot but think, as an untutored mind could comprehend) as his Saviour.
>
> We have had many equal, and one or two decidedly superior to Bessy, and the question is, 'Is it right to let such intelligence be wasted, or worse, be turned to evil without some effort to prevent it?'[37]

During Annesfield's early days, Rev. Wollaston expressed in his diaries a concern about the children's parents. He wondered if they would protest against or agree to the rehoming of their children. Rev. Wollaston reviewed his own question in later entries, declaring how his concerns had been short lived and observing that, from his perspective, more children had come to be at Annesfield than the Camfields were able to accept, due to limited government funding. An ally of Rev. Wollaston, Anne validated his thoughts in the government report:

CHAPTER 1: BESSY

> The objection many people make, that it is cruel to take their children from them is not a solid one; because the children left to the parent's management, or non-management, soon cast off all submission, and all care or love for the parents, so that when the latter become old and helpless, they are almost wholly neglected.
>
> When on the contrary, the children are brought to school, the parents see them whenever they like, and their children are taught to treat them with kindness and consideration.[38]

The historical assumptions made by Rev. Wollaston and Anne disregard the impact of colonial settler efforts aimed at restructuring the social lives of Minang people, including disharmonising family networks and disrupting access to traditional lands. The breakdown of family life and lack of access to food and cultural resources would have led many parents to make decisions about their children that appeared on the surface consensual, but were in fact acts of survival. It's a history that Bessy's descendant families and kin look back on and relate to with respect to personal experiences and memories of mission living.

At Annesfield, Bessy took on all that was offered to her and used her colonial and Christian education to forge a future within the colonial settler society in which she had been placed. Bessy was ambitious as well as tenacious. She sought recognition for her skills and for her accomplishments. She was not ashamed of settler curiosity, such as the keen interest shown her by the parishioners at the St John's Church. An accomplished organist, Bessy was remembered in church for her wide-brimmed hat decorated with a red ribbon. It was noted by those in the congregation that as she played hymns, the only visible and distracting sign of her was the hat with the ribbon.

Bessy relied on both Anne and Henry for family love and affection. In later years, she would mention in her letters to Anne how her mother and father had been close at hand, even working for a period of time at Annesfield. Despite having her parents nearby, it was evident that Bessy sought the approval and respect of her settler guardians. In many ways, she had come to depend on the Camfields' guardianship, particularly since the colony had become an ever-changing place for Minang people and their families.

Anne took responsibility for Bessy's journeys away from Annesfield. The first, in 1864, was a long sea voyage to a model school in Sydney, where Bessy had been sent on the advice of Perth's bishop, Mathew Hale. Bishop Hale regarded with interest Anne's progress at Annesfield, especially her teaching success with the children covering English literature, history, geography and mathematics as well as specialised subjects considered to be useful to girls, such as sewing, craftwork and music. Anne wrote of Bessy's activities in Sydney:

> On being taken by friends to the Eastern Colonies, she on one occasion played the hymns for the afternoon service on the Organ at St Phillip's Church, Sydney, when there was a full congregation, and she for some time, two years in all, played the Harmonium, an instrument with two key-boards, at Albany Church, because there was no one in the place who could play it better, and who was willing to do so. Her knowledge and practice of music has made her useful. She is now earning her living very creditably as a teacher in a native school in Gippsland.[39]

When Bessy returned to Annesfield from Sydney, she became Anne's assistant teacher and also a salaried church organist. In Anne's eyes, she was a role model for the other children at the institution.

In June 1867, three years after her first trip, Bessy embarked on a journey with four other young women from Annesfield that included her sister Ada Flowers, Rhoda Tanaton (or Toby), Emily Peters, Nora White and Nora's infant son, Charlie. Voyaging more than 1,300 nautical miles, they made their way to the Ramahyuck

CHAPTER 1: BESSY

Aboriginal Mission nestled close to the Avon River in the Gippsland region of Victoria. The inter-missionary arrangement was for the women to marry Christian Aboriginal men living at the mission. A couple of years earlier, the same trip had been made by two other women raised at Annesfield: Caroline and Anna. The arranged marriages never took place as, on arrival to Melbourne, they were taken by typhus fever and passed away at the Melbourne Hospital.

In letters to Anne at Annesfield, Bessy described their experience leaving Annesfield, introducing the individuals they met during their travels:

> My dearest Missie,
>
> I know you will be glad to hear that we arrived quite safely & had such a nice voyage…We went to Church [in Adelaide] on Sunday morning… The service was beautiful. Oh! the music & singing was delicious, they sang the Amen after everything. In the afternoon we went for a walk & we met the clergyman, he said that he would see us tomorrow (Monday).
>
> They came yesterday & took us up to Adelaide [from the port], fancy dear Missie was it not kind of them? We went into the Legislative House & into the Assembly room, & then we went into the museum. There were such a lot of birds & all sorts of things, it was so pretty.
>
> …After we had gone to the gardens, we saw a tiger, a bear, all sorts of peacocks; there was a white one, a lama & ostrich the place is laid out beautifully, I only wish that you were with us.
>
> …my love to poor dear Mother & tell her that Ada & I are quite well…
>
> From your grateful & loving B.[40]

In Melbourne, the five Annesfield women met the Rev. Friedrich Hagenauer. He was a Moravian missionary who had moved to Australia from Germany in 1858 with the purpose of establishing the Ebenezer Aboriginal Mission situated near the Wimmera River in northwestern Victoria. In 1862 he arrived in Gippsland and the following year set up the Ramahyuck Aboriginal Mission Station. In September 1867 he wrote about the success of Ramahyuck:

> It gives me great pleasure to state that the spiritual condition of the Christian blacks in general is a good one, and that Christian knowledge is also increasing among those who are not yet baptised. The religious meetings held daily and on Sundays are generally well attended, and all of them form a well-organised congregation.
>
> …There are now
> a. 13 Baptised aborigines.
> b. 7 Candidates for baptism, under special instruction.
> c. 5 candidates for baptism besides, who make very little progress.
> d. 35 Aboriginals live in houses, a civilised life.
> e. 76 Aborigines are on the station.
> f. 13 Little children come to school.
> g. 8 Young men form an evening class.
> h. 2 Of my men had been baptised at the Government station on the Yarra.[41]

In June 1867 Bessy wrote to Anne about their first meeting with Rev. Hagenauer, detailing how her first impression was one of amusement. She also communicated that love be sent from herself and sister Ada to her mother and her brother Harry:

CHAPTER 1: BESSY

> My own dearest Missie,
>
> …On Saturday morning as [we] were coming to the pier I was looking out for Mr H [Hagenauer]. After some time we saw a gentleman with a dark beard, when he saw us he smiled & shook his hand. I could not help laughing; he looked so funny…
>
> We went to the Scotch Church yesterday…In the afternoon we went to the Sunday School & Mr H spoke to the teachers & scholars about his mission station, when he had done speaking, Mr Menzies told them that they wanted a harmonium at Gippsland. I asked the children to save up their pence & shillings to buy one.
>
> …will you please give my love to my poor dear mother & Ada's too, & tell her we are all quite well and I hope her arm is getting better, I must not forget her…I do not forget Harry…[42]

Bessy's new home at Ramahyuck replicated the design of other Aboriginal missions across Victoria, appearing like a well-ordered township. There was a house for the Reverend and his family, a store for supplies, a vegetable garden, potato and arrowroot crops and an orchard. At Ramahyuck the residents became the builders of timber homes that replaced traditional bark huts. They were taught to read and to write, and sang German songs and hymns translated into English.[43] In 1865 James Fitchett (or Fitchet) and Charlie Foster built a church as instructed by Rev. Hagenauer. Both men had been chosen by Rev. Hagenauer to be the husbands of Anna and Caroline from Annesfield.

> The first convert, James Mathew Fitchet was baptised. This first convert had given true evidence of a change of heart, and his whole life showed that he served the Lord. On the 29th of April of the same year,

> the second convert, 'Charles Jacob' was baptised by myself, and both young men were admitted to the Lord's supper, by their own desire and after further instruction, two months later. Thus the Lord helped wonderfully, and established the first aboriginal church in this district.
>
> ...We had expected that these men should soon have been married to native Christian women from Mrs Camfield's Institution at King George's Sound. These girls arrived in Melbourne, but soon afterwards both died...[44]

Rhoda Tanaton (or Toby) and Nora White became the replacement brides from Annesfield for the Christian converts, James and Charlie.

> In June of the present year, we had the great joy to see again some Christian black girls arrive in Melbourne and here, from our esteemed friend Mrs Camfield, to be married to our young Christian men, and on the 12th of July two couples were married in our church, on which occasion there were about 60 blacks and about 200 whites present.[45]

Bessy, Ada, Nora, Rhoda and Emily all lived under the authority of Rev. Hagenauer, who was known to be a man with a commanding personality and paternalistic by nature. In the missionary management of both Annesfield and Ramahyuck, marriage was a common concern shared by Anne and Rev. Hagenauer. In 1872, English writer Jane Millet reflected that:

> Mrs Camfield's chief difficulty is how to settle her girls in life, for when grown up the inevitable question arises, whom are they to marry? They cannot, after the training they have received, take a savage husband; and

CHAPTER 1: BESSY

> though I believe two of her pupils have married ticket-of-leave men, yet the prospects held out by such alliances are poor rewards for adopting Christian habits, and but sorry inducements for retaining them.[46]

Anne suggested to Rev. Hagenauer in their correspondence that Bessy would be suited to marriage, if this was to be arranged, to a Moravian missionary or someone with high social regard and Christian standing. Anne believed such an arranged marriage would complement Bessy's Christian education and faith. However, Rev. Hagenauer was opposed to the idea of an interracial marriage and he rejected this suggestion, staying true to arrangements that he had initiated in the past whereby Christian Aboriginal women married Christian Aboriginal men. He decided that the women from Annesfield would marry Koori men who had been baptised and were living at Ramahyuck under his authority and that of the government. Though a suitable husband had not been found for Bessy prior to her leaving Annesfield, it became apparent Rev. Hagenauer had a clear vision of the role that she would play under his rules, writing:

> [Bessy's] help in my school will be very much valued and will bring her into a field of usefulness, which I trust will last all her life…and if it would be God's will that she should marry here, she would be better off than if she might fall into some hands of certain white men.[47]

Unlike Nora and Rhoda, it happened that Bessy, her sister Ada and also Emily were not obligated to marry soon after their arrival at Ramahyuck. It was arranged that they would live in the missionary home with Rev. Hagenauer, his wife Louisa and their children. In a letter to Anne, Bessy described this domestic arrangement involving her care for Louisa, along with the Hagenauer children, Theo and Cissie:

> I am trying to be a comfort to Mrs Hagenauer. I dress the children and make their beds; then it is breakfast time. We have prayers at the Church, and then it is school time. In the afternoon I have Theo and Cissie…Mrs Hagenauer is such a dear lady. I sleep in the nursery with the little children.[48]

Bessy's emotional attachment to Anne and to Annesfield is conveyed in her letters, and is clearly demonstrated in her excitement and joy at the prospect of Anne and Henry visiting Ramahyuck:

> Oh what do you think, dear Missie? I thought you were coming here and I worked myself into such a state that I was continually looking out for you across the river and at the gate to see if I could see a carriage, and I looked in the newspapers to see the names of the passengers. I hope you won't laugh too much, dear Missie, for I hope you will soon come and dear Martie too.[49]

Bessy's life was deeply seated within the daily activities of Ramahyuck. In early letters, Bessy wrote positively about Rev. Hagenauer to Anne, and Hagenauer wrote to Anne kindly about Bessy, commenting in one particular letter that: 'Bessy Flower[s] is entirely in our family and we are pleased with her; we are very fond of her…We all rejoice to have her with us, and I feel it will do her much good'.[50] This favourable reception of Bessy and her exceptional skill and usefulness at Ramahyuck would not be lasting.

Bessy did not agree with all of Rev. Hagenauer's ideas about her future on the mission. Marriage was just one such issue. In November 1867 Bessy received a marriage proposal from a colonial settler who was working on Ramahyuck as a builder and general labourer. Though Bessy had been living on the mission for five months, there had been no marital arrangements made. Rev. Hagenauer was strict and socially controlling of all the residents. He disapproved of Bessy's proposal to marry a white labourer on her own terms. He swiftly made his own arrangements for Bessy. Rev. Hagenauer wrote to Anne about the issue of Bessy's marriage and stated with paternal conviction that:

> It is true few of them can read and write, but if the young man is good in general, he would be a good husband to her and she could still take charge of our school.
>
> I hope that she [Bessy] will get over this present temptation. On the whole however, I believe that it would be best to get her [Bessy] married by and by in order to get her out of future temptations for I do believe that, as now the springs of love in her heart is opened and she is evidently in great trials on that point, that the only remedy is to get her permanently settled.[51]

While Rev. Hagenauer went in search of a suitable Koori Christian convert, Bessy was sent to the Lake Tyers Aboriginal Mission about 137 kilometres further east in the Gippsland region. She lived there for a short period of time under the guardianship of Rev. John Bulmer. Meanwhile, Rev. Hagenauer sought advice from a fellow missionary, Rev. Friedrich Wilhelm Spieseke, at the Ebenezer Aboriginal Mission and he agreed with Rev. Spieseke that Donald Camcron would be a more suitable husband for Bessy.

Donald was a Wotjobaluk man. He came from a family known to Rev. Hagenauer through his first missionary role at the Ebenezer mission. For the arranged marriage, Rev. Hagenauer baptised Donald at Ramahyuck's church and, on 4 November 1868, Donald and Bessy were married.

Following their modest wedding, Donald and Bessy worked together in Ramahyuck's schoolhouse. This fitted with Hagenauer's plans to build a boarding house on the mission for children taken away from family care. A member of the Victorian Board for the Protection of Aborigines reporting on the progress of the Ramahyuck Mission on Lake Wellington wrote that there were 29 Aboriginal people living there: 17 children and 12 adults. The historical report also described the boarding schoolhouse:

> There is a large schoolroom, with five bedrooms and one sitting room attached, similar to the school and bedrooms at Coranderrk. The schoolroom is also used for the dining room for the children. One of the bedrooms and the sitting room is occupied by Bessy Flower[s] and her husband, and two of the bedrooms are occupied by twelve of the children; all was clean, and everything was in good order…most of the children can read and write a little; at present they are taught by Bessy Flower[s].[52]

Bessy and Donald worked hard to care for the daily needs of the children at the school, which for Bessy involved teaching them basic writing and reading skills. This changed in early 1869, when Rev. Carl Christian Wilhelm Kramer returned to the mission to fulfil a teaching role that he had begun in about 1864. Rev. Kramer had left Ramahyuck in June 1866 to take on a position at the Lake Hope Mission in South Australia.

Bessy was well regarded as a teacher, and in the years that followed Rev. Kramer's return, a sense of hopelessness pervaded the letters that she wrote to the missionaries and to the Board. In particular, Bessy's correspondence began to detail the struggles produced by mission life, such as inadequate access to paid work, housing shortages, family health issues, stringent rules and regulations, and personal challenges that were beginning to arise within her relationship with Donald.

CHAPTER 1: BESSY

Over the years of their marriage from 1868 to 1895, Bessy and Donald had eight children.[53] The eldest child was Annie Magdalene (known as Magdalene or Maggie), followed by Nellie Grace, Louisa, Ada May, Donald Boyd, Haines Adolphus, Mena Blanche and Keith Flowers. News of Louisa's birth appeared in a letter from Bessy's brother Harry to Captain Alfred Darby on 6 October 1873:

> 'Bessie has another girl she was baptised last Sunday her name is Louisa. Maggie loves her very much she always wants to nurse it. She won't go to school without kissing it.'[54]

Having the responsibility of a growing family added to the discomfort of Bessy's Ramahyuck experience. Care for her children became increasingly difficult, with food and clothing systematically regulated on the mission and often inadequate for their needs. All Aboriginal residents received food rations and an allocation of clothing, blankets and other necessities. They had to make do. They were also forbidden to leave the mission for any reason without the written permission of the governing missionary. The rules were strictly enforced, with punishment meted out for any disobedience. Any contact with members of the outside community was discouraged. It could be surmised that mission living had taken on the stifling system of a government prison.

Bessy was an educated and accomplished woman. She was an admired teacher and skilled organist who, by the people that she respected and who in return respected her, was treated cordially within social parameters determined by Christian values. She considered Annesfield her home, writing fondly to Anne when in the eastern colonies, 'Never mind, I must work hard & then it will be all the sweeter when I come home to help you & be your right hand always'.[55] This societal confidence was in stark contrast to what her life was to become: an overworked mother, a wife of a philandering husband, often homeless, and a woman reduced to begging for food and shelter for her family from those who had once expressed admiration for her worthy skillset and social qualities.

Bessy's original ideas and positive imaginings of how life on Ramahyuck would be after departing Annesfield began to change. Her thoughts returned to Albany, especially her longing for the place that she had regarded as home. This yearning found its way into a letter to her friend Captain Darby in April 1872. Darby had captained the *Charles Edward* steamer in 1867, which had transported the Annesfield women from Melbourne to the Gippsland Lakes:

> It is getting very cold now in the mornings & the evenings. It will now be five years since we [Bessy and the other four Aboriginal women] came to Gippsland, it seems much longer to me, it is our home now for good, but I never thought it was to be my home.[56]

After this time, there is a strong sense of regret and despair that emerges in Bessy's letters. Life as a mother had been for her both joyous and heartbreaking. By 1872, Bessy had birthed two healthy daughters, Magdalene and Louisa, but she had also suffered the loss of an infant daughter Nellie Grace, which Bessy communicated to Captain Darby in April 1873, writing:

> Did you know Captain I lost one of my children, it was the youngest Nellie Grace, so have only the one Annie Magdalene who goes to school, she is a spoilt little rouge I am afraid. I am very happy when I think of dear wee Nellie for I know she is safe with the Lord Jesus…[57]

The passing of Nellie Grace was followed in 1874 by the death of Bessy's younger sister, Ada, who at the time was only 21 years old, married to James Henry Clark and with a young child, William. In another letter to her friend Captain Darby, Bessy wrote of Ada's death:

> I must tell you about my sister's death you wished to know the cause of it. She had an abscess under the arm & afterwards a cold on her chest poor dear! She suffered very much, but I believe she is safe in heaven. She only left one child, a boy who will be six [?] years old in November.[58]

Bessy also mourned the passing of children born to the other Annesfield women and those children born to other Ramahyuck women. 'There was a burial here yesterday', she wrote, 'it was the burial of a little child'.[59]

By August 1879 Bessy confronted the reality of her marriage breakdown. She issued a request to the Victorian Board for the Protection of Aborigines that she live away from Donald, who she accused of having a relationship with another Koori woman at Ramahyuck. This infidelity had struck a heartfelt chord with Bessy and she asked Rev. Hagenauer and the Board for permission that would allow herself and her children to move to the Lake Condah Aboriginal Mission located in western Victoria.

Once again, Hagenauer demonstrated his disapproval. He was extremely critical of Bessy's desire for autonomy, and equally of her decision to leave her husband and to take her children. He reported to Captain Page, the secretary of the Board:

> The black woman Bessy Cameron has left Ramahyuck yesterday, as she does not want to live with her husband anymore. Before she left she burnt his best clothes and abstracted his bankbook, no doubt with the intention to get his money from the savings bank. She said she was going to you to ask if you would forward her to Condah [Lake Condah Aboriginal Mission].[60]

Both Donald and Hagenauer persisted with claims that Bessy failed in her domestic duties and, accordingly from their observation, was 'not a good housekeeper'.[61] They perceived her to be emotionally erratic and unreasonable in her demands aimed at keeping her children both safe and happy. While it happened that Bessy returned to Ramahyuck, for a time afterwards she maintained in her arguments with all that she was moving to the Lake Condah mission and taking both her daughters and her son with her. Donald petitioned the Board for their children to be left at Ramahyuck's boarding house, which had been set up for children taken from the care of their parents or their extended family.

> My wife just returned from Melbourne, & tells me that you had given her a place at Lake Condah; well perhaps I can do nothing if she goes she may, but I humbly beg you and the Board not to remove my children from Ramahyuck, I have put them in the boarding house, and they are happy & cheerful, & well cared for, if they should be taken away, it will be for misery, for my wife is very careless of house keeping.[62]

Though Bessy was issued a pass granting her permission to leave the grounds of Ramahyuck, as was required of all Aboriginal people living on a mission, she would only live at the Lake Condah mission for a relatively short time. The unwelcoming attitude of the missionary in charge ensured that Bessy returned to East Gippsland in search, once again, for a more positive and satisfying livelihood. Daily survival for herself and her family was a constant undertaking.

In time, Donald and Bessy reconciled despite Donald's ongoing relationship with a Koori woman belonging to the Pepper family and with whom he had two children. Bessy and Donald battled tirelessly with the Victorian Board for the Protection of Aborigines, as was the case for many Koori families. They constantly asked for help in finding paid work and a place in which to live. At times they were

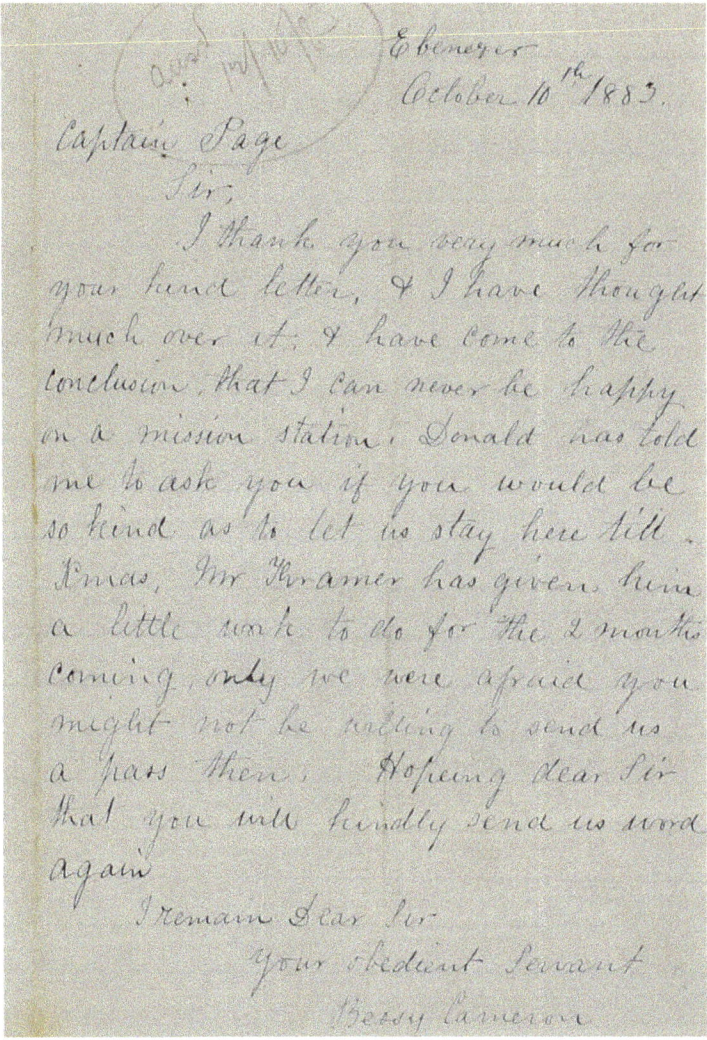

Figure 9 Bessy letter, 1883. Collection: National Archives of Australia, Correspondence Files, Central Board for the Protection of Aborigines, B357 item 177.

forced to lead transient lives that left them without a permanent home. They were moved between missions operating in different parts of the state and constantly battled to support their family. These challenges became a heavy burden to carry as is evident from the letters that Bessy wrote to Captain Page, who represented the secretariat authority of the Board:

> I hope you will allow us to stay on this station [Lake Tyers Aboriginal Mission] it comes hard on the children and myself wandering about without a home, and I feel it more as I had a good home when I was young.⁶³

Bessy's struggle with mission life continued. She experienced daily hardship and was often refused support by both the Board and Rev. Hagenauer. In a letter to the Board on 4 August 1884 Bessy wrote: 'I am very sorry to see that we cannot get any rations, it would have been such a help to us, as we are such a large family'. One of the only solid structures of Bessy's life was her family.⁶⁴ She even took on the care of her grandson Roy (Magdalene's son), who the Board had suggested be transferred to an industrial school.⁶⁵

After battling for more than 15 years with both the Board and Rev. Hagenauer for better living conditions, Bessy's life came to an end at the Bairnsdale Hospital. She had made a trip from Ramahyuck to Bairnsdale to visit Maggie (Annie Magdalene), her eldest daughter, as well as Emily Brindle (née Peters), a friend who had made the original trip with her from Annesfield. After spending only several days in Bairnsdale, Bessy died on 14 January 1895. Her death certificate reports a life-threatening case of peritonitis that was experienced over a period of 48 hours.

The passing of Bessy was mentioned in the *Australian Weekly* on Friday 25 January 1895 and in the local *Gippsland Times* on Monday 11 February 1895. The *Gippsland Times* wrote:

> Aboriginals' settlement at Ramahyuck will regret to learn that Mrs Bessy Cameron who for many years was organist in the church, died recently at Bairnsdale. Mrs Cameron, like most of the Aboriginals looked much older than she was, being only 47 years of age. She was on a visit to her daughter and died after a short illness. Mrs Cameron's

CHAPTER 1: BESSY

musical talent was considerable, and she was very proud of having been asked to play before Sir Henry Loch and Lord Hopetoun when they visited the station.[66]

With emotional insight, the *Australian Weekly* reported that: 'the general happiness of the natives of Ramahyuck were moved to grief at the unexpected death of one of their number', further adding that Bessy's passing 'has caused a profound sensation among the Aboriginals of the whole district'.[67]

Upon her death, Bessy's historical portrayal in the archive came to an end. Despite the newspapers reporting on Bessy's death and recognition given to her educational and musical abilities, there was no mention of how Bessy's husband and her family and her friends had mourned her passing and celebrated her life. The only correspondence providing family interaction with funeral arrangements was a letter from the Board authorities to Donald, asking that he contribute financially to the expenses of his wife's burial.[68]

Bessy, a Minang woman originating from the Great Southern, was buried in the old Presbyterian section of the Bairnsdale Cemetery, away from her birthplace and the traditional country of her ancestors. Practices of mourning and acts of remembrance by her descendant families and kin would become the force for unifying family and for giving momentum to a storied experience of cultural reclamation and spiritual return.

Figure 10 Alfred Hawes Stone c.1800s. Reproduced from the private album of Dorothy Croft, Perth, Western Australia, 2010.

CHAPTER 1: BESSY

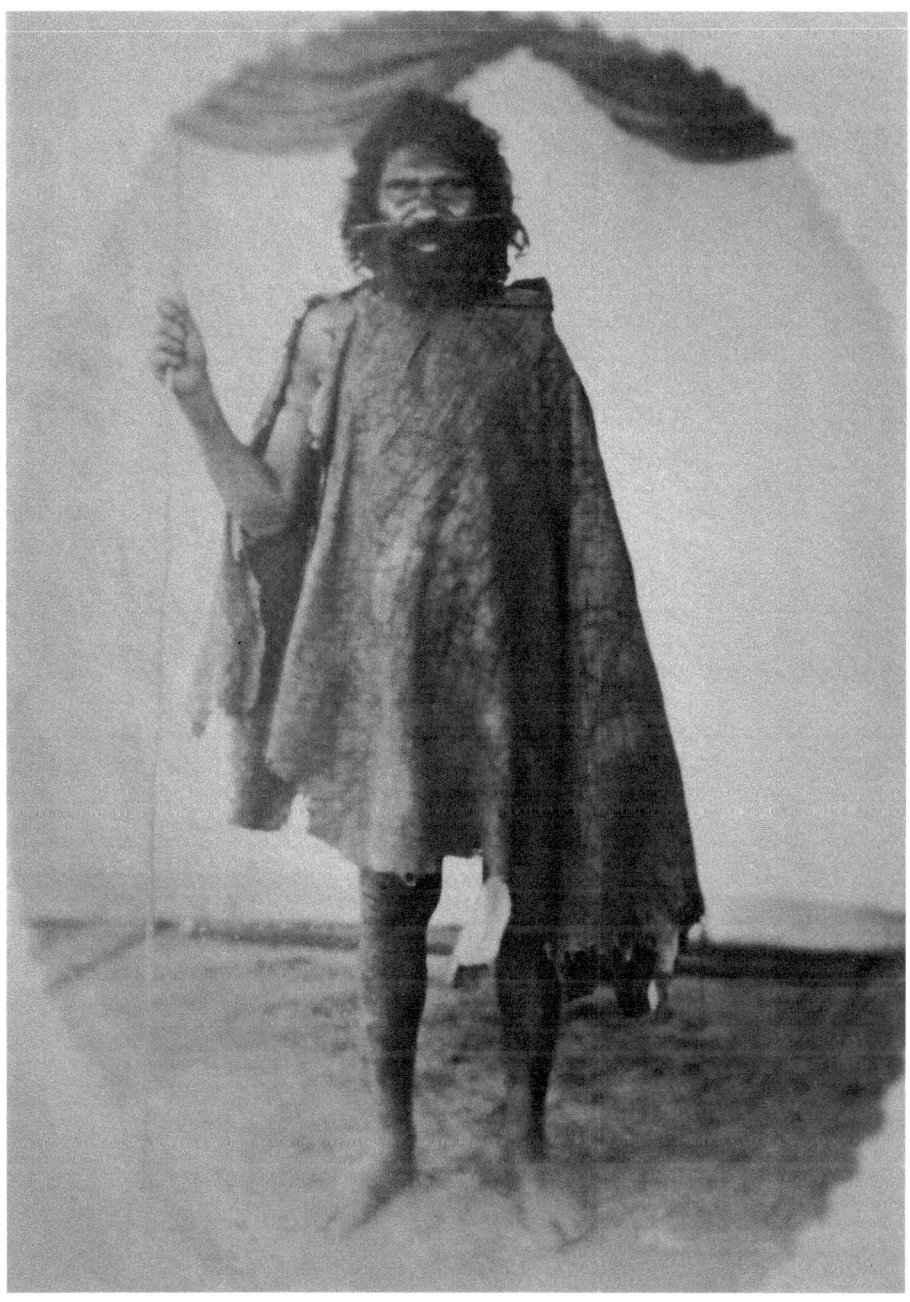

Figure 11 'Daak-in', Alfred Hawes Stone album. Reproduced from the private album of Dorothy Croft, Perth Western Australia, 2010.

Figure 12 Australian First Peoples. Reproduced from the private album of Dorothy Croft, Perth Western Australia, 2010.

Figure 13 Australian First Peoples. Reproduced from the private album of Dorothy Croft, Perth Western Australia, 2010.

CHAPTER 1: BESSY

Figure 14 Annesfield Native Institution, King George Sound, Western Australia, c.1850–60s. Collection: State Library Victoria.

Figure 15 Anne Camfield c.1860s © Alfred Hawes Stone. Collection: Battye Library, State Library of Western Australia.

Figure 16 Anne Camfield and Bessy Flowers c.1860s © Alfred Hawes Stone. Collection: Battye Library, State Library of Western Australia.

CHAPTER 1: BESSY

Figure 17 Annesfield Native Institution, King George Sound, Western Australia, c.1850–60s.
Collection: State Library Victoria.

Figure 18 Anna, Annesfield Native Institution, King George Sound, Western Australia, c. 1860s. Collection: State Library Victoria.

CHAPTER 1: BESSY

Figure 19 Avon River, East Gippsland, Victoria c.1900s. Collection: Strathfieldsaye Ramahyuck Album, University of Melbourne Archives.

Figure 20 Rev. Friedrich August Hagenauer and Christiana Louisa Hagenauer, c.1908 © Tom Humphrey. Collection: State Library Victoria.

CHAPTER 1: BESSY

Figure 21 Annesfield Native Institution women in Victoria, c.1860s–70s.
Collection: State Library Victoria.

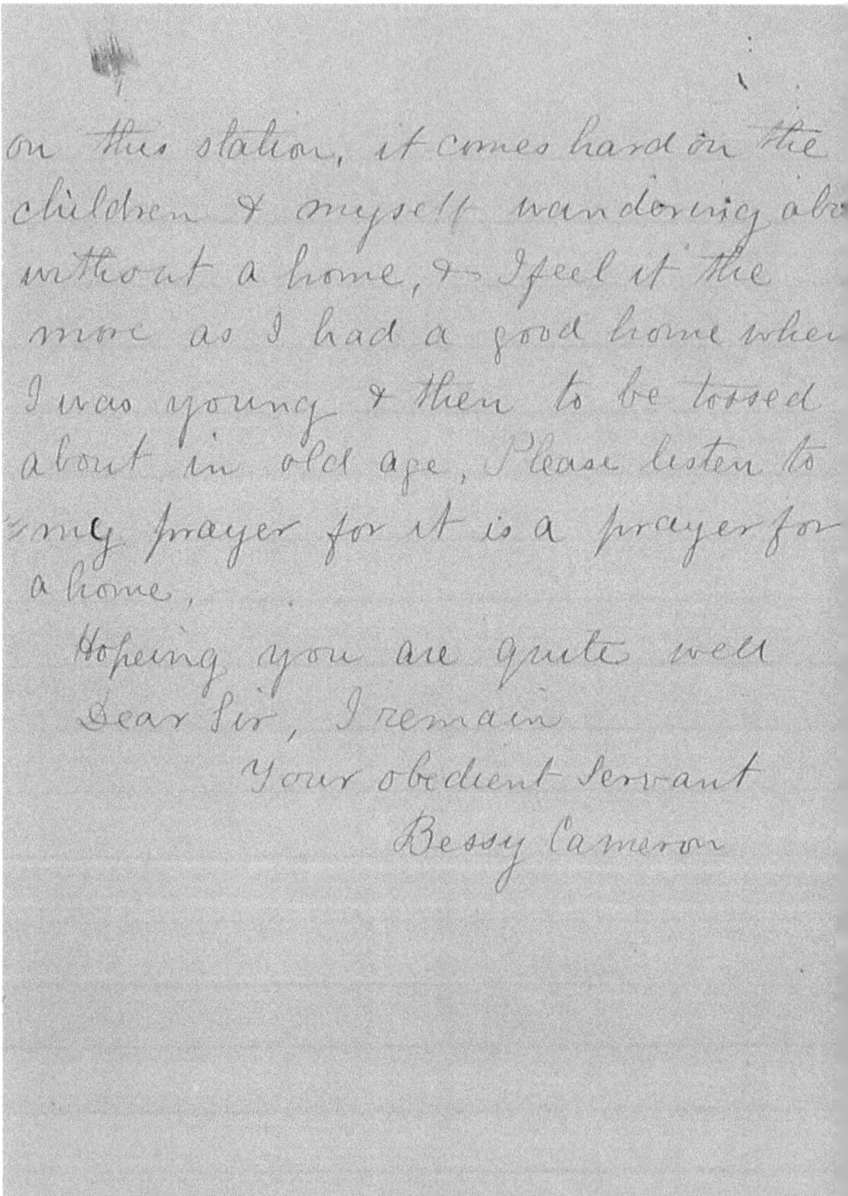

on this station, it comes hard on the children & myself wandering about without a home, & I feel it the more as I had a good home when I was young & then to be tossed about in old age. Please listen to my prayer for it is a prayer for a home.

Hopeing you are quite well Dear Sir, I remain
    Your obedient Servant
        Bessy Cameron

Figure 22 Bessy's letter to Captain Page, 1884. Collection: National Archives of Australia, Correspondence Files, Central Board for the Protection of Aborigines, B357 item 10, p. 8.

CHAPTER 1: BESSY

[8]

Lake Tyers
May 15th 1884

Captain Page
   Dear Sir

I hope you will be so kind as to listen to my petition, & allow us to live on the station. I have tried to living on our own earnings & it wont do. Donald has not been earning regular wages, & it takes all he earns to pay for our food, he said when he had paid what we owed he would go to Ramahyuck, but I wont go there, perhaps you might say why did we not stay at Ebenezer, but dear sir, I would rather have seen my little child in her coffin than in another fit, & if you were a father you would feel the same. I hope you will allow us to stay

Figure 23 Ramahyuck Aboriginal Mission, Lake Wellington, Victoria, c.1906 © Harry Beaumont. Collection: State Library Victoria.

CHAPTER 1: BESSY

Figure 24 Bessy and Donald Cameron c.1870s. Collection: Mitchell Library, State Library of New South Wales.

Figure 25 Annie Magdalene and Louisa Cameron c.1870s. Collection: Mitchell Library, State Library of New South Wales.

CHAPTER 1: BESSY

Figure 26 Ramahyuck Aboriginal Mission residents, East Gippsland, Victoria, c.1900s.
Collection: University of Melbourne Archives.

Figure 27 Mena Blanche Cameron (pictured left), Lydia Gilbert, Annie Harrison, Ramahyuck Aboriginal Mission, East Gippsland, Victoria, c.1900s. Collection: University of Melbourne Archives.

Chapter 2:
The Bryant family

When the Bryants first saw Bessy's 1860s portrait, they shared how any memory of her had been lost from family stories over the generations. The experience of seeing the photo, rediscovering her history and meeting Western Australian kin for the first time fostered a deepened sense of self and unity between the Bryant families.

The Bryants wished to celebrate and culturally commemorate Bessy's life through known shared bonds of family connectedness. They wanted to engage ways of recuperating and restoring a place for their ancestor within collective and meaningful stories of family and culture. Bessy's great-granddaughters and their families decided on the terms that would direct the return of their ancestor's memory to their personal stories of identity. This included the involvement and stewardship of other community knowledge holders and their families to generate understandings of past and present cultural affiliations with history.

Bessy's past existed in the archives and in records curated by notable historians, who wrote about Aboriginal histories and from these accounts compiled insightful biographical information. They were useful histories when having to trace different geographic locations and timelines pertinent to ancestors' lives. However, maintaining Bessy's story as one that was exclusive to a western and gendered historical narration proved to be limiting and largely out of context to the visceral landscape of living Bryant kin and their social interactions, expressions of endearment and acts of meaningful remembrance that provided important sustenance to the building of future legacies of memory and identity.

Understanding the circumstances of how an ancestral memory had been lost to the Bryant family story meant reintroducing a past captured through letters and historical photos. These first steps towards reinvigorating historically mislaid kinship knowledge brought to the forefront a contemporary story of identity culturally defined by the principled belief that one's ancestors are walking in front of family and kin, rather than behind oneself and trapped within the stillness of a distant past.

In August 2010 I met Phyllis Andy (née Bryant) in the regional town of Lakes Entrance, east of Melbourne and in the Gippsland region. The Thorpe family had passed on information about Bessy's living kin in the early 2000s during research exploring the history of their ancestor Nora White. This knowledge allowed the mapping of family networks that linked the Bryant family to Bessy through the lineage of her eldest daughter, Annie Magdalene (Maggie). The meeting with Phyllis was important for beginning a conversation about her relationship to Bessy's past from the perspective of a great-granddaughter. Undertaking research outside of an archive was about locating a time and space in which alternate family perceptions of Bessy might exist and also be shared.

It took many weeks of persistent phone calls before we spoke to one another. Phyllis's first response to the introductory call was layered with caution. Speaking through a filter of everyday busyness, there was hesitation about talking to an unknown person who was knowledgeable about the Bryant family. At the end of the conversation we agreed to meet in person and to continue talks about her great-grandmother, Bessy. Part of the meeting would involve a lunch that was being held for Koori Elders.

In the morning that followed, I made the three-hour drive from Melbourne to Lakes Entrance. I imagined hearing from Phyllis family stories about Bessy that

CHAPTER 1: BESSY

were handed down by her parents. The plan was to use Stone's photo of Bessy as an entry point to our meeting. When we met face-to-face there was limited time for introductions and for explanations about why I held a growing interest in the Bryant connection to Bessy. Feeling somewhat pressured to explain how I came to know about their ancestor, I used historical photos to map the research carried out so far and also to declare my interest in this Aboriginal history. On a table in her office, I laid out for Phyllis two different collections of photos. One collection included Stone's 1860s portrait of Bessy and the second collection comprised early 1950s photos of children who had been raised and schooled at the Lake Tyers Aboriginal Mission.

Intrigued, Phyllis examined Bessy's childhood portrait, but her attention was quickly drawn to the children pictured at Lake Tyers. It was these photos that stirred an immediate interest and action. Taking in hand some of the photos, Phyllis began looking at people and places representing a mission upbringing that was familiar to her. Phyllis had lived at the mission as a child, and it was a history that I came to know well from the stories that she would tell me and the memories shared over time by other senior Bryant family members.

The Lake Tyers photos offered a gateway into Phyllis's past of growing up on a mission. Her experience with the photos had the effect of returning me to the days of recording Koori stories when working at the Koorie Heritage Trust Cultural Centre (The Trust) as part of a family history service. I shared with Phyllis the story of taking back photos in the early 2000s to Ivy Marks-Tregonning, a Koori Elder woman who had now passed on. During the visit with Aunty Ivy, the same photos taken by Vera Bennett, a teacher at the mission school in the early 1950s, had been returned to her for the first time. Ivy's response was memorable and insightful to the energetic exchange that photos can elicit. Sitting down at her kitchen table at her Lake Tyers Trust home, she pointed to a girl pictured in one of the photos. She had screamed out loud with joy, declaring to all in the room that the girl who stood among the other schoolchildren from the mission was herself aged about 10 years.

With a different photo from this collection, Phyllis similarly identified by name a group of girls who appeared dressed for a birthday party and who wore upon their heads paper crowns that were individually decorated. The girls pictured were Phyllis's sisters Emma, Rita and Gladys. Phyllis explained that Emma and Gladys had passed away, but that her elder sister Rita was still alive and would be at the Elders' lunch. The Bryants, I quickly learnt, were a large family of 13 siblings in Phyllis's generation. Among the other photos from the Lake Tyers mission were other children known to Phyllis, including her brother Mickey Bryant.

Figure 28 Bessy's great-grandchildren: (3rd from left) Emma Bryant, (4th from left) Rita Bryant, (7th from left) Gladys Bryant, Lake Tyers Aboriginal Mission School, East Gippsland, Victoria, c.1949–51. Collection: Lakes Entrance Regional Historical Society.

This act of naming siblings inspired more reflections about the Bryant family. But time for elaborations and context was limited as the Elders' lunch required focused attention. During the drive that we shared to the lunch venue, I noted the photos had

CHAPTER 1: BESSY

Figure 29 Mickey Bryant (right, 3rd row from the front), Lake Tyers Aboriginal Mission School, East Gippsland, Victoria, c.1949–51. Collection: Lakes Entrance Regional Historical Society.

made an impact on Phyllis. She told me how some of the Elders attending the lunch might themselves be in the Lake Tyers school photos or, if not pictured, they might recognise and identify by name other people belonging to the mission families.

Upon entering the Elders' lunch at the Lakes Entrance RSL, I kept the photos out of sight in a bag, looking first for the familiar face of any Elder I had met in other visits. In a short time, I did see a face and the feeling of being an outsider to this lunch lifted. Though many years had passed since our last meeting, I recognised Uncle Billy Tregonning. When working at the The Trust, I had travelled to the Lake Tyers Trust – known locally as 'Tyers' – with a Koori colleague, Len Tregonning, and during the trip was introduced to his uncle and aunt – Billy and Ivy Marks-Tregonning. We had gone fishing together in the waters surrounding this place, and I could recall Billy and Len laughing heartily at me as the local pelicans came up very close, loudly expressing their curiosity.

With this memory in mind, I approached Billy and reintroduced myself. I then handed him an old black-and-white photo of Ivy as a girl. The photo evoked Billy's fondness of someone very dear to him who had since passed, but I also observed, from the stories that he shared on this day, a continuing deep sense of loss, grief and loneliness.

Billy asked that the photo be shared with Gale, Ivy's daughter. Gale was also at the lunch and, while she was looking at the photo, I told her about the first time that her mother viewed this same image, which had led to a story about Gale's birth. Ivy had told me about the stormy night in which she walked heavily pregnant to the midwife's home. She talked of the strong winds that had wrapped around her in the darkness, and why she then felt compelled to name her girl Gale. 'Gale, that's the name I gave the baby', she had said to me, laughing.

The same photos that Ivy had seen in the early 2000s now made their way around a room of Koori Elders. As they looked into the faces of mission schoolchildren, I asked if any of the children were familiar by sight and could be clearly named. During the lunch no names came forth, the photos being circulated while the Elders chatted among themselves, triggering personal memories rather than identifying information. It was insightful during the lunch to recognise how the practice of not remembering held an agency of its own, and required both social and emotional validation as would normally be given to experiences of remembering.

After the lunch, I sat with Billy on the entrance steps to the RSL. He talked about the six years that had gone by since Ivy's death and how many people had asked him to write up his life story. He laughed at such an idea, telling me of tragedies in his life, which caused emotional pain to linger as he aged. Billy's laughter in this moment was not in jest, but a testament to the depth of personal hardship. Belonging, he said, after reflecting on parts of his life, was the key to Koori survival. This statement led back to the photo of Ivy as a girl at the mission and to discussions about the complexities of identity. Billy told of Ivy's link to the northwest of Victoria, country belonging to the Wotjobaluk people, and how this connection had become contentious because of her childhood years spent at Lake Tyers. At The

CHAPTER 1: BESSY

Trust, it was usual for Koori families engaged with the political issues of Native Title to question or challenge the validity of another's claim to ancestral lands as defined by cultural terms.

Figure 30 Ivy Marks-Tregonning (back row, third from left), Lake Tyers Aboriginal Mission, c.1949–51 © Vera Bennett. Collection: Lakes Entrance Historical Society.

Figure 31 Rita Bryant (4th from left, standing), Lake Tyers Aboriginal Mission School, East Gippsland, Victoria, c.1949–51. Collection: Lakes Entrance Regional Historical Society.

Later, back in the car with Phyllis, I heard a similar story. Unfamiliar with the Bryants' ancestral connection to Gunai-Kurnai country, I listened attentively to a politics of Koori identity involving a personal story about belonging, and also of not belonging. Finding ways to comprehend Koori politics had been a significant part of my cultural education at The Trust. Based on these years of cultural instruction, I felt compelled to ask Phyllis if she was speaking about her experience of Native Title discussions that had taken place over the years in East Gippsland.[69] She responded to the question with laughter. Not because she considered Native Title to be a humorous topic, but rather that we were able to talk openly with one another in regard to non-Aboriginal people's political influence on Koori identity.

Over past decades, Native Title legislation has contributed largely to family disagreements about rights to ancestral country and has been the instigator for family division and fragmentation. Phyllis spoke about some of these scars created by the factions and frictions between Koori people who had grown up together as family on the mission, but who were divided by the processes of Native Title. It was this discussion that led her to talk about belonging, but also its counterpart experience of not belonging.[70]

It was evident from time spent with Phyllis that Bessy's connection to Western Australia's southwest was an important history and one that the Bryant families could engage with to enrich their cultural identity. The region of East Gippsland is not Bessy's ancestral country. Her marriage to Donald Cameron, a Wotjobaluk man from northwestern Victoria, meant that the Bryants were legally excluded from Native Title discussions on the country in which they were born, Gunai-Kurnai country.

I left Phyllis with a printed copy of Stone's portrait of Bessy and visited Vera Bennett at her home in Lakes Entrance. I hoped that, as the photographer of the Lake Tyers mission school photos, she might name some of the children, and perhaps help bridge gaps in memories with stories from her time as a mission teacher between the years 1949 and 1951. It turned out that she was able to confidently name some of the children, including the Bryants.

Exploring Bessy's past through the perspectives of her descendant family required making time to visit them at their homes. Two weeks after the first visit,

CHAPTER 1: BESSY

Figure 32 Vera Bennett (née Hanlon) playing the piano, Lake Tyers Aboriginal Mission School, East Gippsland, Victoria, c.1949–51. Collection: Lakes Entrance Regional Historical Society.

Figure 33 Drawings, Lake Tyers Aboriginal Mission School, East Gippsland, Victoria, c.1949–51. Collection: Lakes Entrance Regional Historical Society.

I returned to East Gippsland. It was early September and heavy rains were causing widespread floods. In the car, as I began the trip from Melbourne, I listened to a radio announcer painting a grim outlook for travel along the Princes Highway. Feeling somewhat concerned, I called Phyllis from the side of the road to figure out if continuing the hours-long trip was plausible. The river, she told me, was certainly high, but the road she believed was passable and from lived experience and local knowledge, it was unlikely to flood. Taking her advice, I kept on driving. The rain eased along the way and it was possible to view the river swelling though not yet spilling over its banks.

Phyllis was feeling unwell upon my arrival so, in the waiting room of the health clinic in which she worked, I sat with two younger Koori women, showing them the Lake Tyers photos to see if they could identify any of the people pictured and if they knew of anyone related to Bessy. For this trip, copies of the photos were displayed in two hardcover books. One book held the photo of Bessy as a child as well as the photo of Anne Camfield with Bessy and the second book held the 1950s Lake Tyers school photos. The young women, who were sisters, were curious about the photos representing their family history and they invited me to their family home in Lakes Entrance. At the family home I met with their mother and father who remembered many of the children and allowed names to be noted for the first time with the photos.

This particular collection demonstrated how photos from the past could be used as cultural objects helpful for piecing together family networks in relation to living descendants. Knowing more about the events and people portrayed in the photos was only a possibility through time taken to engage with families and family knowledge. It was evident that by activating memories about lived pasts, the people historically pictured developed a visibility within the social meaning engendered by family. In contrast, the archive preserved singular views of the past. In this respect, Bessy's history represented a chronological story and not a dynamic and adaptable story of kinship signifying the subsisting binds of responsibility that socially connect ancestors to the living.

The meeting with Phyllis helped emphasise why relinking Bessy's past with

CHAPTER 1: BESSY

Bryant family living history was important. Phyllis held no memory of her great-grandmother. In order to return Bessy to her family, there first needed to be acknowledgement of lost and absent memories. Back in the archives, I began the work of exploring the collections at Museums Victoria. It was here that I found photos of Phyllis with some of her siblings at the Lake Tyers mission. To know the Bryant family story would be to know something more about Bessy's history. With photos in hand as prompts, interviews were made with senior Bryant women at various times over the years. The process allowed for shared memories to be the conduit for socialising a space in which Bessy could be repositioned as one of the family, rather than captured in time as a historical figure.

***

The Lake Tyers Aboriginal Mission, situated about 130 kilometres from Ramahyuck, is a place that features in Bessy's story and, in contemporary times, continues to be the home of some of her descendants. One descendant with a relationship to this place is the late Betty Hood (née Bryant), who was the daughter of Margaret Bryant and William Johnson Lewis Hood. Betty grew up at the Lake Tyers mission and spent many of her childhood years in the care of her grandparents Keith and Esther Bryant, or Nan and Pop as she called them. Betty was the great-grandniece of Bessy. The stories told by Betty about living at the mission and at 'The Bluff' capture the spirit of the Bryant family. Speaking about her experiences growing up, Betty recalled the following memories while sitting at the kitchen table in her Bairnsdale home:

> I remember mostly my grandmother [Esther Bryant]. I knew her as my mother, not my mother because my grandmother was the one who grew me up.
>
> She grew me up as one of her children, and I used to go to school with my aunties. I classed them as sisters, Phyllis, Gina [Regina], Julia and Roma. I went to school with all of them and their brothers, and all I can

remember is having a good time with all of them and being with their big family. I can't remember anything about me mother looking after me, just that I was with the Bryants.

I can remember the day that Grandmother, Nan Bryant, said, 'Margaret's your mother,' and I said, 'No she's not, you're my mother,' and it took me oh, about 13 or 14 years to call my mother 'Mum' – 'Mmmmmum' and [they would say] 'Oh Betty's found her mother!' 'Shut up,' [I'd say] and I used to get a stick and run after them and hit them…I would say, 'Nan, they're teasing me.' She used to take me for a long walk, with a chaff bag in the search for basket grass.

I went to school at the mission. I remember we used to get soap and scrub it on the grass and skate, and we would go to school and line up and get our numbers to our towels and all march down to the bathroom – pile in there, all the girls in one room and all the boys in the other part, have our bath, and then we'd be the cleanest kids out there.

The day that I was at school I couldn't wait for our cocoa and jam, bread and jam. That was lovely.

When it came to time for our medication, fish oil – that was a no-no for us kids. Tasted horrible. Yes, that's what I remember, and I remember climbing pine trees in the schoolyard and climbing up that way and sitting up there watching the trawlers on the water and that was our little excitement, and when they'd say, 'Know where the kids are?' it would be 'They're up the tree there.'

We had like a stairway going up there, so no one could go near us. But they used to tell us to come down and when we came down they'd give us a cheeky slap. They was looking for us, Uncle Mickey Bryant and the others, because we had to get home, get home and take the billycans to the dairy, hang 'em up for our milk.

CHAPTER 1: BESSY

They made butter out there [at the dairy] and Grandma [Nan Bryant] used to boil the milk and take the cream off and thicken it up. That used to be for our jam, for our jam and scones. No such thing as buying it [the cream] in bottles, nah, just scooped it all off the top and fixed it up, and that was for our cream and scones we had.

I couldn't wait to go to school, I used to love going to school. They used to make us clean up all the time, and we used to do the chores. But we loved our little games and going out, like rabbiting and catching up with the other kids, our relo's [relations], and playing up in the pine trees, and playing in the swamp.

School was good, but I didn't know much.

[The road to Lake Tyers] was all just wriggly roads in my days, wriggly roads and corners, and just a bit of a hump and cross the creek, nothing else, just a track, just a really windy old road and you never thought you'd get out of there, just corners and corners and 'Are we just in the same corner? Haven't we come past the corner, no.' There's no such thing as a straight road. It's all just gravel, nothing.

I felt we were a long way away [from the towns of Lakes Entrance and Bairnsdale], but we had no choice. We had to stay where we were. The only thing that kept us going was heading down to the jetty, swimming and mussellin' and waving to tourists. We didn't even worry about our parents going into town, because it wasn't our part to go into town. We had to stay at home. Our parents had no cars.

We were in our own world. There was just one thing, the old truck, 'cause we used to walk all the way you know up the road to get a ride in [to Lakes Entrance], so we could have some excitement. A big mob of us, just us Lake Tyers kids, we would go, walk out to the road and catch him, get in, and all sit on the back screaming around, that was our entertainment.

NO LONGER A WANDERING SPIRIT

I can't remember if there was a gate [at the front of the mission], but years before that, they used to padlock the gate. I'm just trying to think what we used to do, we always chucked cloth [over the barbed wire fence]…they used to padlock the gate, you had to ring up, so they had to come up to the gate and let you in, that's all I can remember. [They padlocked the gate because] they didn't want outsiders in, white fellas I'm talking about. I'm just trying to think how they used to ring up out there, I can't remember, but I know the gate was locked.

[I don't remember tourist buses coming in], no not the buses. The only tourists I remember would come to the mission on the lake. They used to chuck money in the water. There was a nice old shed and we used to just dive in, eyes open and grab our money, pennies. We would get a good amount of money.

Yeah, [the Lake Tyers Church], we used to go up to the point and meet the old minister, Mr Henry. There used to be a little mob of us that would go and meet him and carry his suitcase 'cause we knew our tickets was in the suitcase, our little tickets. We'd get tickets for being good, little bible tickets. We used to walk along with him, one carried the suitcase along the way, 'Oh I've got a "sisal" over here', grab it and cut it, strip it, and then we eat the nut inside it.

Yeah, we walked and walked until he got to the Sunday School and all our names were down on the books, and we'd follow him for all hours, around to every house, he'd go visit every house. It was a good Sunday school. I loved it.

[Sitting in a church as a little girl] felt like home. We had someone there to talk to us, telling us about God and angels. I don't remember believing it, but it was lovely to sit there with all the other kids. We were good behaving kids. We was good kids. Then when he finished he'd visit every house and he'd go home in the dark, and I don't know,

CHAPTER 1: BESSY

we used to walk him back up to the point, me and my sister, and he'd row a boat across the other side.

That was just the good old days, I like running down there and walking home with him and walking him back. We didn't have much fishing in those days, grownups, that was their job. We just did prawning, swimming and musselling.

[…]

[Our home on the mission] was nice, comfortable. I'm trying to think where Mum and Dad had their place. I've got a map of everybody houses, where the houses were and everyone living in them. I have to get all these things together. Nan and Pop's house, I don't know how we slept in there. I can remember a room Nan used to have me, and me and all the other girls, her daughters, in a room, in a two-bedroom place. I was living with all the Bryants in a house, I didn't stay with Mum and Dad because Nanny wouldn't let me stay with Mum and Dad…Mum couldn't look after us I suppose. She was too young.

We left [Lake Tyers mission] when Pop started building at The Bluff. He started building when they gave him the okay for the wood and stuff for him to build a house for all his sons and daughters. We used to live down at The Bluff and we used to live in the bush, and then the timbers started coming through, and that's when Pop designed and built his own house.

We used to go in the bush and make our own tracks. We'd go and find our food and have a good drink of creek water, and then go home with a bellyache.

Yeah…I liked the mission. When we moved and I had to go to a white school, we had to behave ourselves in different ways. But we all got on, and we managed.

[I felt at home on the mission] but there was a lot of fighting sometimes amongst the grownups…We had our freedom…But we had to be in bed by a certain time and we all stuck together and played together, all the boys and girls with no arguing, and we used to race each other home, and up to the billycans to the cows to get our milk. Early in the morning, we used to get up early and go and get milk without spilling it…

You know we had a lot of freedom out there. I used to like when it was the girls' turn to have their bath, and the boys went to get some wood, no bathtubs just those 44-gallon drums, and they'd make a fire around that [the 44-gallon drum] and fill it with water. They used to have those old things, you put water in, and drag it along with an old dray, and they'd go house-to-house wash for the kids and bath. An old dray and an old big drum to fill up the tanks.

I wish I could go back there [Lake Tyers Aboriginal Mission]. I had good days out there. We had our freedom.[71]

Figure 34 Betty Hood, 2011

CHAPTER 1: BESSY

***

The older members of the Bryant family are the last generation to grow up on a mission. Their perspectives about daily mission life helped them understand Bessy's experience of mission living. Betty's sense of freedom stemmed from a child's perspective, but for adults trying to secure wages and raise healthy children, the reality was very different. There was dealing with the locked gate and also the barbed wire fence, as well as general frustrations.

On 15 May 1884, Bessy wrote a letter to Captain Andrew Page about her own desire for freedom. She had been living in East Gippsland for nearly 17 years under the authority of the Board for the Protection of Aborigines, of which Captain Page was the general inspector and secretary between the years 1877 and 1890. Life had been difficult for Bessy and Donald and their family, and in the letter, Bessy speaks of both financial hardship and the need for a home. She reflects upon Annesfield and the safety that she felt living there, comparing this sense of security to a life in which her family was forced to move from one mission to the next. She wrote how this transient life was hard on her and the children and how the outcome was one of wandering and without a place to call home:

> Dear Sir,
>
> I hope you will be so kind as to listen to my petition & allow us to live on the station. I have tried living on our own earnings and it won't do. Donald has not been earning regular wages & it takes all he earns to pay for our food, he said when he had paid what we owed he would go to Ramahyuck, but I won't go there, perhaps you might say why did we not stay at Ebenezer, but dear Sir, I would rather have seen my child in her coffin than in another fit & if you were a father you would feel the same. I hope you will allow us to stay on this station, it comes hard on the children & myself wandering about without a home & I feel it the more because I had a good home when I was young & then to be

> tossed about in old age. Please listen to my prayer for it is a prayer for a home.
>
> Hoping you are quite well,
>
> Dear Sir, I remain your obedient servant
>
> Bessy Cameron[72]

While Phyllis also held fond memories of growing up at Lake Tyers, she often spoke about what it meant for her to belong and, on the flipside of this feeling, to not belong. This was because the administering body of Native Title through its power of determining who holds Native Title rights according to the legislation had excluded the Bryant family from Gunai-Kurnai negotiations. Bessy's children were born in East Gippsland, including Annie Magdalene, her eldest daughter, who was the mother of Keith (Pop) Bryant and therefore Phyllis's grandmother. Despite this connection spanning more than 100 years, Native Title legislation determined that the Bryants could hold rights only over country that was derived from the birthplaces of their known ancestors, Bessy and Donald. Bessy being a Minang woman from the southwest of Western Australia and her husband, Donald Cameron, a Wotjobaluk man from northwest Victoria, their descendant families were rejected as Native Title holders to Gunai-Kurnai country. Under the legislation, traditional connection to land is an issue of kinship.

This lack of recognition by western law of Koori connection to the lands on which one was born politicised Bryant family identity. It contributed to experiences that challenged western legitimacies of not belonging. To be Koori is to know the family one is born into, and to know the origin of country deep-rooted with ancestral spiritual legacies. Who you are and where you come from rests within the social structures of community living, whereby loyalties, values, beliefs and kinship responsibilities are culturally transmitted and carried forth between the generations.

Phyllis's practice of connecting to Bessy's history was through a personal story that mediated concepts of belonging and of not belonging that were real to her. She explained why this was the case in context to the movement of her ancestor between two different places revealing that, 'We were born in country, so therefore we've created some history…and so when I think of great-grandma, I think of my own life'.[73] Phyllis shared what it meant to be culturally connected to country and why it was important to carry forward in story and in daily life a sense of belonging within the Bryant family. These are some of her reflections recorded at her home and which speak to feelings of belonging and the need to know where your ancestors are buried. Phyllis:

Figure 35 Phyllis Andy, 2013

[It's] being on that ground, the same ground she [Bessy] was on and that she walked on. The ground always connects us, or the dirt, or whatever it is you know it as. It's just being there and knowing she was there. I think I would get a feeling of why she was there [at Ramahyuck]. She went there into the unknown [mission], and it [her future] was an untold thing.

She achieved so much in being there [at Ramahyuck] and I think for us to be there and to experience this historical place is important. I know it'll be difficult because it's deemed now as private property, but the cemetery's there, and you're allowed to access the cemetery.

Being over there [in Western Australia] would give us a real feeling of belonging. I know we don't belong to this country [in East Gippsland], but feeling she was there, and we too are there would be significant to my identity. I think it's all about connecting and experiencing that connection in real time…feeling where we belong, and knowing that she [Bessy] was from there.

Never have [I felt I belong to this country]. People make you feel welcome as an Elder, but the Native Title legislation has really messed things up. But I'm glad it has, because it forces you to ask yourself: where do you belong?

My strong ties are really heading back to my Mum's country into the Wimmera [Wotjobaluk country]. I feel, 'Well you lot, if we're born in country, I think I should go and be buried in my Mum's country', but even though she's here in Lakes [Entrance]. That's how I sort of feel, but I don't think my kids would do that because I've already got my plot here.

I do [feel] a strong connection to the Wimmera, more than anywhere. As I keep saying to people, we know we don't belong [in East Gippsland], so therefore I don't fancy being laid to rest in a foreign country. But whether that will happen or not is up to the kids. They'll probably see it fitting that I go down [am buried] with their dad and I've already bought the plot, but never mind, we'll see [laughs].

Oh, [Bessy] would have had the same kind of feeling that I got [about

CHAPTER 1: BESSY

being buried in East Gippsland when her ancestral country was in Western Australia]. I feel she was more welcomed in this country than I, in a way. But [then] there was none of that Native Title that challenged who belonged where and to what country. Before Native Title everybody just belonged in Australia and then suddenly these little maps of who you belong to and where dampened that. I think she might have wanted to be buried back in her country, but nobody would have thought about it in that time.

Your home is where the heart is, so her [Bessy's] heart belongs to Western Australia, [my] heart belongs to the Wimmera…My connections keep drawing back to the Wimmera…it's [my] Mum's country and [I] feel really at home there. When I've gone there for funerals, it's a real quiet, relaxing atmosphere. I get a sense of belonging and I'm proud to be on my mother's ground, her homeland.

When Margaret [Phyllis's sister] was with us she'd tell us stories about what she did up there [in the Wimmera] as a kid. But East Gippsland here, well The Bluff is our home, and this is where we belong. I don't know whether it's a sense of belonging that I feel, but it's a home, and this is where we'll stay because it's…what we've made home and… [where we've] reared our children, in this country. Even Donald [Bessy's husband] was from that country [the Wimmera] too. [It's] very interesting…But he came this way…[to Ramahyuck in East Gippsland].

[The Wimmera] it's, what do you call it? I don't know if the word is 'desolate' or not, but it's beautiful! I think it's the tranquil feeling I get from this place. Although it's a hot climate [laughs], it's just funny, or uncanny why I feel that way towards this place.

I can't explain it, I don't know [it's more than just Native Title]. Maybe it's the passion about Mum and how strong a woman she was. Everything she did was for her children and never for herself and she was such a strong woman, as all mums are, but you just feel her power and maybe my sense of feeling sorry for her because she left, left her country. She probably found East Gippsland a better place to bring her children up, which is why we're the way we are. And maybe Dimboola [a town in the Wimmera] wasn't a good place to rear up children, I don't know.

[Our memories are often tied up in a place.] I just wish I had the privilege Margaret had to be roaming that country. She never thought about it in depth, but the stories she would tell us were just magic.

[That was my] eldest sister Margaret, she was born at Lake Tyers [mission], but then went back up that way to live. She said Grandfather would take her out onto the salt lakes and camp…She said they lived there for weeks on end, just Grandfather and her, and the brother, and she just adored it. And then they'd bring the billycan back filled with salt and that was their supplies for whatever time they needed, until they went back again [laughs]…Those memories are just magic. Then there'd be camps somewhere there by the river, you know, and they had a house but he [my father] would never stay in that house. He would be in a makeshift hut by the river, just carefree and free.

Because when you're in places like this [a modern house in Tyers] you feel so closed up and it gives you nothing. I know when we were up here [as children with our parents] we had a beautiful home, but we'd still go and find a spot out in the bush to sleep because it was just out in the stars, under the little stars and, yeah, nothing to close you in except the warmth of the fire. It was beautiful times. Those things you can't do that nowadays [when busy with grandparent responsibilities]. You can't go up into the bush and sit quietly or make a fire…just sit there and get the warmth and the glow from the fire. It's a feeling that gives me security and cleanses my mind so that I can go forward into

CHAPTER 1: BESSY

Figure 36 Joe Bryant with sister Julia, c.1958–60s © Bryant family.

the next day's challenges, or to meet the next year's challenges. The warmth and the glow of the fire can do that all for me [give the sense that you are connected to a place], and not being enclosed or…feel I'm all closed in…

NO LONGER A WANDERING SPIRIT

CHAPTER 1: BESSY

Figure 37 The Bryant family, c.1960s. Collection: Bryant family.

NO LONGER A WANDERING SPIRIT

The history about Bessy is powerful – what she did within colonial settler society and how she shaped herself into a leader in our community is inspiring. I can relate to this history [in terms of] how she wanted to be received in the world. She was passionate about helping and supporting her community such as her teaching and learning and giving people an education. I feel like some of that has rubbed off on me. My passion for helping people has come from her.

My kids get cross when I'm working way past the times that they think I should. They think I'm a nine-to-five person but really I'm not when communities are in [need] of my assistance. I give regardless of the time…So, what she did back then with that boarding school and the educational side of it, I feel there's a big part of me there too. What she did is in a similar context to what I am now doing today. She was part of the church, so I'm part of the church, and it's a big part of the church I'm part of [as an Anglican minister] and you just feel that a lot of the good she did is instilled in me, and the rest of the family too.

I know that I'd give heart and soul, if someone were in need, so it's all of that, you know, giving. She's really left a legacy and there's a generational hand-me-down that I feel. I've always been out there helping people and I feel like that was the same thing she did. She… taught them to be the best person one could be and people saw the good in that. White people all saw the good in that, because they supported her and encouraged her along the way. We share many interests in our chosen work I've found, which is scary [laughs] [because of her distant past] but beautiful as well. It's just a natural thing, and it's good that I can accept that feeling from her and therefore connect back to her history and what she did at Ramahyuck for the Ramahyuck people.

I can understand the passion that she had for people in general and missions are small, you know, and your work is often spread far and

CHAPTER 1: BESSY

wide. Our communities are huge. But I manage to reach out to those people to support them in whatever they endeavour to do or what their requirements are…

I'm a community development worker. It's a big jargon, but it just means helping local Koori people. And I'm also an Anglican minister. The two jobs are similar, in every context of the word, because I'm forever engaging and helping others. There's no difference between the two roles except that you get paid differently from one organisation to the other…It's all about people, helping and supporting, and even if it is six o'clock on a Friday afternoon, or if you want to get home you can't turn your back on them.

And whether that's in my priestly realm or in my work as a development worker, I cannot close myself off to people, because why am I there in that role? Why do I carry that name? So I need to be there for the people. When I was sick, I was out for two months…and I only went back to my job yesterday with the Elders and it was like, 'It's so great to have you back!' and I walked into the office of another department and they said, 'Geez it's good to have you back.' So I got all these hugs and they said, 'When you weren't here nobody was engaging.' Yesterday [at the Elders lunch], there were a lot of stories and lots of laughter. There was fun and there was happiness…

Lots of laughter – there was this one fellow, Uncle Billy Tregonning. He took me back a bit [into the past] because he started to talk about us as kids, growing up at The Bluff, and what he and the brother did at The Bluff. He said, 'I'd like to have a feed of possum. I'd love to have a feed of possum.' I kept thinking that he was telling me all of this because our connection was part of his being at The Bluff and engaging with me brother, and of course us girls who would go there to annoy them.

NO LONGER A WANDERING SPIRIT

All those times, swimming in the lake and coming across to The Bluff was about staying days being part of the family group. The missions were always locked and closed places. You couldn't have your freedom. We were really lucky to have that sort of freedom at The Bluff. With [Uncle Billy] talking about it yesterday I was thinking, 'Why was he talking of it?' But maybe it was because he hadn't seen me around for some time and he had a very sad loss...had lost three important people, his ex-partner, his stepdaughter and then his sister, all in a couple of months. So that emotion might have been coming out, and he didn't really have anybody to sit down with and talk to. So he decided to talk to me about it...I sat and talked with him and it was just so beautiful to hear those stories come back...

He [Uncle Billy] talked about when he was a kid and what he did at The Bluff. We used to have a lot of guys come to The Bluff. My brother would go out and bring them in. He'd go down to Morwell alone, come back with all these boys. Because he'd be telling them stories about what The Bluff was about, so they wanted to come and experience it. And it was so good to have all of these boys come along. We had boys in the family, brothers, but they [other boys from other areas] became the extended brothers in the family. And then the girls were the same. They heard so much about what we did up here, they wanted to come and be part of that freedom. Because towns were always closed-up spaces and the mission was closed. They wanted the freedom that we were experiencing at The Bluff.

That key word is just being together. They were all connected family members, so I couldn't have a relationship with them. But I don't think they were looking for a relationship, they were just looking for brotherly and sisterly love...that's the atmosphere The Bluff created for us.

CHAPTER 1: BESSY

[We] went to school and did the normal things, our chores, our weekend work, but there was time to have fun. We [siblings] made that time to have fun, so walking the lakes to go to the carnival, or to go and see what was happening in Lakes [Entrance]. You know, buy a hamburger and a bottle of soft drink and then walk back home. We didn't look for cars, we walked as a group and we got home quicker because half of us would be running along, playing games and chasing or playing catch-up games and that meant running and we were fit kids too...

We lived on the mission [Lake Tyers] in about the fifties. I was born in Orbost in 1951 and seven, or maybe five, of us went back to Lake Tyers. It was something decided upon through the Protection Board [Board for the Protection of Aborigines]. You go back there, or you lose your kids – that sort of scenario. So we'd gone back and then there was this assimilation thing that came in and if you weren't that black-skinned person then away you went. And I'm talking black, black and not this colour – not my colour black known to be half-caste or quarter-caste.

We ended up on a farm and living there for some time and then we moved from that farm down to The Bluff in a humpy. We had no running water. It was a bark humpy made with bags for the door and bags for the window to keep the cold out and a beautiful fireplace.

You just took things as they came and, yeah, sleeping on the dirt. You were carefree and happy and had your freedom. We left running water, electricity and all sorts of stuff at Lake Tyers. As you can see in the papers the Protection Board gave Dad some timber to bring back over here to build and he built it, The Bluff, a two-bedroom place.[74]

....

***

The introduction of Stone's portrait of Bessy to Phyllis and other members of the Bryant family began to shift personal and family feelings about belonging and not belonging. The historical photo worked to place Bessy within a colonial past. It also evidenced sovereign Minang connections. How one's sense of belonging might be culturally extended became integral to the Bryants' reclamation of Bessy's memory and the creation of a newly made narrative that recognised personal Bryant histories. Phyllis's recurring reflections provided insight over time to family issues of belonging and of not belonging. She also reaffirmed the value of returning to family heritage photos:

> I feel strong about where we belong when I hear about Bessy. Though we were born in country, we don't belong, because this is not our country, it's Gunai-Kurnai country.
>
> Bessy's life and what she has done here in East Gippsland has made us feel part of this land. Her story has connected us to one way of culture, and a life that respects where we come from as Koori families and people. I think about this when I look at the photo of my great-grandmother.
>
> The picture saddens me because she was sent away from her home at a young age. I feel she looks lonely, though her composure speaks of a power that she would have been given through her education and the Christian ways of her lifestyle.
>
> Bessy was a determined young girl and she was courageous to have travelled into what was for her a foreign country. But her willingness and obedience made this journey in her life possible.
>
> Obedience, because we had to be obedient to all of the white people, they were our teachers and they were the ones that we weren't allowed to disobey because of the government policies in place. They were the ones that were going to teach us our future, which was to become her future.

CHAPTER 1: BESSY

> In her letters Bessy has signed them, 'Your obedient servant'. I have greatly admired the way in which Bessy showed the potential to learn and to become a leader. They are qualities I feel inside of me.
>
> We were a lost people, but now we can connect both to our great-grandfather's country, the country of the Wotjobaluk people, and our great-grandmother's country, the country of the Minang Noongar people.
>
> We've finally found where we belong through Bessy's tribal country and it is important to feel that and for me to connect to this sense of belonging. I know where I am connected, and it feels nice to know that one day I may stand on that ground she was from, with a feeling of welcoming and belonging.
>
> Because that's the most important bit for me, where we all belong. I think visiting her country will give me a blessed inner feeling, to go back to country to find out what that's all about and to learn about her childhood. I've always wondered about what tribe she was from and now Minang connects us all to her, as her descendants.
>
> I can proudly now call myself a Wotjobaluk and Minang woman.[75]

Despite the emotional challenges of a lost ancestral story, the Bryant family continued to explore, imagine and assert with courage a space for themselves within the historical records of colonial governments, churches and welfare authorities. How the Bryant family chose to enact identity with cultural meaning provided context to the ways in which histories might be thought about, revitalised and creatively shared.[76] Extending upon the experience of cultural heritage reconnection to the unification of two families led to a first meeting with members of the Flowers family in Western Australia.

Figure 38 Children at the Lake Tyers Aboriginal Mission School, East Gippsland, Victoria, c.1949–51. Collection: Lakes Entrance Regional Historical Society.

Figure 39 Pine trees, Lake Tyers Aboriginal Mission, East Gippsland, Victoria, c.1949–51. Collection: Lakes Entrance Regional Historical Society.

CHAPTER 1: BESSY

Figure 40 Bryant family, Lake Tyers Aboriginal Mission, East Gippsland, Victoria, c.1949–51. Collection: Museum Victoria.

Figure 41 Bryant family and other children, Lake Tyers Aboriginal Mission, East Gippsland, Victoria, c.1949–51. Collection: Museum Victoria.

Figure 42 Entrance to the Lake Tyers Aboriginal Mission, East Gippsland, Victoria, c.1949–51. Collection: Lakes Entrance Regional Historical Society.

CHAPTER 1: BESSY

Figure 43 Lake Tyers Aboriginal Mission, East Gippsland, Victoria, c.1949–51. Collection: Lakes Entrance Regional Historical Society.

Figure 44 Congregation, Lake Tyers Aboriginal Mission Church, East Gippsland, Victoria, c.1949–51. Collection: Museum Victoria.

Figure 45 Lake Tyers Aboriginal Mission Church, East Gippsland, Victoria, c.1949–51.
Collection: Lakes Entrance Regional Historical Society.

Chapter 3:
The Flowers family

In September 2010, the search for Bessy's living relations in Western Australia began. To help locate family networks, first contact was made with the Albany regional office of the Department of Indigenous Affairs. It was here that I spoke with Robert Reynolds, who at the time was the senior regional heritage officer and knowledgeable about local Noongar cultural sites, histories and local family groups. Robert helped with introductions to Noongar Elders and senior family spokespeople connected to the Great Southern region.

The house that had once been Bessy's childhood home with the Camfields was a destination of interest after the five-hour drive from Perth to Albany. Robert had emailed instructions on how to get there and the historical photo of Annesfield acted as a visual aid. Attempts to match the original building pictured in the photo with the contemporary homes on Serpentine Road proved to be more difficult than first thought. Many of the houses in the area displayed heritage and period features but were disguised by contemporary renovations. The Annesfield photo depicts an old stone home set among dry grass with large boulders resting nearby. There are a group of children and several adults standing near the building bordered by a neat picket fence.

Unable to find the house, Robert and his wife Vickie answered my call and in their car led the way to the house. I remember thinking that there was nothing remarkable about Annesfield in a first viewing. The building appeared very similar in character to other houses lining the street and seemed to blend into the modernised town designs. Wanting a closer view of the house I walked down a side street that led to the rear of the building and to the open spaces of a garden. Old pine trees stood tall and straight in a line across the grass, and bushes of white daisies were in flower near the veranda. On closer inspection, it was possible to see more clearly the resembling features between Annesfield in the historical photo and the now heritage-listed building.

In the historical photos, Annesfield is depicted as two joined buildings. The main building has four small windows and the adjoining building a second floor with an outlook through a small window to the garden. Though some refurbished parts of the building when compared to the photo were no longer recognisable, I was filled with curiosity to go inside and asked Robert at our next meeting if this would be a possibility. He agreed it would be worthwhile and took on the task of locating Annesfield's current owner for permission. It was discovered that Annesfield was owned by a retired farmer and, though heritage listed, it was for sale.

In a book Robert lent to me titled *Old Albany: Photographs 1850–1950*,[77] Noongar people were represented through historical photos as fringe dwellers. Not given a place within the British colony, they appeared as misfits and disassociated from the emerging colonial society. At Annesfield, Bessy was largely separated from a cultural way of life and, instead, she was immersed within colonial ideals that were attached to the value of education and the capacity to work hard. What was her relationship to Minang traditional culture? How might a child living away from her biological family and community kin negotiate the reality of a settler home?

In the archive it details that Bessy's mother played a role as a domestic servant in Annesfield's daily operations. What might the experience have been to witness a daughter and the other children being raised by Anne Camfield? Such questions fostered other thought-provoking inquiries that engaged the emotional

CHAPTER 3: THE FLOWERS FAMILY

toll of colonial influence upon cultural beliefs and values. History was limiting, particularly when taking into consideration how emotions that could generate deeper understandings and awareness of past events were generally not retrievable from the colonial record.

Exploring inside Annesfield and bearing witness to the place where Bessy had spent a large portion of her childhood was about imagining answers to questions through personal experiences of identity. It would be an opportunity for her descendants and kin to activate a set of perspectives that provided a different context from which Bessy could be remembered and culturally expressed.

Bessy mediated with skill different constructs of everyday settler social life and mission living. Her Minang family connections had been almost entirely lost to her, and when she was moved to eastern Victoria her life was constrained and economically stunted by the imposition of mission rules and regulations. At Ramahyuck her letters clearly demonstrated that she was challenged by decisions made by Rev. Hagenauer, his authority often placing her within the restrictive parameters of mission life. This paternalistic guardianship failed to acknowledge her ability to reside successfully in both an Aboriginal world and a colonial settler society.

On a return visit to Annesfield, the old clothesline out the back was being spun around by the wind and the surrounding streets were quiet. I walked once again through the old pine trees standing tall in the garden. There was no fence that marked the boundary of the yard but a single wooden gate oddly presented the property perimeter. The back garden was similar to a park with its open space of undulating green grass. Looking with greater attention at the house that was once Annesfield, the newer additions became more obvious. It was not difficult to imagine a time when Bessy was within the rooms of this place and playing the piano or reading a book, as she loved to do. Nor was it a strain to visualise on the outside Bessy playing with the other children at Annesfield. The reality of being away from family and in the care of people like the Camfields would become an experience that Bessy's living descendant families and kin would relate to when they reflected on her past and sought to understand all that had taken place.

In Albany for research, I was invited by Robert to attend a series of Noongar family history workshops and used this experience to share information about searching beyond the archive for Bessy's story. The first workshop was at a local cultural Keeping Place. Present was a group of women Elders and senior family spokespeople. The Welcome to Country was expressed through stories that engaged the natural elements of water and air. Significant to the telling of one story was the movement of mist arising from the ocean and across the lands, the mist described as being the tears of ancestors.

Figure 46 Mist, Albany, Western Australia, 2010

Following the Welcome to Country, a colleague of Robert's from the Perth office spoke to the group about archival records relating to local family histories. He was part of a dedicated family history unit and explained the privacy laws that regulated access to records, particularly the sensitive information collected by child welfare agencies.

The access to individual and family records, particularly for the Stolen Generations, was familiar territory to me from my work at the Koorie Family History

CHAPTER 3: THE FLOWERS FAMILY

Service at The Trust. I listened intently to those present expressing to the speaker the need for Noongar families to access their own records as well as those records about their ancestors. The records in both state and national archives continue to play an integral role in linking historical material culture with living practices of heritage culture.

With an interest in learning from the Elders present if Bessy existed within their stories, the portrait of her taken by Stone in the early 1860s was projected on a large screen for everyone to view. Enlarging the historical photo in this way energised the group and they responded enthusiastically to other photos of Annesfield featuring Bessy as a girl when in the care of the Camfields, together with the photos of Bessy with her husband, Donald Cameron, and the photos of her two children, Annie Magdalene and Louisa, which were taken at the same time as Bessy and Donald's photo.

As these historical photos were projected, I spoke to the images with extracts from Bessy's letters that she had written to Anne Camfield, Rev. Hagenauer and members of the Victorian Board for the Protection of Aborigines. The letter readings allowed Bessy's historical voice to enliven the photos, illuminating aspects of her life. As she wrote about such key events, Bessy's personal tone often revealed her feelings about particular experiences. An example of this was her enthusiasm when en route to Ramahyuck and the early years spent living at the mission. It was an eagerness for adventure that diminished within a short period of time at the mission, when her life became one of struggling for survival. Bessy's concern for her family, and the pressures of providing food and shelter for her children, struck an emotional chord with the women Elders at the workshop. It inspired them to tell their own stories about mission life and to reveal their personal efforts to raise their children under trying circumstances and financial duress.

In a conversation that followed the photo screening, one of the women Elders referred to Melva Flowers. She lived, they said, in a local Albany nursing home. They suggested she might be the person with knowledge about Bessy since she carried the family name. The next day, I presented the same photos to a different group of Noongar community members in the regional town of Katanning. As in the previous workshop, the reading aloud of Bessy's letters gave context to the people and places in the photos. This time senior members of the audience told stories about living at Gnowangerup, a former mission located near Katanning. I was directed on this occasion to the local home of Clara Flowers, who had known about the workshop but was unable to attend.

Before returning to Albany, I made a visit to Clara's home. A tall Noongar woman wearing a brightly coloured beanie answered the door. She listened politely as to the purpose of my visit. She then moved our conversation into the garden, and then to her front gate, and then to the car in the driveway. In plain terms, Clara said she was unable to answer questions about Bessy. This was because it was a story that belonged to the paternal line of the Flowers family. Clara's connection to the Flowers family was through marriage, and in the absence of her late husband, Seymour Flowers, the responsibility and right to speak about issues concerning Flowers family business resided, she said, with one of her sons named Ezzard.

Clara's respect for her husband's lineage and hesitation to offer cultural information was understandable. In the past, giving information to strangers or government officials about family members often had dangerous consequences for parents, grandparents and extended family. The removal of children was a strategic and cruel government practice aimed at pulling apart families. The political basis of being taken away from family was often related to the heritage of parents and even grandparents. Clara confirmed that it was Ezzard who was the right spokesperson for any information that concerned Bessy. However, she did not share how to contact her son so that I could ask more questions about his ancestor's history.

In Albany, at this time of year, the humpback and southern right whales return to the cooler seas of the southwest with their calves. They often appear in sight of the beaches, as they enjoy the sanctuary of both Oyster Harbour and King George Sound, where the waters are abundant with rich food for their growing young. For millennia these magnificent creatures have migrated between northern and southern seas, appearing in the writings of early European explorers, but before such time vividly within Noongar oral histories. I kept watch for sightings of the whales as I waited for a meeting with Ezzard.

In the meantime, at the Albany library, I searched records from the Albany History Collection in the hope that they might list Bessy's date of birth and the name of her parents. The late Bonnie Hicks was a local historian who recorded in her writing Bessy's tribal name as 'Quinnupp'. But emplacing Bessy within a Minang history before she came into the care of Henry and Anne was impossible using the library's records and other sources. In a previous search of the library's collections, I discovered the names of two boys with the surname 'White' in a microfilm listing local baptisms. They were possibly related to Nora White, one of the five women sent to Ramahyuck from Annesfield. The cultural identities of all children at Annesfield were dissolved in the Christian act of 'purification' that was baptism. The baptismal records failed to indicate a person's previous name, heritage or their birthplace, which made invisible an enduring and relational connection to traditional country and kin.

In terms of Nora White, her displacement became apparent in questions asked by members of her descendant family. On more than one occasion over the years they had asked where Nora was from. Such a question warranted a definitive response as the answer would reveal culturally important information: where one came from and the family one belonged to. Not providing this information for Nora White's descendants had led to research that traced through time Bessy's lineage and connections to country. The continuing presence of traceable Flowers kin in the southwest was not the case for the other women, Nora, Rhoda and Emily, who had been sent from Annesfield to Ramahyuck and never returned to Western Australia.

Frustrated by such gaps in history, I once again visited the Albany library to review for a second time historical baptismal records. I gave myself the task of tracing the boys' birthplace with the surname 'White'. If substantiated through the official records, there was a chance to reconnect this history with relations perhaps still living in the southwest. The archive of Aboriginal historical records began to show its limitations for cultural truth telling. No link between the two boys and Nora

White could be found beyond a surname shared on the baptismal certificates. It's likely that Anne kept journals with entries detailing background information about the children in her care. If such documents have at all survived, they have never been donated to a public archive or made discoverable for research. I considered the many challenges presented by research that sought to restore people's links to ancestral country and to living family.

After a week spent in Albany and asking questions about Bessy in an attempt to locate her Minang kin, I finally met Ezzard Flowers. Robert called from the department office. 'Ezzard Flowers is here', he told me, 'and he's willing to meet with you to talk about Bessy Flowers'.

***

When I arrived at Robert's office, I walked into discussions about ongoing cultural heritage projects. Robert had known Ezzard for many years, but had only partial knowledge about his relatedness to Bessy. Beyond reciting information that had been generated by historians, there was no Noongar or Koori person who could speak of Bessy at this time from oral knowledge, or as part of family memories and remembrance practices strengthened by social declarations of recognised cultural identity.

I waited for Robert to finish working for a formal introduction to Ezzard, despite us having already met over a cup of tea in the office kitchenette. I was struck in our first meeting by the considered thought Ezzard gave to everything that he had to say about his connection to the southwest region. Many of the other Noongar family names mentioned throughout our conversation were unfamiliar to me, but I began to formulate in my mind the relationships between family groups and the missions located north of Albany and near the towns of Tambellup and Katanning, such as Gnowangerup. I sat with Ezzard, drinking more tea, and talking more about his ancestor unearthed in the archival research.

This intercultural exchange was unscripted. I simply told Bessy's story as I had come to know about it from her letters, colonial correspondence and Stone's portrait, which sat on the table and at the centre of our edifying discussion. I

CHAPTER 3: THE FLOWERS FAMILY

sought Ezzard's opinion about the research involving Bessy's colonial experience and which had required access to records at various state and national archives. The quest to understand her past had led me to Albany, and a search for her family. We exchanged ideas about steps forward in the reclamation of Bessy's memory, including engagement of other members of the Elder Flowers family and written cultural permission and consent.

When compiling a biography, the usual practice of historians post-research is to curate key life events in chronological order. However, I was more interested in family stories that represented Bessy through less structured processes of remembering kin and as productions of knowledge orally exchanged. To understand Bessy as part of Noongar history, I needed to hear from Ezzard where the memory of his ancestor was emplaced within a personal story of identity.

Ezzard was aware of my visit to his mother several days earlier and of my movements within family circles of his Wirlomin and Minang community. Family knowledge is political and represents a complex network of relationships, especially to one residing outside of community-based interactions. Not surprisingly, family cultural knowledge revealed information about family connections that were protected by community members, such as Ezzard's mother.

Ezzard was the member of the Flowers family granted the authority to speak about his ancestor. Such care and responsibility could mean granting, or denying, an outsider's access to Bessy's past and family cultural business. This had been the experience also when talking with Bessy's descendants in Victoria and those who were family to Nora White. Essential to these conversations about ancestors and identity were understandings about the cultural and political dynamics of contemporary Koori family relations and the social structuring of their communities. The success, or even failure, of intercultural conversations depended on having this knowledge from a place of respectful understanding.

Ezzard and I also engaged the idea of Bessy's spiritual return home. We considered in our first conversation and in subsequent talks what this might mean for the Flowers family, but also for her descendants, particularly her surviving great-grandchildren. Up to this point, the final destination of the research had not been fully determined. As it was to unfold, both family groups would be responsible for directing the research through decisions made over time about the cultural form that would shape and inform ancestral reclamation and memory restoration.

Ezzard had followed from a distance the path I had taken in the previous days meeting members of his community, many of who were family. He waited patiently until our office meeting. To arrive in an Aboriginal community without knowledge of family networks was a challenge. In Victoria at The Trust, I always travelled with a Koori colleague who would make the introductions to Elders or senior family. Before I left the office, Ezzard suggested I attend a gathering. It was with the cultural heritage group. There was a meeting on the weekend, he said that, at a culturally significant site. The site was several kilometres out of town and, as I drove there on Sunday morning, I was quietly surprised to enter an urban housing estate. Was this the entry to a heritage site? As I came closer to the nominated meeting point, the ocean's edge came into view. Ezzard was there to meet me and led me to a group of Elders and senior knowledge holders representing the Albany Heritage Reference Group Aboriginal Corporation (AHRGAC). The group gathered on a regular basis to inspect the fish traps created thousands of years ago.

The AHRGAC is made up of 10 Noongar families from the Great Southern and they speak for Minang people on matters of culture and heritage. I walked in the company of this group along a track following the water's edge, while listening to stories about the ecological care of this place. There were eight fish traps intact and each circle of rocks was a physical reminder of ancient Minang traditions and the continuing cultural presence of Minang people.

This area was once river country, I was told by one of the Elders, who then explained that the ocean had found its way further inland, making the production of fish traps a useful method to source ocean food. Following the pointed finger drawing attention to one of the fish traps that was slowly disappearing underneath the rising tide, I heard about the method used for its construction. As it was told, first, the smaller rocks were placed on a bed of sand, followed by the placement of larger rocks and then the filling-in of large gaps with branches and brush. This meant that the smaller fish were able to escape, while the larger fish were entrapped and collected for eating. Discussions about preserving this site of highest cultural significance circled around me.

The experience at the fish traps provided an understanding about responsibility to country and to the preservation of culture. Why this place continued to be meaningful to everyday Noongar lives was brought home when an Elder said to me during the group's inspection of the site, 'We talk about landscapes, not just isolated spots'. I took this to mean that the fish traps were part of a much larger cultural existence and, therefore, were considered vital to webs of knowledge and cultural practices. This process of storytelling, and learning by witnessing and listening, was why I had made the trip to Albany. It provided a chance to be a participant within exchanges of knowledge developed over generations and instrumental to processes of keeping culture strong.

Walking along the trail in sight of the fish traps, there was an opportunity to communicate the story of Bessy to members of the group. The story began with the historical existence of Annesfield and then the sea journey of Bessy and the four other young Aboriginal women from the institution to Ramahyuck. Although the community members I was talking to were not directly related to Bessy, her story brought to the surface personal stories of mission childhoods. As experienced throughout the continent, mission living in the Great Southern and the fragmentation of many families were memories held inward of the heart. I realised how the history of Bessy belonged in many ways not just to her direct lineage, but also to all Noongar families. Her history was a point of access for collective experiences to be respected, held in story and listened to, which meant that the meaning of Bessy's past was never isolated in a singular reading or cultural interpretation.

Transmission of Bessy's past as recorded in the archive invited the group to retrieve and activate stored memories. My part was to listen, as they had listened. The exchange generated a space for direct and honest conversation, such as the question to me: 'You've got knowledge, don't you?' Our exchange navigated the complexity of impactful experiences on community cultural structures. I was reminded not to focus on Bessy's story at the exclusion of other Noongar narratives that engaged memories of dislocation and removal from family and country. They said to me, 'You must know your audience', explaining that Bessy's life history was no less important than other Noongar stories of childhood removal from family, hardship, survival and cultural performances of resilience. Bessy grew up at Annesfield, an institution for Aboriginal children, and the European influence on her life that involved Christian teachings was also the experience of many Noongar and Koori children and that of Aboriginal peoples from across Australia.

After the fish traps inspection was completed, and as the wind and rain began to set in, we gathered at the back of a large four-wheel drive to eat sandwiches and to drink tea. As we did so, I wondered what the next steps would be in this research and, though quiet during our walk, Ezzard provided an answer to these thoughts in the form of a question: 'You know where this Annesfield place is?' From our earlier conversations, Ezzard was aware I had been to Bessy's childhood home, a place that was unknown to him despite his years of living and working throughout the southwest. He decided it was time for him to experience the former 'native' institution and his ancestor's childhood home.

When we arrived at Annesfield, Ezzard lingered behind me in the shadow cast by the overhanging rooftop. We were both uncertain as to how two strangers with the purpose of requesting entry to a private residence would be received at the door. I had known Ezzard for only two days, and in this time, discovering together an entry point to Bessy's past had taken on a social immediacy and cultural agency that the written word disappoints, even today. I knocked on the door and we waited. Eventually, the insistent door knocking paid off and a woman opened the door. After her initial enquiries as to who we were and the purpose of our visit, I let the history of Bessy flow like a well-rehearsed theatre script. The woman agreed that we could enter the house on the condition that both Ezzard and I first gained permission from the owner. Initially this request made our hearts sink. Was it going to be possible to locate the farmer and the property owner, let alone also gain his approval to go inside the house and experience the former institution firsthand? Fortunately, good news followed. The farmer, as it happened, lived only a short walk away and in a house located behind Annesfield. Once again, I was given the job of knocking on a stranger's door.

This time it was an elderly man who answered. In few words, I told him how it was Bessy's connection to the nearby property that was the reason for our visit. He invited us inside his home. Ezzard and I sat at the kitchen table and listened to the now retired farmer talk of the positive and congenial relationships between his family and the past workhands on his farm in the Albany region who he referred to as the 'Aborigines'. In the periodic silences that followed, I imagined Ezzard and the farmer in a process of calibrating personal memories informed by very different experiences of the past.

One year on, when I was sitting with Ezzard to record his life story, I understood with greater sensitivity his feelings of reservation and discomfort when first meeting with the farmer and sitting in his home at the kitchen table. I listened to Ezzard talk about how his ancestors and other Noongar people helped clear the farming lands for colonial settlers, including how the Native Welfare Department granted leave for Gnowangerup Aboriginal Mission residents to do this work mostly unpaid.

I considered these relationships of power disparity in the context of the process to restore a memory of Bessy, and the role of persisting Flowers family narratives of identity. As a wadjella woman, a Noongar word meaning white person or European, I was navigating the use of Bessy's history as a tool for negotiating and mediating entry for Ezzard into the childhood home of his relative. This go-between role generated greater awareness about the vulnerabilities residing within cultural reclamation practices, and the mutual concern and care that is needed. The polite conversation continued with the farmer and, by its end, permission to enter the house was granted. We returned to the former Annesfield home and went inside.

As previously observed, the building was divided into two conjoined residences. In the first section we attempted to find physical evidence of historical Annesfield among the now modern living spaces. The woman we had first met at the front door happily shared information about the institution derived from a personal investigation into its history. This included details about the purpose of each room and the employment of people with Chinese heritage who supported Anne in her domestic care of the children.

A door from the first section of the building leading directly to the second section was closed off, but access was still possible from another doorway located outside the main house. We took the concrete steps of faded green paint, which led up into a series of emptied rooms. The first level was a large rectangular room with a red fireplace at one end and two cast iron pots layered with dust resting in its hearth. Locked away in one of the cupboards was a Chinese gong that was apparently used to announce mealtimes. Peeling plaster on the walls revealed red bricks as well as ornate wallpaper showing the design and style of past eras. This room, we were told, had been the dormitory where Bessy and the other children had slept.

While inside Annesfield our conversation was limited. We were absorbed by the building's history and our own imaginings. Respecting this silence, I decided to capture Ezzard's interactions with this place through images rather than conversation. Taking photos became my method for making sense of what Ezzard was internalising. It also recorded my role as a witness, situated on the fringes of his cultural experience. I pictured Ezzard exploring inside the home. I observed him as he moved from room to room without speaking a word. Though the second section of the building was mostly empty, Ezzard appeared deep in thought and preoccupied with all that couldn't be seen. The photos taken at this time depict empty rooms without domestic objects or people. They also portray Ezzard perceiving an unseen but ever-present past.

Once we had completed walking room to room, Ezzard shared some of his process, saying that he had been imagining Bessy's life using the stories that I had shared with him about his ancestor's experience of living in Anne's care. Bessy's letters gave insight into how she had felt about her childhood home and also her relationship with Anne. Ezzard said that he had also been giving emotion to Bessy's life story by drawing on personal experiences of mission living and the emotional

CHAPTER 3: THE FLOWERS FAMILY

scarring of being separated from his family.

Ezzard led the way up the stairs. The staircase appeared as though ocean blue, a colouring that was caused by the sunlight filtering through the stained glass. I followed closely behind and used my camera to digitally record the potency of the moment. In the rooms, at the top of the stairs, was a bedroom. It was partially furnished and featured a newly installed bathroom. To someone else, these spaces might have been as they were: a bedroom, a bathroom and an empty dining room. But the experience of being in these spaces and imagining Bessy's past from our differently situated viewpoints seemed to offer something more. As a way of remembering such considered experiential observations, I photographed Ezzard looking to the outside through a small window. In view were the backyard pine trees and, in the distance, the township of Albany enveloped by hills, beach and ocean.

I was conscious not to intrude on Ezzard's thoughts while venturing throughout the rooms that represented elements of Bessy's history. Once downstairs I asked him to share what he had felt, and he told me:

> It feels good, positive energy going through the place. Just reflecting back to when Bessy and the kids probably would have been here. It feels lonely. Probably would have been lonely back then, especially with the people who took care of her and stuff and to actually know now where this place is…is also very hard for me as well, and to hear some of the stories we just heard…[78]

His voice then trailed off, returning us to the quietness of contemplative thought. From Ezzard's process of reflecting, he appeared to be consolidating the history of a distant kin with that of his own story of growing up on the Gnowangerup Aboriginal Mission, and stories from other missions throughout Western Australia. He lucidly unified positive elements of his past with challenging life events that had caused sadness. Despite not knowing Bessy's history in its entirety, as it existed in the archive, Ezzard acknowledged when in Annesfield that he believed his ancestor's relationship with Anne to be one instilled with affection and admiration.

Though now a modern home, Ezzard considered the old Annesfield residence to be a heritage site with cultural value, and as an explanation of this worth, he paralleled the care of the fish traps and the continued custodianship of this cultural history. While he finished his time at Annesfield, I took photos of the bright orange flowers blooming in the garden. We left the site making a plan to meet in the regional town of Tambellup, where he was living at this time with his family.

***

Figure 47 Sand, rocks and salt water, Albany, Western Australia, 2010

CHAPTER 3: THE FLOWERS FAMILY

Figure 48 The former Annesfield Native Institution, Albany, Western Australia, 2010

Figure 49 Ezzard Flowers at the former Annesfield Native Institution, Albany, Western Australia, 2010

Figure 50 Empty stairs, the former Annesfield Native Institution, Albany, Western Australia, 2010

Figure 51 Ezzard Flowers at window, the former Annesfield Native Institution, Albany, Western Australia, 2010

CHAPTER 3: THE FLOWERS FAMILY

Figure 52 Wallpaper, the former Annesfield Native Institution, Albany, Western Australia, 2010

Figure 53 The main room, the former Annesfield Native Institution, Albany, Western Australia, 2010

Figure 54 Ezzard Flowers, the former Annesfield Native Institution, Albany, Western Australia, 2010

CHAPTER 3: THE FLOWERS FAMILY

A key experience of family history research is about bringing people together, and this can often involve a shared barbeque. The first stop before the drive to Tambellup was, therefore, the local Albany supermarket. Tambellup is a small country town that's about 220 kilometres north of Albany. It has a population of about 3,000 people. One way to get there is to take the road that passes by the Stirling Ranges, rather than the main highway. Taking this route, the landscape was ever changing. Once past the ranges, the country opens up to farming land and as I could see at this time of year, paddocks seeded for harvest. It was only a month into spring and the ground appeared dry and dusty with the rains yet to fall.

In Tambellup I met Ezzard and members of his family at a park equipped with a barbeque area. This was a meeting place that was near to, but also away from, the family home. To help in the creation of a family tree, Kooramyee Cooper had made the trip from Melbourne. Kooramyee is a Yorta Yorta woman with connections to Wotjobaluk and Wamba Wamba people through her maternal lineage. The surname Cooper is a cultural link to the Cummeragunja mission and to the traditional lands of Yorta Yorta people. Influential to Kooramyee's life have been strong leaders such as her father Blue Gum Cooper and her uncle Wally Cooper. Working together at The Trust, her expertise in Koori genealogies helped many Stolen Generations to locate and access many different kinds of government records that were essential for restoring family links.

Kooramyee often shared why keeping family knowledge strong within oneself and as part of community social histories respected the intergenerational passage of stories about ancestor links to their traditional country and to kin. She often said that understanding ancestral connections to country through family bloodlines was to respect the spiritual presence of ancestors, who she described as stepping alongside their kin in the living world. Kooramyee talked in detail with Ezzard about his Flowers lineage and family networks. While they engaged in this discussion of kinship I took family photos, as a different method for making sense of, and remembering, how the people gathered at the park all fitted together as family.

In relation to taking these particular photos, I'm not able to recall the exact question that took me across the road and into the home of Carmel and Melva Flowers. The young women were the granddaughters of Melva Flowers who was mentioned to me at the family history workshop in Albany. After hearing some of Bessy's history and the reason for visiting Tambellup, Carmel and Melva asked for photos to be taken of them with their children, and also with their mother Sedeena.

The women and children were happy to be photographed and the process of photo taking demonstrated the deep affection existing between them all. The intimacy of family energised our interaction of moving to different locations both inside and outside their home for the photos. In the lounge room I was invited to look at family photos framed and hanging on the wall. The people pictured in them were introduced by name spoken aloud. I tried to retain the names told to me, which represented relatedness between members of the Flowers family. The connections would make more sense when shared as part of Ezzard's stories about his family and kin. Our meeting was lively and enjoyable. Particularly when taking photos of third-generation little Melva with her grandmother Sedeena.

Figure 55 Sedeena Flowers, Tambellup, Western Australia, 2010

CHAPTER 3: THE FLOWERS FAMILY

Figure 56 Carmel Flowers, Sedeena Flowers, Melva Flowers, Tambellup, Western Australia, 2010

Figure 57 Carmel Flowers, Melva Flowers, Tambellup, Western Australia, 2010

NO LONGER A WANDERING SPIRIT

Figure 58 Top to bottom: Carmel Flowers, Sedeena (Nina), Little Melva Flowers, Tambellup, Western Australia, 2010

CHAPTER 3: THE FLOWERS FAMILY

Figure 59 Little Melva Flowers, Tambellup, Western Australia, 2010

Figure 60 Left to right: Ezzard Flowers, Melva Flowers, Carmel Flowers, Sedeena Flowers, Anthony Flowers, Tambellup, Western Australia, 2010

Meeting the Flowers family in Tambellup inspired a visit to the most senior family member, Melva Flowers. Melva was a Minang Noongar woman and, at this time, Bessy's oldest surviving Flowers kin. When I met her, she was living in a residential nursing home in Albany. Leading up to the visit, I wondered what stories might arise once I had shared the journey of Bessy from Albany to East Gippsland. When I sat with Melva, however, I found that she had laid many memories to rest. In her senior years she had chosen to keep many parts of her past carefully internalised and emotionally secured and without need for their storying. This quiet disposition and freedom from gifting to another openly shared reflections was not conducted as an act of fortified defiance, but in my experience of our time together, one of pride, dignity and self-preservation in old age.

Time spent with Melva was lively with discoveries, even though our conversation avoided exploring her past. Rather than sharing personal stories, Melva contemplated with a deep curiosity Bessy's life as it was shown to her through historical photos. With slender fingers and brightly painted pink nails, Melva gracefully touched the faces that peered back at her from the photos pasted in a book. 'Old-fashioned', I heard her say as she turned each page to view the places and people that had figured in the history of her ancestor, such as children at Annesfield and young Koori families from Ramahyuck. When I offered Melva pictures of both her daughter and grandchildren that I had taken when in Tambellup, she recognised their faces in an instant. She examined the photos, the moment given merit in the care that was taken to remember and cherish the younger generations of her family.

With Melva, I waited for the taxi that was taking her out for the day. As we sat together, I watched as she clipped and unclipped her white handbag, each time looking at the Flowers family photos I'd left in her possession. We parted company in the same way that we met. There was no talking about the past, just simply a shared enjoyment of looking at photos. Melva demonstrated how there is value in silence as well as in story. Not all memories she instructed through her actions were readily available for sharing, especially in the older years of one's life. Paying attention to the past for Melva was a very inner and private act. There were no stories shared about the past while turning the book pages with photos of Bessy, a distant kin who was lost to her memories and those of the Flowers family. Rather, Melva focused in her final years on the meaning to her of present-day living family.

The opportunity to meet members of the Flowers family was a step forward, despite not locating familial memories of Bessy. From this visit to the southwest of Western Australia it was clear that the pathway to be followed was to unite the two family groups representing two different cultural communities. Interpretations of the colonial archive in real time and with respect to present-day experiences of historical places featured in the archive was proving to be a culturally productive process to reconcile personal memory with that of Bessy's history.

Figure 61 Melva Flowers, Albany, Western Australia, 2010

Figure 62 Melva Flowers, brightly painted nails, Albany, Western Australia, 2010

Figure 63 Melva Flowers looking at photos of Bessy, Albany, Western Australia, 2010

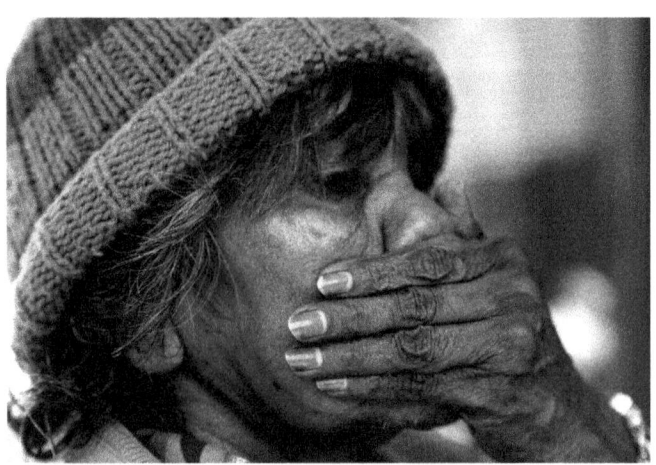

Figure 64 Melva Flowers laughing, Albany, Western Australia, 2010

Chapter 4:
Two families united

In East Gippsland there were two places significant to the family retrieval of Bessy's story from the past. One was the original site of Ramahyuck and the second was the Bairnsdale Cemetery. Since first meeting the Bryant families, a consistent topic of discussion had been the final resting place of their ancestor and what it might mean to memorialise and acknowledge her life. To know where ancestors were buried was to keep intact connections to an intergenerational story of identity.

Knowing that the Bryant family were exploring Bessy's mission past and seeking information about where she was buried, Kooramyee Cooper had offered to assist with the preliminary investigations. At this time she was working for a Koori agency that was responsible for connecting Stolen Generations with members of their family and traditional country. As part of consultations for a family reunion, she had driven to Gippsland in the early months of 2011 in search of the historical Ramahyuck site. When she finally found its location, all that was visible into the distance were farmland paddocks and herds of grazing livestock. The only evidence that remained of the historical mission was an area of fenced ground reserved for the cemetery. This first trip that Kooramyee made was followed by a return visit by us both.

Early on a Sunday morning Kooramyee arrived at my house in Melbourne. The trip to Bairnsdale was to visit the old mission and to try and solve the whereabouts of Bessy's grave. Once inside the car, Kooramyee was quick to tell me that her Nan was coming along for the ride to East Gippsland. I followed the wave of her hand to the back seat of the car where I could see a large blue box, but not an elderly woman. 'She's there in the box', she told me, all the while laughing and leaving me to wait for a story of explanation if one was on offer. I discovered, as we began the drive, that inside the box was earth Kooramyee had collected from a grave belonging to her nanna, Kathleen Colger, who was buried at the Balranald Cemetery.

Kooramyee was intending to place the dirt on her Uncle Max's grave as a mark of respect and in accordance with cultural knowing regarding a restless spirit. Uncle Max, she revealed, wished for his final resting place to be in Balranald, a regional town on the New South Wales side of the Murray River and a country of meaning for Yorta Yorta and Mutti Mutti people. However, his immediate family had decided to bury Max at Mooroopna Cemetery near Shepparton, a town with a large community of Koori families, including his own. On the back seat of the car, signifying Nan Colger in spirit and as one with her country, the blue cardboard box testified to the depth of this moral cultural obligation to the dead. For Kooramyee, it was important to uphold her uncle's request to be buried in a place where he felt a strong sense of belonging, even if that meant taking a collection of dirt from country to where he now rested.

Talk of death, dying and cemeteries continued along the Princes Highway. We also spoke about the importance of finding Bessy's grave and the experiential knowledge to be gained by retracing the route that Bessy had taken from Ramahyuck to Bairnsdale two days before her death in January 1895.[79] On leaving the Princes Highway, we followed the narrow bitumen roads that passed by paddocks where sheep or cattle grazed. As far as we could see, there was no road sign indicating the way to Ramahyuck. Finding the site depended on Kooramyee remembering the roads travelled on her first trip.

CHAPTER 4: TWO FAMILIES UNITED

We drove along for some time seeing nothing besides the long stretches of wire fencing and the fresh growth of wild grasses. A flock of birds flying overhead caught Kooramyee's attention and we followed where they were headed. She laughed aloud saying how these birds would lead the way to Ramahyuck. Birds and creatures of various kinds are known for their roles as messengers and their presence is seriously regarded, such as with the pair of mountain ducks doing a fly-pass and the two wedge-tailed eagles that were gliding around the edge of the bush in near sight.

When I travelled through country with Koori colleagues from The Trust, they would acknowledge the significance of a crow sitting on a roadside fence post or on the branch of a tree, describing it as an omen. One crow meant joy, two crows a foretelling of bad luck and three crows indicated the imminent death of a close relation. Crows were also considered at other times to be a guide through country, and so it was at a farmer's gate that Kooramyee and I came to a stop, the dirt road ahead covered with potholes and puddles from the recent rains.

Whenever I have visited the sites of former missions and reserves, the journey has often taken me along unsealed dirt roads that branch off a main road. The drive to these roughly surfaced roads was always beyond the outskirts of town, meaning that the residents had a considerable distance to travel to go anywhere, particularly during historic times when travel away from the mission was not only slow because of methods of transport, but often prohibited and strictly limited by the official permissions needed to leave the mission. The sense of isolation generated by travelling along these unsealed dirt roads often brought to mind the adage 'out of sight and out of mind', an attitude adopted at those times by paternalistic protecting authorities. Keeping Koori people separate from settler communities was part of everyday missionary control and management, a regulation influenced by restrictive acts of parliaments as well as the gospel teachings imposing a Christian, duty-filled way of life.

On our drive along the dirt road to Ramahyuck there were no visible remnants of such a past. Once out of the car and standing in a farmer's paddock, we made our way along a track overgrown with knee-high wild grasses. Kooramyee picked up a large stick to beat the ground. 'Keeping away the snakes,' she told me, 'and waking up the old people, so that they know we're here, walking on country'.[80] Eventually, we arrived at a large clearing among a cluster of eucalypts. This area of trees and dried earth was the Ramahyuck Cemetery. In the late 1960s, Italian-Australian anthropologist Aldo Massola wrote of Ramahyuck that, 'An old peppercorn tree is all that remains of Hagenauer's efforts'. He also described how the old cemetery was situated on a hill and that buried there were not only Aboriginal people from the mission, but also early settlers and their families.[81]

The pepper tree was no longer visible, and in addition to Massola's descriptions was the electrified fence that now outlined the cemetery's boundary. The fence was designed to create a barrier, it seemed, between the cattle grazing nearby and the historical graves of Ramahyuck Aboriginal residents and local settlers. Looking from the fence line and across the vast stretch of farming land, the trees at the edge of Lake Wellington could be seen. The electrified fence deterred any idea of walking to the lake, so we returned to the middle ground of the cemetery and inspected the only headstone remaining, which was a memorial to Nathaniel Pepper. Nathaniel was a Wotjobaluk man from the Wimmera region in northeastern Victoria. An evangelist and teacher, he received his Christian training from Rev. Hagenauer and Rev. Friedrich William Spieseke while living on the Ebenezer mission. The connection with Bessy's history is that Nathaniel married a young woman, Rachel Wardekan (or Warnedeckan), who had also been raised at Annesfield. Rachel was admitted into Anne's care in 1852 at seven years of age and she lived at Annesfield until marrying age.

The single marked burial site contrasted with the reality of other unidentified graves. A series of Rev. Hagenauer's letters indicated that other burials at Ramahyuck Cemetery had taken place, such as those of friends and kin of Bessy, including Nora Foster (née White), one of her children who died from 'teething complications', Rhoda Fitchett (née Tanaton/Toby) and, within five days of Nathanial Pepper's death, Bessy's baby Nellie Grace from teething complications. At this time, death certificates were not generally issued, but documented within the missionary letters

CHAPTER 4: TWO FAMILIES UNITED

is that 80 Aboriginal people and 16 colonial settlers were buried at the Ramahyuck Cemetery between the years 1863 until 1908. For many years wooden crosses had marked the graves of these Ramahyuck residents. By the time of our visit, it was only the eucalypts that collectively marked those buried in this country.

The importance placed on respectful treatment of the dead by Aboriginal kin was evident in a cultural ceremony in August 1983 where historian Phillip Pepper, a descendant of Nathaniel, planted a tree to mark the grave of an unknown Brayakoloong woman whose remains had been found by the Crowns Land Department during the work of rabbit eradication in the area. Pepper sought state government permission for the custody of the more than 500-year-old skeletal remains so that he could perform a dignified burial and change the common circumstance of an Aboriginal ancestor being kept within a government department container.[82]

In 1984 Gunditjmara Elder Jim Berg and Ron Merkel QC issued an injunction to take legal action against the University of Melbourne for the return of the Murray Black Collection. This consisted of Aboriginal skeletal remains taken from five burial sites on the New South Wales side of the Murray River and, after collection, stored in steel cabinets in the anatomy department of the university with each bone given an identifying number. The case was eventually successful and the skeletal remains with identifying provenance were returned to their country of origin.

In 1985 skeletal remains of 38 ancestors from a Museum Victoria collection were wrapped in cloth and bark and carried by 38 people in a Reburial March to their final resting place in the Kings Domain Gardens. The plaque on the boulder marking their final resting place states, 'Rise from this grave, release your anger and pain as you soar with the winds back to your homelands. There find peace with our Spiritual Mother the Land, before drifting off into the "Dreamtime"'.

***

Ramahyuck closed down in the early months of 1908. Rev. Hagenauer had retired and one of his sons had taken over management of the mission. At this time, the Victorian Board for the Protection of Aborigines was dealing with the financial viability of the missions and reserves in Victoria and a declining population of Koori people, caused mostly by ill health and harsh living conditions. The Board had tried over several years to relocate the Aboriginal residents of Ramahyuck to Lake Tyers, which was situated further to the east. This coastal-based mission was under the management of the newly appointed Captain Howe, who was directed by the Board to replace the longstanding Anglican missionary Rev. John Bulmer.

Hagenauer died aged 80 years on 28 November 1909 at Lake Tyers. He spent many years devoted to his role as the religious superintendent for Anglican missions at Lake Tyers and Lake Condah as well as two Presbyterian missions. He was influential in this supervisory role, as seen with his appointment as the acting secretary and general inspector for the Board from 1 July 1889 until 1906. His readiness to implement government policies of the day and the effects of these policies upon the lives of mission residents is a history that continues to resonant within the thoughts and feelings of Bessy's descendant family members and kin.

Situated at the heart of this trip to East Gippsland was finding the best practice for cultural reclamation of Bessy's memory. This required forming relationships with descendant family and kin, and finding ways to engage with Bessy's past that created meaning and value when shared between each other. The impact of lost memory and the emotional reality keenly attached to the process of bridging expanded gaps in time were states of wellbeing that were constantly being negotiated.

Upon leaving the Ramahyuck Cemetery, Kooramyee and I travelled to Bairnsdale and to the cemetery where the records indicated Bessy had been buried. Driving along the old Gippsland highway that ran parallel to the Princes Highway, it was not difficult to imagine this road as being the same route Bessy had taken to visit her daughter and grandchildren several days before her death on 14 January 1895. Was it an arduous trip for Bessy upon a horse-drawn buggy? Had she been feeling unwell for some time? On Bessy's death certificate, her cause of death at the age of 46 years lists failing health from gallstones for two years and then peritonitis, the inflammation of the abdominal tissue, for 48 hours.

CHAPTER 4: TWO FAMILIES UNITED

At the Bairnsdale Cemetery, and in search of a grave that had been identified by Kooramyee to be that of Bessy's, the past felt tangible rather than distant and inaccessible. There was more to Bessy than historical caricaturing. She was socially apt and equally determined and willing to speak out against colonial government servitude and injustice. Her descendants and kin engaged with these qualities, which were also recorded in the archive when they sought connection to their ancestor through personal lived experience. Reclamation of ancestors by present generations was about knowing one's family and where one belonged. As we left the Bairnsdale Cemetery talking about responsibilities between the dead and the living and issues of culture and identity, Kooramyee remarked upon the burial of ancestors. She said that:

> Knowing where your ancestors are buried is important because I can be on my country, and my spirits [cultural guides] know where they are…they are safe in the arms of the ancestors.
>
> Country has to know where their children are. If country doesn't know where their children are, then country is not well. People are not healed, and country is not healed.[83]

With Bessy's Bryant families, our conversations often circled around death and feelings of loss for members of family and for other community members who were regarded as kin. Family memories of Bessy were absent and this loss was yet to be fully recognised and respectfully expressed as a united family. Beginning the return drive to Melbourne, the light rain that had started turned quickly into a torrential downpour. Barely able to see the road as the rain fell on the windscreen, Kooramyee said: 'They are tears of joy…tears of joy because Bessy is happy to be found.'[84]

***

Several months passed by during which time Kooramyee had arranged a family reunion for a Stolen Generations woman from Victoria who fitted into the Bryant and Flowers family network. The reunion in September 2013 became the first meeting between members of the Bryant family and their Flowers kin.

Some members of the Bryant family who were taking part in the reunion travelled from Melbourne to East Gippsland. On the floor of the minibus, among bags of clothes and food supplies for the coming days, lay a grey marbled headstone. The carved inscription read 'Elizabeth Cameron, 1849 Albany WA – 14.1.1895, Noongar Woman'. The Bryant family reunion was about restoring broken family connections for a Stolen Generations woman who was related to this family group. The event was an opportunity for the families to welcome this woman home to the traditional country of her ancestors in East Gippsland, which on this occasion was the Lake Tyers Trust, formerly the Lake Tyers Aboriginal Mission.

The reunion was the formal Stolen Generations business of a dedicated Victorian organisation for the re-establishment of cultural ties for Koori people who had been separated from their family and community. As part of the gathering, it was possible to share the story of Bessy to a larger number of Bryant family members. The childhood portrait of Bessy was once again central to conversations about the extensive social life of memory. To know Bessy was to witness how her family drew upon family relationships to place and to people, and the ways in which knowledge of culture and identity was asserted.

The family reunion was specific to the Bryants' connection to the Lake Tyers Aboriginal Trust. This place was where the Bryants had spent a large part of their childhood, and where family members continued to live in the present day. Attachment to country that was once a mission symbolised the powerful link to country where ancestors had established tribal boundaries. For the Bryants, speaking of the connection between people, and between people and country, was a natural part of the emotional welcoming home granted to a woman identifying as a member of the Stolen Generations. It was also integral to the welcome given to Ezzard Flowers, who had made his way to East Gippsland with the support of Yorgum, the Western Australian Link-Up agency. Supporting Ezzard on this trip was a senior community member, Russell Nelly, a strong cultural figure and renowned Elder living at this time in the Great Southern.

The research efforts to locate Bessy's grave had motivated Ezzard to find help in travelling from Western Australia to Victoria to unite with Bessy's descendants and his kin. This was a first trip to East Gippsland and an opportunity to connect with the country where Bessy had lived after departing from Annesfield, and where she had died and been buried. He felt excited about the family reunion but also apprehensive. Ezzard confided that going into another Aboriginal community not your own, even if you were yourself Aboriginal, was not easy. He explained that there are as many cultural differences as there are similarities within different family groups that coexist as a community and with responsibilities to each other.

The face-to-face meeting with the Bryant family carried along with it an air of expectation. Together, as a family, he imagined that answers might be unearthed, which would add to the layers of history that were now becoming known about Bessy. Where the family travellers were staying in Lakes Entrance and not far from the Lake Tyers Trust, there was a sense of restlessness about the reunion to take place the following day.

The following morning at the Lake Tyers Trust was very lively and also emotional. This trip was the first time I met Betty Hood (née Bryant) and her sister, Glenis Solomon (née Bryant), after they were picked up in one of the minibuses driven by Larry Levi from their homes in Bairnsdale.[85] It was also the first meeting for Ezzard and Russell, who sat listening to the Bryant women Elders talk about their childhood experiences at the mission.

Making the decision to detour from the main road leading out to the Lake Tyers Trust, Larry had taken everyone on board to see one of the places often spoken about in the Bryants' stories – The Bluff. At this site were the remains of a two-bedroom family home that had been built by Keith Bryant, a family figure who was a grandson to Bessy. Betty was enthused by the memories that surfaced in her mind as the bus followed the familiar roads returning her to the past. She told heartfelt stories about clothes-washing days at the nearby natural springs, and then hanging the wet clothes out for drying over tree branches and low-lying native shrubs. She reminisced about the days spent trapping possums in the bush along with the other Bryant children, and she talked about her relationship with her Nan and her Pop, who were Esther and Keith Bryant (Keith being her mother's brother).

A passenger on the bus, Ezzard sat listening to these stories. He watched from the window as places passed by with storied explanations animating childhood memories. He felt part of the storytelling process that was helping him to connect with his ancestor who had lived in this country since she was a young woman. When the bus arrived at the Lake Tyers Trust, members of the community walked from their homes on country to warmly greet Ezzard and Russell. They actively demonstrated without shame that kinship matters, displaying this in real time with eager and tender hugs together with an exuberant curiosity about their newly discovered kin.

Such a family welcome was unscripted. There had been no prior rehearsal for this performance of genuine love and care, or an earlier family discussion to work out how this particular event should unfold. I, like Ezzard, had been nervous during the lead-up, though for a different set of reasons. I had been responsible for returning Bessy's history to both families who were now meeting for the first time, and Ezzard was among kin he'd never met before. To accept and respectfully acknowledge family relatedness when feeling a long way from home appeared to cause a degree of insecurity. Any doubts or uncertainties, however, were washed away when one of Bessy's great-granddaughters, Regina Wilkinson (née Bryant), took a step towards Ezzard and without hesitation embraced him with open arms, a trail of tears appearing on her cheeks as she did so. The emotional greeting continued as she turned and took Russell's hand in her own. He was sitting on the steps of the minibus and was visibly moved by the intense and raw emotions being produced by the family unification.

At the Lake Tyers Trust, photos of ancestors started to be circulated. Betty could be seen carefully retrieving several small envelopes from her handbag. Her family were quick to gather eagerly around her. In one hand she held proudly a

CHAPTER 4: TWO FAMILIES UNITED

series of black-and-white photos. They were examined up close and then used as props to tell stories that brought into the present moment members of the Bryant family who were no longer living. The names of these people were called aloud. The call out to their spirits endeared kisses to be bestowed with affection on their pictured faces. At other times a photo of family was held aloft in the air like a trophy won at a sporting carnival. There was a sense of reverent celebration and a feeling of being victorious. Dignity and pride for dead kin and for living family were all on display. The recognition of kin-relatedness between the two family groups stood up against any historical appropriation of kinship suffered at the hands of colonialism and that of settler interventions upon everyday family lives.

I went about taking photos of Betty and others who examined with heart the Bryant family photos. There was no exclusion of family who had passed over to the spirit world. With zoom fixed on the camera, it was possible to capture the creases of time visible on the worn prints, as well as the aging hands of the person who held them so gently. One of the old photos that pictured Keith and Esther Bryant appeared faded with time. The edges were scuffed and torn from human handling. This photo energised the gathering, as did the portrait of Keith pictured on his own. Holding the photo towards my camera, one of Keith's children, Regina, insisted that this moment with her father be documented.

Before the Bryant reunion, historical photos had helped generate dialogues that gave access to practices of cultural identity and belonging within the social sphere of the everyday. It was moving to witness the use of photos by the Bryant families to bring ancestors and their loved ones into the present. In a conversation with Betty that would take place a few years after the reunion, I discovered that when she was a young woman she had owned a box Brownie camera. With this camera she had taken photos of different family members, such as Keith and Esther Bryant, and in her words had kept them safe over the many years that had passed. She told me that, 'No one was allowed to touch them, [I] put them in my grandmother's stuff, and no one was allowed to touch them'.[86]

Figure 65 Glenis Solomon and Betty Hood, Lake Tyers Aboriginal Trust, Victoria, 2011

Figure 66 Glenis Solomon holding a photo of Keith and Esther Bryant, Lake Tyers Aboriginal Trust, Victoria, 2011

CHAPTER 4: TWO FAMILIES UNITED

Figure 67 Betty Hood with Bryant family photos, Lake Tyers Aboriginal Trust, Victoria, 2011

Figure 68 Keith Bryant with daughter Emma. Collection: Bryant Family.

Figure 69 Betty Hood with Esther Bryant, c.1960s. Collection: Bryant Family

CHAPTER 4: TWO FAMILIES UNITED

Figure 70 Russell Nelly with Glenis Solomon, Lake Tyers Aboriginal Trust, Victoria, 2011

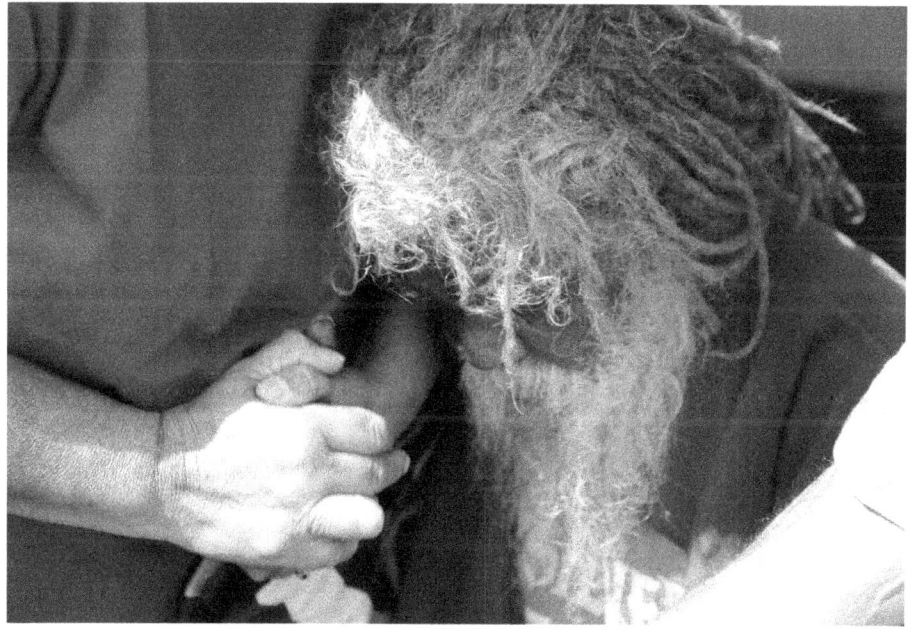

Figure 71 Russell Nelly with Regina Wilkinson, Lake Tyers Aboriginal Trust, Victoria, 2011

Figure 72 Russell Nelly, Lake Tyers Aboriginal Trust, Victoria, 2011

Figure 73 Russell Nelly with Betty Hood, Lake Tyers Aboriginal Trust, Victoria, 2011

CHAPTER 4: TWO FAMILIES UNITED

Figure 74 Church, Lake Tyers Aboriginal Trust, Victoria, 2011

Figure 75 Top row from left: Alfred Solomon, Colin Hood, James Mullett, Thomas Hood, Margaret Bryant. Middle row from left: Aidan Finn, Flo (Marion) Hood, Betty Hood, Carmel Hood, Glenis Solomon, Teniesha Hayes. Front row from left: Jake Finn, Tyson Hayes, Joe Mullett, Elizabeth Mullett, Toorloo Arm Hall, Victoria, 2011

Figure 76 Back row from left: Rita Hood, Madge Hood, Joseph Johnson. Front row from left: Jeffrey Walter, Deacon Johnson, Toorloo Arm Hall, Victoria, 2011

Figure 77 Back row: Colin Hood. Front row: Flo (Marion) Hood, Betty Hood, Glenis Solomon, Toorloo Arm Hall, Victoria, 2011

CHAPTER 4: TWO FAMILIES UNITED

Figure 78 Flo (Marion) Hood, Toorloo Arm Hall, Victoria, 2011

Figure 79 Glenis Solomon, Toorloo Arm Hall, Victoria, 2011

At the nearby Toorloo Arm Hall for lunch, the family storytelling continued and, as requested by the senior Bryant women, group photos of the Bryant family were taken. Each person would later be identified by name with help from the Bryant family. After lunch, the family drove to the Bairnsdale Cemetery. The cemetery was Bessy's final resting place but the location of her grave, as time revealed, would continue to be unknown. It was a difficult task for the Bryant families and for Ezzard and Russell to engage with acts of remembering an ancestor whom they had never met. More than a century had passed since Bessy's arrival at Ramahyuck. To reconcile a past that had been fragmented by colonial settler dispossession, finding ways to confidently meld both modern and traditional practices of remembrance became a cultural requisite.

Gathered at the Bairnsdale Cemetery, there existed initial indecision about how to mourn an ancestor who had been absent for generations from their memories and, therefore, family story. The colonial dislocation and dispersal of family throughout the region and also in areas beyond meant that ceremonies for mourning ancestors who were without burial sites known to their living relations needed to be discussed and decided upon. The Bryants had grieved for and buried family and loved ones at the Bairnsdale Cemetery, and it was this familiarity of practice and place that they drew upon to mourn but also recognise the life of their ancestor.

At the cemetery where the families had congregated, there was no open pit of earth prepared for a formal farewell and the placement of a coffin. There was no funeral hearse on standby or preacher to provide guidance as to what to say or do. By a general rule, funerals are a tightly orchestrated affair which tend to follow a set mourning ritual with expected graveside behaviours. On this occasion at the cemetery there was a different kind of ceremony at play. It appeared to exist outside of Christian or other religious practices of acknowledging and mourning the dead.

The Bryant families, alongside Ezzard, were seeking to reclaim a relationship between themselves and their ancestor. The emotional performance of mourning Bessy was one way of bringing back her memory to their lives, with meaning for

CHAPTER 4: TWO FAMILIES UNITED

each individual but also for family and community. The act of grieving played a large part in family expressions of reconciling the past in the present, as did having to negotiate feelings of shame and self-judgement related to the cultural neglect of caring for ancestral memories.

Phyllis spoke about the feelings of shame that she experienced in not knowing where her great-grandmother had been buried. 'I just felt so ashamed…if it was about knowing where she was, why didn't I do anything about it?'[87] She questioned why the location of her ancestor's grave was information not passed on through the family, particularly by her father, Keith. There was a genuine concern expressed about where family members were buried.

On the advice of a Koori from East Gippsland (who has now passed), Kooramyee identified for the families what she believed to be Bessy's grave. Unfortunately, with more research it would later surface that the records were inconsistent and an error had been made despite the intended goodwill. The Bairnsdale Cemetery Trust explained in later correspondence how the original cemetery records had been lost or accidentally destroyed. This meant that burial numbers over the decades had been duplicated. The Trust affirmed indisputably that identifying Bessy's grave from historical records was not possible.

At the cemetery, the coming together of family and kin at the graveside symbolised both a farewell and a welcoming home. Decisions were made about where to lay the headstone purchased by the Stolen Generations agency to replace the rusted iron cross, numbered 1215. The Bryant families stood in sombre silence. Breaking the silence, Ezzard called out a prayer to respect his ancestor with ceremony the cultural way: 'Kia Kia, Noogiting Wirren, Minang Yorga, Minang Boodja'. Phyllis stood at his side and offered her words, weaving her role as an Anglican minister with that of her cultural heritage as a great-granddaughter of Bessy. She prayed aloud for all to hear, 'May you rest peacefully Great-grandma, in the heavenly Dreaming'.[88] Ezzard then explained to all present what he had said in Noongar language to respect and honour his ancestor:

> I called back to country, and I'm sure that's what she [Bessy] would have heard growing up in Albany, prior to coming out here.
>
> I told her that Uncle Russell and me have come here from the Albany region, Kinjarling, Noongar boodja, Noongar country, and hopefully that will strengthen her spirit, and she can rest peacefully now.
>
> Because I know in some of her letters her heart was longing and yearning to come back home to Albany, to see the beaches and the banksias, but that wasn't to be and even though it's a sad story, it's also an amazing story.
>
> Because, even though she come over here on her own, she's got family here and it's been good for me to come over and make that connection, and to come and see her, and to let her know that everything is okay and that the family here is what we've come together for. We've all got that one link and that one strong connection.
>
> We should be proud of our past, and of our history, and of this Noongar woman that we all share our history and memories with. So thank you for embracing me for the last couple of days, and welcoming me into your hearts and into your homes. I'll cherish it, because I'm sure she would love that and I know that it will be ten-fold when you come over to Albany, as well.
>
> I think it's important – the legacy that she's left and the legacy for you to carry on. It's a powerful legacy for everybody here.[89]

Phyllis elaborated on the short prayer offered for her great-grandmother:

CHAPTER 4: TWO FAMILIES UNITED

> I feel like I've followed in her footsteps in my leadership…her church works and where I am today [make for synchronicity]. I think it might have been [my choice to be an Anglican reverend] through her guidance, and the strong woman she is.
>
> I just feel that I'm always there – out and about in community and my community knows that I'm always there to help them, whenever the need is…and maybe I got that strength from her. Maybe she is living within me because I feel very strong [when I think about her]. I did read about the works that she did, and so maybe she is re-living in me…giving out that strength to the people she loved so much, and cared for. I'm a big part of her, and I'm so proud to know that.[90]

Addressing the Bryant family at the cemetery, Russell spoke of cultural responsibility to family:

> It's a sad time, but at the same time it's an exciting time, for you people here in Bairnsdale, Victoria – for us, me and Ezzard, to come over and to share with you a piece of our family.
>
> We don't know what tomorrow is going to bring. We don't know what next week's going to bring. But we do know that each of us has a responsibility to ourselves, to our family, and then to the wider community.
>
> I'm going to tell you now, you people, the very fact that we're here shows you what love is. Love means leaving one side of the country to come and share with you.
>
> I can say more.
>
> But I know a piece of my heart is here, a piece of Ezzard's heart is

> here. I'm a Law-man, an initiated man. I go Docker River and I go right through the centre. I'll always come back to here.[91]

On completion of these shared words, the process of family commemoration continued with the placement of fresh flowers on the ground. Hands were placed on the earth. Phyllis said in a later conversation, 'It's a proud time knowing that we found our great-grandmother at last'.[92]

Once again, passing around old photographs of family, along with the presentation of Keith Bryant's death certificate, added to the family performance of restoring ancestors to the present. Also circulated were photos picturing Bessy as a girl at Annesfield and the Bryant family members when they were children at the Lake Tyers Trust. The childhood photos produced laughter within moments of self-recognition, and a longing for family who were no longer living, such as Keith and Esther Bryant.

The loss of Bessy's memory within the Bryant and Flowers families was returned to a performance of living history through photos, memory and story. Stirring up past memories effactually emplaced Bessy within a present context, her Gunai-Kurnai and Wirlomin and Minang families reinstating for their ancestor a place of family pride and dignity, while also reasserting the need for keeping strong legacies of family connections.

In a conversation with Russell Nelly that reflected on this social dynamic of kinship, he expressed why it was important for Bessy's family to engage with history and to create memories for cultural futures. He said: 'the effects of this life are still being felt today by her [Bessy's] people. I feel like I can empathise with Bessy, because we, as Aboriginal people, are spiritual and it's how we understand whatever we have.' For him, to appreciate the life story of Bessy was to believe that 'there is hope and there is inspiration that can be gathered from [her] life'. Russell was not suggesting that the process was going to be easy, however. As experienced in East Gippsland, the meeting of both family groups connected to Bessy became a

CHAPTER 4: TWO FAMILIES UNITED

cultural interaction between individuals and family that was physically, spiritually and emotionally demanding. Russell asked, 'Are the families prepared to go over their history? It's a big project', particularly when, as he described, 'the past is indelibly etched on one's life. In the future…we tend to dwell on the past to draw our resources and strength from, we have to…'[93]

The conversation with Russell was influential to an interview with Ezzard that explored his personal history. Our conversation helped to generate an understanding about what was taking place from his cultural perspective. This included the emotional toll and consequence of receiving Bessy's returned history. Russell explained that Bessy's descendants and kin would have to deal with the past, and what had happened to their ancestor throughout the duration of her life. He said that they would deeply feel the history of her story and that the impact would be beyond a state of mere curiosity. Comprehension of Bessy's past meant experiencing her life not as a fable or as a make-believe history, but as a life that had once been lived in real time. The stepping back in time by her present-day kin would be emotional and, as Russell expressed, he believed that the experience would 'make a lot of people cry'.[94]

***

Engaging with a history that had previously been silent to descendant family and kin, the Bryant and Flowers families found intimate and meaningful ways in which to speak back to Bessy's past. They reclaimed a truth through contemporary knowledge, language, kinship and generation of shared memories. This experience, among family, of heritage reclamation was essential to restoring self and community identity, dignity and emotional strength. It also established cultural reasoning for maintaining and preserving physical, cultural and spiritual relationships to the country of ancestors. Understanding these concepts of living culture came to be particularly potent in Betty's engagement with photos of her Bryant family. Attachment to family as an expression of family remembrance is about knowing why reclamation matters.

Betty Hood was the eldest Bryant descendant of Bessy when the reunion took place. Her mother was Margaret, and Bessy's granddaughter and Keith Bryant's sister. Betty grew up with Keith Bryant and his wife, Esther (née Marks). Esther was a Wotjobaluk woman from northwestern Victoria, which was Donald Cameron's ancestral country. Keith's mother was Bessy's eldest daughter, Annie Magdalene (Maggie), who was photographed as a child with her younger sister Louisa some time in the 1870s.

Betty's love of photos led to her being the family photographer for many years. I spoke to Betty in 2013, several years after the reunion, to explore why she first started taking photos, and her role in caring for a small collection of the Bryant family photos which had appeared at the reunion. Betty shared the following reflections:

> It was Grandma [Esther Bryant] who got it for me [a Kodak Brownie]. It was a box camera from a second-hand shop. Nan, she bought it for me for a couple of shillings, and then I went out and got a film and started muckin' around with it. Started taking photos of little brother, the other brother with his dog at The Bluff, and Aunty Emma and Pop, and the parties out there.
>
> [This photograph of Nan and Pop], that's taken at the Red Bluff, The Bluff. I was about 12 or 13, I think. That's when we got off the mission. I took it [the photo] because I liked mucking around with the camera. No one else did, they just liked running around in the bush and killin' possums.
>
> I took [lots of photos] of the mob here because I got 'em all together and said, 'I'll go and take a photo and see how it comes out.' They didn't believe that I was gunna take all the other ones. That's the mob where they're all looking straggly [referring to a photo of kids with unkept hair and clothes dirty from playing rough out in the bush]. But then a roll of film didn't cost much. Cost a couple of dollars to get them printed out, a few shillings in those days.

CHAPTER 4: TWO FAMILIES UNITED

[I like being a photographer.] I thought I was going to be one because I was always muckin' around with this funny little Kodak box camera. I like taking photographs, you know, of people sitting or looking different…

[It was important to photograph the family] because they wanted to look at [photos] of when they were little, and so I kept them in something that belonged to me, and no one was allowed to touch them. Put them amongst my grandmother's stuff…She used to say, 'Well let's go and look at the photos of them when they was young', and 'Look at 'em all straggly there'. Yeah they were straggly. They was happy…even though they was snotty-nosed straggly little kids.

I just can't picture [Bessy] properly. All I see is this old lady…As soon as she comes closer [the image] fades away from me and when I wake up…I can't picture her anymore. It's different with the photo of Nan and Pop, that's stuck in my head and I can picture them all the time. I can just see them two sitting there at The Bluff. I can still see that picture in my mind.

[Bessy] just feels like some lady that's gone that I can't even picture anymore…I've got to look at the photographs and try and picture in my mind that she's family. Sometimes I just shut it out because my mind is not going to go back to her anymore. It's like wind blowing into a box and shifting all the pages, that's the way it is with me. The wind blows and all the paper pages are gone, and I can't come back to it.[95]

…I can't fix it by myself unless I've got someone to help talk it through with, 'Yeah, this' one belongs here to this one, or this one over here belongs to that one'. And I'll start making the conversation and then kind of finish it and then we leave it for another day, another day and that day never comes, it's gone.

[Bessy] feels like a ghost. [Nan and Pop never talked about her but] Pop used to tell us ghost stories. We used to get scared and cuddle up together, but he never talked to us about his family, not that I know of...

[When I see some of these old photos] I say, 'Who's all these people?' 'I don't know, I don't know', and I say: 'I saw the photo of so-and-so, connected to Pop Bryant.' Pop Bryant, he's the only man left in Victoria [who would have had the role of family storyteller] with us, we'd tried to [talk to him], but [he said], 'Go away, go away.' But he never used to talk about Nanny Bryant [Bessy].

When Pop was alive he could have found his grandmother's grave himself. I'm getting involved at the last minute now when I'm getting ready for my own grave. Probably, I'll meet my great-nanna up there and be walking around, 'Are you a Cameron? Are you a Cameron? Finally met you in death, after [my] death.'

Seeing the past means the past is still with me. I took them photos down off the wall [before Betty went to hospital] and they're locked in the cupboard and I want them back on the wall so I've got something to keep me going. I can walk past and say, 'Hello Nan', 'Good morning Pop'. I wish I could go back to the past because I had a happy time with them.

The only thing that clears my mind is seeing my Grandma and Grandpa, that's something that I hold on to. Oh, I can walk around, leave the pictures there, 'Love ya Nan; love ya Pop.' The bits of paper... it's a history book to me but that's real, that stays in my heart. It makes me feel good [to have taken the photos] and it's something to treasure. If I go and get a book and sit down and read it's just history to me and I can't get my head around it...I can't follow it and I can't find the answers on my own.

[Photos help me remember in a different way than books.] I can run around and tell [Nan and Pop], 'Oh it's a lovely day', and I can put the billy on for them and little things like that...It's stuck with me because

CHAPTER 4: TWO FAMILIES UNITED

them the two that reared me up.[96]

The unification of Bessy's families created opportunities for them to imagine her living at Ramahyuck and in the Gippsland region. Respecting interconnections between kin and significant sites on country also mobilised a process of self-examination through stories of identity that, when openly shared, expanded the questions being asked about Bessy's past in context to Bryant and Flowers family futures.

Figure 80 Betty Hood, Toorloo Arm Hall, Victoria, 2011

Figure 81 Julia Hood, Toorloo Arm Hall, Victoria, 2011

Figure 82 Back row: Frank Hood, Jason Hood Senior, Leslie Briggs, Jason Hood Junior. Middle row: Kyle Hood, Julia Hood. Front row: Olivia Hood, Curtis Hood, Toorloo Arm Hall, Victoria, 2011

Figure 83 Left to right: Phyllis Andy, Rechelle Andy, Jake Lee, Jacqueline Andy, Ashley Conway, Toorloo Arm Hall, Victoria, 2011

CHAPTER 4: TWO FAMILIES UNITED

Figure 84 Left to right: Chantelle Hood, Jeffrey Walker, Regina Wilkinson, Janelle Bryant, Toorloo Arm Hall, Victoria, 2011

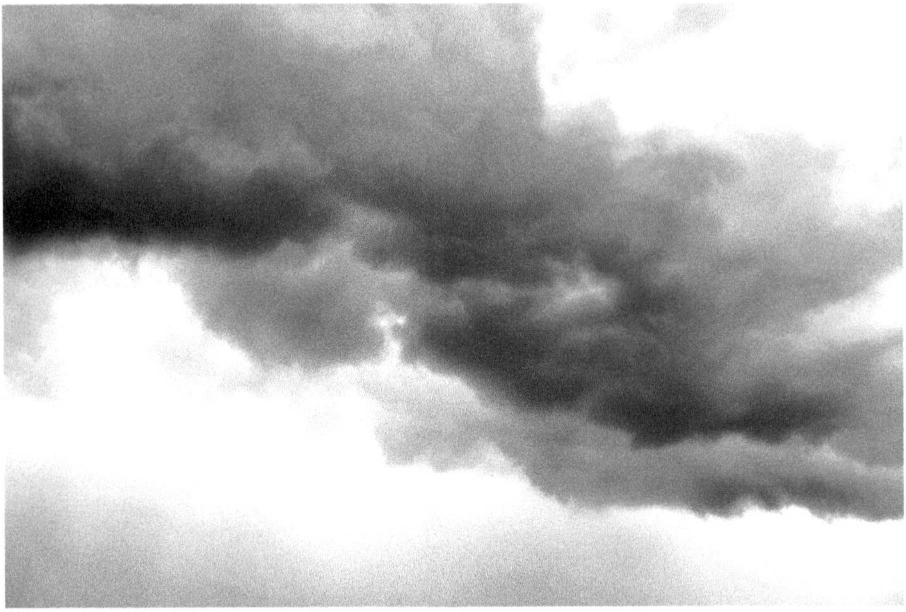

Figure 85 Clouds, Bairnsdale Cemetery, Victoria, 2011

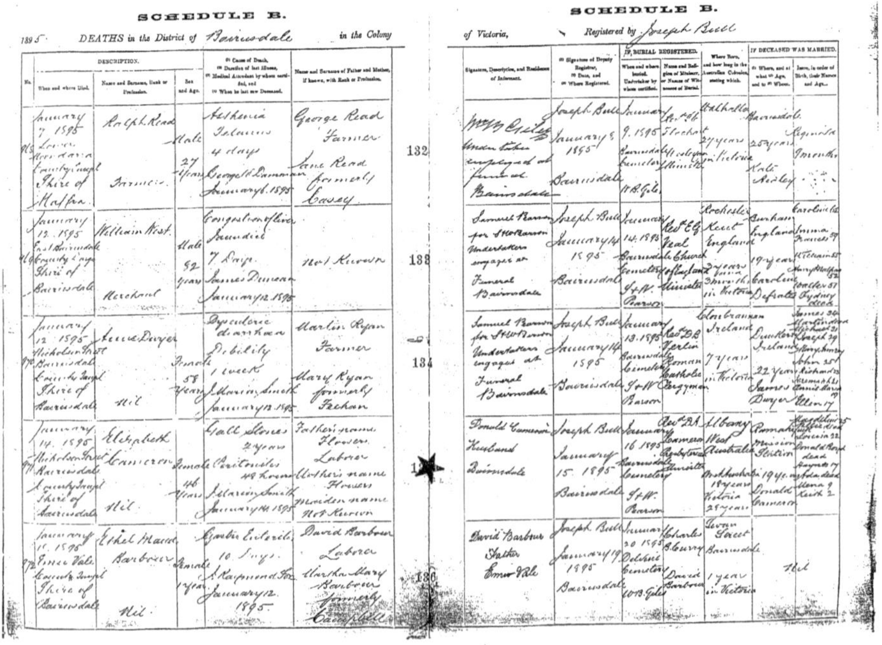

Figure 86 Bessy Cameron Death Certificate, 1895. Collection: Melbourne Archives.

CHAPTER 4: TWO FAMILIES UNITED

Figure 87 Phyllis Andy, Bairnsdale Cemetery, Victoria, 2011

Figure 88 Phyllis Andy, Bairnsdale Cemetery, Victoria, 2011

Figure 89 Grave 1215 not located in the old Presbyterian section and listed on the cemetery map as belonging to a young girl buried in the 1900s, 2011

CHAPTER 4: TWO FAMILIES UNITED

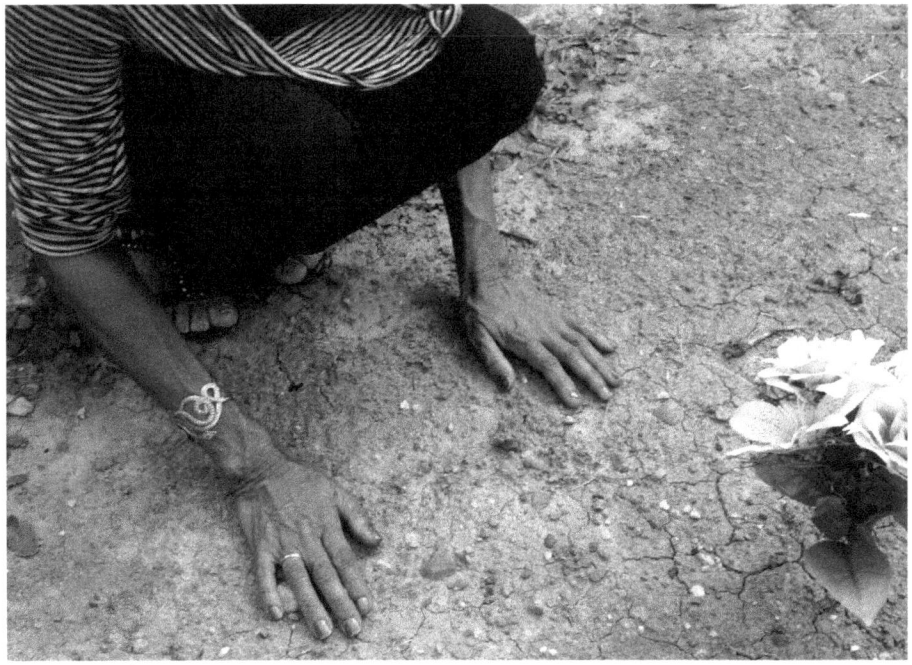

Figure 90 Flo Hood, Bairnsdale Cemetery, Victoria, 2011

Figure 91 Ezzard Flowers, Russell Nelly and Betty Hood, Bairnsdale Cemetery, Victoria, 2011

Figure 92 Ezzard Flowers and Phyllis Andy, Bairnsdale Cemetery, Victoria, 2011

Figure 93 Regina Wilkinson and Phyllis Andy, Bairnsdale Cemetery, Victoria, 2011

Chapter 5:
Never forget –
who we are and why we're here

In November 2011 I returned to Western Australia to widen the scope of conversation with Bessy's Wirlomin and Minang kin, particularly the Elders and senior knowledge holders of the Flowers family – Donald Flowers and Clara Flowers – and Noongar Elder Hazel Brown. I also planned to interview Ezzard at his request and spend time exploring through story the social and spiritual bond between ancestors and living family.

Donald, at this time, was one of the oldest surviving members of the Flowers family and, for this reason, talking to him about Bessy's past, such as her journey from Annesfield to Ramahyuck, was vital to understanding how heritage might be reclaimed through voices that recognised, through life experience, the ways in which identity was both constant yet ever changing. To create a contemporary story with integrity was reliant upon inclusive yet varied perspectives representing her descendants and kin, which in the case of this trip were Wirlomin and Minang senior relatives with pasts affected by colonial legacies of trauma, and memories prejudiced by both the breakdown and restoration of family connections and social contexts.

Ezzard had called Donald ahead of my arrival and set up our meeting in Moora, north of Perth. Listening to Donald reflect upon his life was about establishing a place for Bessy that existed within his own approach to attaching people from the past to the present. The historical photo of Bessy was the gateway that enabled a passage between the dimensions of the living and the dead. Donald negotiated the loss of Bessy within living memory through stories that he told about growing up on missions in various parts of Western Australia. With Melva Flowers there had been memories laid to rest whether instinctively or out of the pure necessity to be freed from the past. For Donald it was about transforming a settler-colonial product represented by the written history of Bessy into an experience holding personal and family meaning and value.

Pushing to the side what was not known, the focus of our conversation became about the familiar and the deeply understood. Donald's wife, Dolores, known affectionately as Aunty La La, took the lead. Moving from the small table and chairs in the carport she took me inside their home. Here she insisted that I look at their wedding photo on the wall and a montage of other photos that pictured the family growing up over the years. The proudly displayed family photos in the domestic home made the immediacy of emplacing Bessy within the everyday social world of the living tangible and very real. I departed Moora and travelled to Katanning on the Great Southern Highway southeast of Perth where I spent time with Ezzard and Russell Nelly.

***

CHAPTER 5: NEVER FORGET

Figure 94 Donald Flowers, Moora, Western Australia, 2011

NO LONGER A WANDERING SPIRIT

CHAPTER 5: NEVER FORGET

Figure 95 Dolores (La La) and Donald Flowers, Moora, Western Australia, 2011

Figure 96 Dolores (La La) Flowers, Moora, Western Australia, 2011

Figure 97 Dolores (La La) Flowers looking at family photos, Moora, Western Australia, 2011

CHAPTER 5: NEVER FORGET

Before leaving Katanning, Ezzard and I went to visit his mother. My first meeting with Clara Flowers was in 2010 after presenting Bessy's history to senior Noongar family members at the family history workshops. I had met Clara at her home to determine what knowledge about Bessy existed within the Flowers family. When I arrived with Ezzard this time, Clara recalled the earlier visit and she laughed at the memory of keeping me at bay and the clear message given about Ezzard's authority regarding information about the Flowers lineage. For Clara, being the family contact for Bessy's history was not her responsibility and there was also deep sadness when asked to talk about the past, especially in relation to her children. It was painful to remember the trauma experienced by Ezzard when separated from his family and kin as a child.

Clara repeated something I had learned at an earlier time from Melva Flowers. It was the personal decision to tell a story or not to tell a story. Telling stories often involved going back in time. Clara said: 'I prefer to let all of that go' and 'I look forward to what is coming and not to what's backward'.[97] For some people, returning to the past offers no solace and to reflect can mean the reappearance of memories that are permeated with feelings of distress, grief or sorrow. In the case of Bessy's history, it was important for Ezzard to return to the past and from there share a personal story in which she could be culturally emplaced.

On return to Albany, Ezzard took me to the home of Hazel Brown, who was a Wirlomin Noongar Elder and matriarchal custodian of knowledge and cultural stories. Though small in stature and now in her older years also hard of hearing, she was both enigmatic and straightforward in what she had to say about the dynamic forces of culture spanning multiple generations. Hazel told story upon story about Wirlomin families and community life. She explained in detail the history of Wirlomin people and spoke the memories that returned her to mission living and to time spent in the bush. Hazel was born on 9 November 1925 and her legacy of knowledge was of significant value to Wirlomin people seeking family histories or other details about Wirlomin heritage.

Ezzard wanted to hear from Hazel about his ancestry. His knowledge of the

Flowers family and community kin connections had been disrupted at a young age. Ezzard had missed out on hearing the many stories passed down by the old people. He had been disconnected by no choice of his own from communicable oral knowledge of family and cultural ways. The reclamation of this knowledge was important. As the matriarch of Wirlomin histories, Hazel earnestly shared with Ezzard the times in which she had kept company with members of his family, particularly with the old people who were hazy within his lived memory.

In respect to Bessy's story, I asked Hazel if she knew anything about her from the stories handed down through the generations. The photo of Bessy had started a conversation about why family albums were important to finding memories of family. Hazel explained to us how photos helped to emplace family within a story of relatedness, and within a shared community experience. She said, 'Photos help to bring people together, to find out who they are, where they are...'.[98] To know who was family within a community meant knowing one's self. To keep threads of kinship strong was also to know where your ancestors were buried. Hazel discerned that knowing where your ancestors were buried was crucial to one's sense of self and therefore one's identity. In the same way that photos generated memories of family and loved ones, to be acquainted with ancestral burial places meant that 'you can go back, and find them memories'.[99]

Conversing with Hazel made evident that networks of family were an unbroken continuum, as long as people who had passed on were remembered by the living. Time spent with Hazel helped Ezzard fill in gaps he had identified within his family knowledge. He talked about this in the interview about his life story recorded after his meeting with Hazel.

At another time, Ezzard had gifted me a book, *Koorah Coolingah – Children Long Ago*, about the Carrolup drawings made by Noongar children during the 1940s and 1950s, and the work being done for their return from Colgate University in the United States.[100] He had spoken a great deal over the years about this repatriation. Ezzard discussed how he believed there was a connecting experience between the drawings created by children living on the Carrolup Native Settlement

CHAPTER 5: NEVER FORGET

Figure 98 Hazel Brown, Albany, Western Australia, 2011

Figure 99 Ezzard Flowers, Riddles Creek, Victoria, 2012

and his childhood memories of mission life. Operating on similar terms to the missions that were governed by Western Australian authorities under the *Aborigines Act* 1905, the Carrolup Native Settlement had been set up on the banks of the Carrolup River, using the site of a traditional Noongar camp. This history inspired the basis of Ezzard's history that he shared.

He began his story with his birthplace in addition to significant childhood memories that involved his separation from family and community:

> I'm a Wirlomin and Minang Noongar and I was born in 1958 on the Gnowangerup [Mission] in 1958. It was part of the UAM, the United Aborigines Mission.
>
> In 1968 I got sent to Marribank Mission after the death of my father in a car crash, and my mum didn't know because she was with family. She had left us with Aunty. I was at Marribank Mission, and I left in 1972 when I was 14 going on 15, I got sent to Mogumber Mission.
>
> My clan is the Wirlomin and Minang tribes and I'm also a Stolen Generations surviving member.
>
> My father's connection is Minang and my mother's is Wirlomin. Minang covers the Albany region, the Great Southern, and Wirlomin the Central Great Southern region. Wirlomin is a clan in the Goreng group in the Gnowangerup area. There are 14 different tribal groups…that come under the Noongar Nation. Wirlomin is just one of them and Minang is another. The Noongar region has many languages or dialects. There are similarities but they're all different, even spelt differently.
>
> [Being a Wirlomin and Minang Noongar connects me to country], it's a totemic connection. Wirlomin for instance connects me to the curlew, [it's] a small, long-legged bird with big eyes. It makes a very distinct and unique cry. If you were in the bush, you would definitely hear it.

CHAPTER 5: NEVER FORGET

Sometimes, if they hear you coming, they will lie down amongst the bark, or in the bush, and you wouldn't see it because it camouflages itself so well. My other connection is to the eagle, the Waalitch, wedge-tailed eagle. They give me an identity. I know who I am and which part of the Great Southern I am connected to.

A lot of people say to me, 'Stolen? You wasn't stolen.' But if I take something away from you without you giving me permission…is that stealing? Or in my case, what was taken from me, without my permission, or even my mother's permission, was not only my family structure and connection to country, but my identity, culture, my language and customs, which I had to learn all over again to reconnect to who I am.

When I was about six or younger, I lived out in the bush, on the farms with my grandparents. [And] they used to teach me the language, which was part of my growing up, and also knowing where I was by knowing the name of the bush tuckers, and what season that they were around, and how to survive.

[So] that's why our language was very important when we were growing up. But we were not allowed to speak any word of our language when we went to school. We had to speak English, 'please' and 'thank you' and put your hands up, 'can I go to the toilet ma'am or sir' and if we were ever seen in a group and talking in our own language, we would get the cane. I saw it happen plenty of times in school.

When we went to school in mainstream we weren't allowed to speak language and our parents and grandmothers and grandfathers weren't allowed to for fear of being reprimanded. That's how fearful it was for our people to pass on that language, because it was part of the 1905 Act and, of course, with us in Western Australia [having to deal with] the

Chief Aboriginal Protector who knew nothing about Aboriginal culture.

What happened back then is having an impact on the struggles we're having today. [Because] of that confusion around our history and our language when it comes to storylines and songlines that connect us to country. Of course, it's becoming more significant and important now to find out where we come from, so we not only reflect on the past prior to assimilation, but also to our country in regards to Native Title rights within the region and knowing exactly what group you belong to.

…We need to know the bigger picture in regards to everybody who comes from the region, who has the right of passage, and who are the gatekeepers, especially now that Noongar people, and also Aboriginal people right through the country have to prove our Aboriginality.

Nobody else has to prove whereabouts they have come from. Yet we, as Aboriginal people, have to prove where we've come from, simply because of the 1905 Act, which discriminated against fair-skinned kids. The Chief Aboriginal Protector at that time, AO Neville, classified us as half-castes, quarter-castes, quadroons and all that kind of stuff. That's not talking about bloodlines, that's talking about skin groups and that's why we have to prove our Aboriginality and that we're Aboriginal. Why, I don't know.

That's why a lot of the Elders are concerned about the word 'Indigenous'. They feel that it doesn't identify them as First Peoples, whereas Aboriginal [is] connected to country. When you say 'Indigenous', well every person born in Australia is Indigenous. When you say 'Aboriginal' then you know you're talking about the First Peoples.

There is a big difference between 'Aboriginal' and 'Indigenous' and if we look at today's society it's multicultural. Yet the focus is only on the First Peoples. We know times have changed, and we've got to move

CHAPTER 5: NEVER FORGET

with it, but you've also got to know where you come from and who you are, so that you can pass knowledge on to your kids.

That's the thing these days, being accepted and being acknowledged, and for us we need to know where we come from, and who we are…to move forward, because we've come a long way in history. Have a look at the history of Noongar people, at how many bills that were passed, the acts that were made. You'd be amazed how hard it's been for us to maintain our history, our heritage and our dignity and identity…who it is we are, through surviving.

Those of us on the mission, we survived because of where we were put…on the mission. We were lucky that the mission we were in was in the bush. It gave us the strength to survive, and for the ones who went into foster care, or homes in the cities, it would have been entirely different because there wouldn't have been any bush that could connect [them] to something cultural.

Gnowangerup, Moore River and Carrolup were the three major settlements controlled by the 1905 Act and so when the mission in Moore River got full they were sent to Moore River Native Settlement and when Carrolup got full they got sent to Gnowangerup…and vice versa. So everybody was registered like cattle and drafted like cattle or sheep out of their own country where they were born or where their grandmother's country is or their grandfather's.

Today when we look at culture and identity it's important to know where our ancestors and families come from, what line we are linked to, in regards to bloodlines and also kinship lines, storylines and songlines, even totemic lines. They mean that we come from that certain region, and we are to take care of that region or that country and those animals that live within it.

NO LONGER A WANDERING SPIRIT

Gnowangerup [where I come from] is about 120 kilometres north of Albany…Gnowangerup is wheatbelt and farming country in the Central Great Southern region.

It's mallee country, good farming land, and a lot of our grandfathers and ancestors helped clear that land around Gnowangerup and even down around Bremer Bay. Back in those days if the farmers needed a worker, they would get permission through the Native Welfare Department, because Aboriginal people weren't allowed to move off the reserves without permission.

Those missions were sites of assimilation, reservation and segregation and my segregation connected me to the three significant sites, Gnowangerup, Marribank and Mogumber missions. I connected to Carrolup and Moore River through my experience at Marribank, and Mogumber through my segregation and experience as a Stolen Generations survivor. I was born on one mission site, sent to another mission site and then got sent to the other one. All my life I had no say in it, I just had to move because the Welfare said this is where you're going, and that's what I think happened with old girl [Bessy], when she left Albany and went that way [east] to Victoria. She probably didn't have that much say in this movement away from home either.

There were three agricultural schools developed for Noongar boys. One was the old Gnowangerup Mission. Another one, where I got sent to, was the old Mogumber Mission, but because of the closing down of the mission…they formed the mission campus into an agricultural school for boys. Because, when they asked me first when I was in Marribank Mission if I wanted to go to agricultural school in Gnowangerup, I said, 'Of course', because I thought I was going back home. But then some of the boys from the Kimberley also wanted to come down to Gnowangerup Agricultural School and I think there

CHAPTER 5: NEVER FORGET

was about six of them. That filled up the numbers there, so I got sent to Mogumber, further away from home again, you know...And I was yearning for family and being on the mission, knowing where I come from and trying to get back there all the time. From there I just met up with some of the other boys who was on the mission and we started doing this and doing that and ended up being a regular guest of the majesty and all that kind of stuff, in and out of jail.

That period of being on the mission, we were never once shown any affection or given a hug and a cuddle, and they never even prepared us for life outside of the mission. It was rough for us boys, but at least we could live rough. But can you imagine the girls? They never taught them anything. And most of them when they came out didn't only not know where they come from, they'd lost that family contact and connection. Most of their relationship was abuse through alcohol and drugs and jealousy, because they wanted to look for a father figure. Someone to look after them and take care of them...Never been taught anything about the facts of life, babies and all that kind of stuff. They were just sent out of the mission to white house parents. Some did good and others didn't, because of that longing and yearning to be home with family.

And most of our grandparents, my grandfathers and grandmothers, most of them had passed away and the reserve was a scattered and shattered place to be. I had to go through all that again, reconnecting, and most of that three years since being on the mission and going back I had to sit and listen and watch and learn what I had missed out on all that time throughout those 10 years.

We had plenty of opportunities of taking off from school, but none of us ever thought of it. And when that *Rabbit Proof Fence* movie came out and we were watching that, because I was at Mogumber Agri-cultural School...to actually see those girls run away and back up home, tears just started falling down my face, automatically, big crocodile tears. Because they did what I couldn't and I had plenty, easy opportunities. They took off home, went back home to country and they knew where to go because before they left they was told by their mum and their nans, 'Always walk along the rabbit proof fence, or if you ever get lost, follow the rabbit proof fence'. And that's what they did.

But now, for us adults, most of us grandparents now, yet we still have a close bond and connection as brothers and sisters and extended brothers and sisters. And that's the thing we focus back on, the positive thing that we had. Even though we were [shown] no affection or love, we embraced one another as sister and brother, and a lot of people say, 'Well, what was stolen?' Well, that's the sort of stuff that was stolen away from us, without asking us – our identity, our culture, our mothers and fathers, our grandparents who could not pass on what they learnt, because there was none of us there for them to pass it on to, and most of them died of broken hearts, literally.

…A lot of people say, 'Well, our culture's gone'. The only time our culture will be gone, my culture will be gone, is when I'm gone. Because I am who I am, because of where I come from and what I know and where I belong and that's out in the bush…We never lost our language [completely], it's still there and even with our bush tucker, our trees and the stories that are handed down, like Bulla Miel, place of many eyes and also its other name, Koikernerruph, place of mystical clouds. And when we see the clouds rolling in over Bulla Miel, Bluff Knoll, that usually means that there's someone from this country has passed away…But also it's a resting place for where we go into the afterlife, where our spirits go. That's why Bulla Miel, Bluff Knoll, is place of many eyes.

Yeah, [the stories have survived], them ones and others, even the

CHAPTER 5: NEVER FORGET

stories of the stars like the Emu up in the sky and all of its connections. A lot of the kids wouldn't know that today, because they're in the fast lane, going nowhere. Or they're in the city and they've never ever seen the stars or the moon because of the bright lights, or they've never heard the sound of the real night. All they've ever heard is the roar of the city. They don't hear the crickets and the frogs and the birds…and once you get back and want to do that you know, it can only be done if you make that choice. It's about your choice and your decision.

If you believe that your culture is shattered and scattered and finished, or your language is gone, well then you're a dead man walking. But if you believe and know that you can reconnect to your language, to your culture, well then you become empowered. Your spirit leads you…

When we go out to designated sites that [have] story connections and songlines, like fish traps, for example. Over time, the elements, the wind and the water might knock a few rocks over, and we might come along and look at them and go, 'Ahh, fish traps'. Do we leave those rocks there or do we put them back in place and rebuild that structure? Does it have to be in that shape and in that form, or do we need to add more to make it stronger, for it still to be alive and active and breathing?

Because my trip is all about my spirit being in transition all the time, you know, wandering spirit. It wasn't until I'd come back home and sat down and listened and watched and seen what was going on that I realised who I was and…talking with Elders, getting their stories and hearing them speaking about the bush and how powerful it can become. That's built my spirit up, because if we kill our spirit, well then we're dead and that's what our spirituality is all about.

It was really important for me as a Stolen Generations survivor and someone who's been in a mission [to go into the former Annesfield institution]. But…actually that was the first time I'd been there, I didn't even know it was there…I felt really connected to the place and I seen a lot of things in there other than just that empty space.

It just brought back memories of my days as a kid in a mission, in Marribank Mission, and I can only imagine what went on there. Some of the feelings and the emotions was powerful stuff, but there wasn't too much negative stuff that I felt there. But that doesn't mean there wasn't.

I could see them rushing around in their in old uniforms and aprons on and those bonnets or whatever they were called. [But] going in there and making that connection really, really made me feel – oh, really connected me to this story. And then going over to Victoria and doing that stuff down at East Gippsland, Lake Tyers and Bairnsdale, really brought that connection into being. That's when I started to become really emotional you know, because of that, when she went over there and she was still longing and yearning for Albany, but she couldn't come back.

She wrote a lot of letters back to Anne, but she felt homesick. Just like I did. But, with me, the only way I tried to get back home was through breaking the law. Because, I thought, oh well, I'm up here in Kalgoorlie, break the law here and they'll send me back to Perth and I'll be closer to Gnowangerup, and from there I can go down to Albany. But with Aunty Bessy she couldn't do that because she went on a ship out on the ocean and that's a daunting and scary experience for anyone at any time. Travelling from Albany to Lake Tyers mission is a long way.

Just thinking about it now I can hear them saying, 'Bessy, you've gotta go to Melbourne'. She probably wouldn't have asked why, and do a tantrum and say: 'Why can't somebody else go?'

CHAPTER 5: NEVER FORGET

When we went to school, we weren't allowed to question anything. Or we had to put up our hand and ask permission. But because of the 1905 Act all permission had to be written or questions written and presented to the chief superintendent, the carer of all Aborigines, who was Mr Middleton here in Albany. So if [Bessy] wanted to complain she would have had to ask Mrs Camfield, 'I want to write a letter. I want to complain to Mr Middleton that I do not want to go to Victoria on any boat.' Because, as we know she was well educated, she could write letters…

So I take my hat off to her and the other women who went on that boat, not knowing their destiny…There's a powerful story coming from it and I reckon whatever comes out of this will be a powerful legacy. [A legacy of] survival! A story of hardship, a story of the woman she became while she was over there [at Ramahyuck] and survival, that we back here as Wirlomin and Minang people did not know what she'd done over there in Victoria. They need to know her story and what she achieved, it's a powerful story.

[I'm interested in the past] probably because of where I've been and my upbringing. Because, before I got sent to Marribank mission, I was mainly with my grandparents. I wasn't with Mum and Dad all the time, because they used to be doing seasonal work and I had to stay with my grandparents, and when some of the other grandparents went out on the farm I went with them. This was all before going to school, so yeah, I reckon that being with them and watching what they did and hearing what they said probably made me more aware from the beginning, and chiselled a path to what I'm doing now…connecting to who I am and what I'm here for.

[Mum isn't interested in the past anymore.] Probably because, not so much with the story [of Bessy], but probably that disappointment of her not being there when we got sent away. That kind of connection to what Bessy went through and to what we went through, or she [Mum] went through.

I think because [Bessy] was a strong-spirited woman, and a strong woman in general, her spirit was wandering and yearning for country. That's what mine was doing. Even though I'd been a long way from home my vision and my heart and my spirit was still connected to Gnowangerup and that's where I wanted to be.

So I think even though she was over there [at Ramahyuck] she still would've been connected to Albany, spiritually, and physically, because she wrote about Albany all the time…expressing her yearning for Albany.

…For example, if you mention Gnowangerup, I can vision myself being in Gnowangerup and doing what I've done there in the past. That spiritual connection, and if your spirit is strong so are you. When your spirit goes weak, you go weak as well. Once you lose your spirit, well, you lose everything. Spirit is about you being in the moment, being in the past, present and future. Most importantly, it leads you into the future, you make your destiny.

I feel a sense of belonging and connection to my grandfather's family when I hear the story about Bessy, but also a confusion and sadness. I'm proud because of what I've come to know about my ancestor, but confused because there wasn't any of this history spoken about within my community.

I remember looking at the photo of Bessy for the first time. I saw a young girl who had humility, respect and strength, the three main traits that I believe sustained her throughout her life and times from Minang country to Koori country.

Straight away [I noticed] there was no eye contact with the camera.

CHAPTER 5: NEVER FORGET

She doesn't want to be there, but she's showing in her own Aboriginal way that she's respecting the person taking this photo. The picture along with the words made me think about her life of power, but also loss, struggle and dispossession from culture, family and country. I wasn't to know that this photo of a young girl sitting on a stool would take me on a journey from one side of the country to the other.

This history needs to be recognised and acknowledged because it's a powerful human story that speaks about a strong connection between Western Australia and Victoria. Bessy was just a humble, obedient Aboriginal girl learning to survive in a world that was changing for Aboriginal people.

Back in the colonial days, the Christian emphasis was on rehabilitating Aboriginal people. If they could change an Aboriginal's way of thinking and life, well they'd done their cause, which was changing our way of life. Her Christian faith and upbringing along with her cultural values and beliefs would have empowered her for whatever was to come. I think she definitely did remain a true and obedient servant to the higher authorities at the time.

This story has made my spirit stronger. It has connected me to members of my family I didn't know I had and has also put me in touch with Bessy's history and what she achieved during her life in East Gippsland. Her story has now connected me to family, and all of us family finally know where she's resting.

It's a great sense of relief that we found her, and know where she is, and since that day it has been a spiritual journey of remembering, reflecting and reconnecting, from both sides of the country. This story now connects us, and our conversations with one another will continue as we walk forward along the path of Bessy, our Minang Noongar ancestor.[101]

NO LONGER A WANDERING SPIRIT

***

The recording of oral histories and on-country conversations proved to be beneficial for understanding significant issues and discussions involving the cultural and intercultural dynamics of relational research, knowledge exchange, and both principled and ethical dialogues. Working together in an authentic way recognised and respected the diverse expressions of cultural identities, particularly in relationship to kinship networks, dynamic interrelationships between human and non-human worlds, and the social and ecological cross-generational connections to ancestral homelands.

Imagining the past on cultural terms became the creative device for establishing a meaningful pathway of connection between the past and present. Repositioning the custodianship and ownership of a family history from the archive and to the authorial voices of Elders and families representing the Flowers and Bryant families animated how memories of Bessy were kept safe and cohesive within everyday social lives.[102]

The following conversation in 2012 builds upon positive and resilient activations and activisms of family and kin. It provides insight to a respectful intercultural collaboration and gives cultural context for exploring and understanding the complex particularities of identity, as well as the specificities of heritage that are of value to current and future generations:

> Ezzard: …this is what this story is all about, reviving the spirit of Bessy Flowers, and I believe that her spirit is leading us to do this, you know. I think because of what's happened and what we know, it needs to be completed, because her spirit has been longing and yearning for Albany.
>
> For this story to be told back home in Albany where it all happened is significantly important for her spiritual return to country, and that can happen by bringing back the aunties and the other family members

CHAPTER 5: NEVER FORGET

and meeting up with the immediate family from over there and also the extended family as well.

Sharon: What does it mean to collaborate with one another and to have conversations about culture and identity, between you as an Aboriginal man and me as a non-Aboriginal woman? What does it mean for you to share your cultural knowledge with me, as a wadjella woman? Because that's what we're doing, aren't we?

Ezzard: Well, I think the first time we met, when we started talking about it, and when you took me to that place, the native institution [Annesfield], and when you…said what you were doing for the aunties, I think that clarified for me that they respected you and they'd given you the right of passage. So I acknowledged this and accepted it…So that cleared everything for me.

…You were the right person, in the right place, at the right time, doing the right thing for the right cause. Not only just as a wadjella woman but also your academic achievements as well regarding doing this story, you know this history. By the way you went about it, I just knew it was meant to be and so you have the right of passage to the story and we trust you and respect you.

I think also being respectful and I know that you're connected to the story, because I've seen you show emotion and that's only natural. Because it is an emotional story and captures all those feelings and emotions and what happened and where we're going and what's going to be the outcome.

Sharon: So why is it important to have these conversations that mediate between your lived history, ancestral pasts and imagined futures?

Ezzard: I think it prepares us for what is yet to come and how to adapt and adjust towards that and to accept that.

Sharon: What are some of the challenges we face? For me, it's juggling finances and family, the geographic extensiveness of this story and travelling. Travelling from the Victorian Koori community who I knew for over ten years and arriving in Western Australia, driving down to Albany not knowing anyone that was a challenge for me. I was very nervous about that, entering into an Aboriginal community where I had no connections at all. It was very daunting. What are some of the challenges for you in terms of this project, whether they're cultural or spiritual?

Ezzard: I think the most challenging thing would be making family aware of why this story is important and significant. To make sure that not only what I'm doing, but also what yourself is doing is important and that we need time to make sure it all falls into place, appropriately, culturally and educationally and historically.

Coming over [to East Gippsland] by myself would have been daunting enough to meet family, but because I had Uncle Russell Nelly come with me, well I did have one family. And, also meeting you and Koora [Kooramyee Cooper], when you two came over [to Albany], well that gave me something to focus on and to vision.

At least I knew you. But then going down and meeting all the family and you introducing us all and that kind of stuff made it a lot better… Because you was working with them for ten years or so, you also gained their trust and respect as well as mine.

Not only are you the storyteller, but you're the interpreter, mediator and cultural advisor as well [laughs]…You know exactly what the aunties are thinking, you know what I'm thinking and you just relay that interpretation in all aspects.

And not only are we connected to one another through commun-

CHAPTER 5: NEVER FORGET

ication, but I think also through this story here as well. Because the more I speak to you and the more I sit down and do this, we're not only focusing on the story, but I think we're in it. What do you reckon?

Sharon: I think we've become characters in a bigger story. It's no longer the historical story about Bessy Flowers and the four women shipped from Albany to Ramahyuck mission, this story is now about her descendants, her extended family in Western Australia, but also now about me, a wadjella woman and therefore the broader community. It's a story that not only criss-crosses two states of Australia, but also the Aboriginal and non-Aboriginal communities. There's something quite powerful in that.

Ezzard: I think, even though this story is focused on the life and times of Bessy Flowers, I think we also need to acknowledge the other women who came over here as well, and also you – because you've made the connection through the story and you're more or less making it happen.

Sharon: At the same time, I see it as collaboration even though, as you said, I may be the beginning, the middle and the end, I'm also none of that without you and without Aunty Phyllis [Andy] and the other families. So I am all of that, but not in isolation.

Ezzard: …Everybody on both sides would acknowledge you, because of what you've done and how far we've come. So spiritually what you thinking [about the whole story]?

Sharon: I often feel that my relationship to Bessy Flowers is greater than I ever imagined…I heard a story and [initially] didn't even realise I was engaging with it from my own experience. [Yeah] as a young girl who lost my mother when I was two years old and having feelings of not knowing where I fitted in, or that sense of absence, and coming to know why belonging is important to me through a connection to country, the place where I grew up with my family.

So it's interesting when I first heard about this story and imagined the life of Bessy. I've only just come to see that I've planted myself in that story and that I imagined her through my own experiences in life and that has forced me to take ownership of what I have created by pursing this story. [Because] in a sense by imagining something, by envisioning something through our own experiences, we're actually creating and breathing life into the past. I've come to realise how powerful that can be.

Bessy was a Minang woman, her Aboriginality certainly a large part of her identity. She was an incredibly proud, spiritual woman and a caring human being who had the courage to negotiate her way in a colonial world. She represents to me a human story, what it means to love and be compassionate, to be self-determined, to know that you have a place in this world.

Ezzard: ...I felt when you made contact: I'll communicate with Sharon, but I'll just stay to the left a bit, you know. I'll be independent out here. But the more we continued into this the more it has entwined me. Like you said, powerful spiritual connections.

Sharon: I think without being on country, and in the presence of you all, none of this would make sense to me...None of it would make sense just through her letters and the stories told by non-Aboriginal historians. I've only been able to comprehend it all by visiting those sites of significance – walking through the old Annesfield Native Institution, going to the Ramahyuck Cemetery, to her grave in Bairnsdale, being in the presence of those that hold the essence of who she is. This is the first time Bessy's historical narrative has been held in the hands of those who have the authority to speak on behalf of it, on behalf of her.

Ezzard: I think that was a moving moment and an emotional time

CHAPTER 5: NEVER FORGET

when we all did go to her graveside… You've played a real integral part in connecting us, as family.

Sharon: I feel like the connections are real. They've taken place on country and between people who are connected to Bessy through ancestral bloodlines… Being able to situate yourself in time and place with families from both communities was incredibly significant, and no history book can do that. There's something very powerful in bringing histories together, those lived and those still being lived.

Ezzard: To witness two different families coming together for the first time was both emotional and heartwarming. To meet and to embrace, it meant that our connection to a young girl who then became a mother and a matriarch is a connection that I will be able to hold onto throughout the rest of my life.

I will always remember that unexpected moment when we arrived at the site of the Lake Tyers Trust and I got out of the car. All I could see were faces coming to meet me with big smiles, and that just melted away my fears and concerns. Aunty Phyllis just grabbed me and gave me the biggest hug ever and only family can do that when you need it. The family embraces settled me for the rest of the journey and I will never forget that moment.[103]

......

The cultural practices that were being designed to understand and reclaim an ancestral past were becoming clearer. To sit, reflect, acknowledge and understand why country was so important brought forth a spectrum of stories sensitive to poignant, soulful, shameful and challenging memories. Recognition of family connections also brought forward an intermingling set of emotions. Whether a story was 'good' or 'bad', it had the potential to make a piece of paper – history on a page – come to life.

The physical and metaphysical elements of identity derived from *being in place* innovated a new territory for the expression of family authorial voices. Coming together on country in the Great Southern region, the Bryant and Flowers families went about seeking more answers to heritage questions about their ancestor, and by doing so generated firsthand knowledge significant to living heritage that was in keeping with their cultural worldview.

Figure 100 Sharon Huebner, Lake Tyers Aboriginal Trust, Victoria, 2011 © Link-Up NSW.

CHAPTER 5: NEVER FORGET

Figure 101 Sharon Huebner, Toorloo Arm Hall, Victoria, 2011 © Link-Up NSW.

Figure 102 Ezzard Flowers and Sharon Huebner, Stirling Range, Western Australia, 2013 © Kooramyee Cooper.

Chapter 6:
The certainty of love

In February 2013, five Koori women stood together on a pier in Albany as a strong summer wind lifted skirts in the air and wisped hair against faces. The Bryant descendants of Bessy Flowers – Betty Hood, Phyllis Andy, Amy Hood, Regina Wilkinson and Flo (Marion) Hood – had crossed the continent from their homes in Victoria to bring full circle the on-country unification of Bessy's family. After the Bryant reunion in East Gippsland involving Ezzard Flowers and Russell Nelly, there had been talk among the Bryants about a trip being made to Bessy's traditional country, Phyllis having said in one of our conversations that:

> It'd be just wonderful to connect and put the jigsaw puzzle together and to be able to put back the pieces. But also, connecting back to her country, meeting and connecting to her family who were left behind, and that she had to leave behind, no choice of her own.[104]

Bessy had been captured within the pages of a western archive for more than a century and Phyllis wanted to shift the focus away from the written records and back to everyday family practices of remembrance and memory-making, as she described the visceral process to be. Part of this practice would involve visiting sites that were significant to Bessy's childhood past.

Figure 103 Foreshore, Albany, Western Australia, 2013

Figure 104 Betty Hood, Regina Wilkinson, Amy Hood and Flo (Marion) Hood, Albany, Western Australia, 2013

CHAPTER 6: THE CERTAINTY OF LOVE

Figure 105 Phyllis Andy and Ezzard Flowers, Albany, Western Australia, 2013

Figure 106 Russell Nelly and Regina Wilkinson, Albany, Western Australia, 2013

At Ezzard's request, everyone met on the first morning in Albany at the Princess Royal Harbour, located within King George Sound. His idea was that everyone was to stand at the same harbour from where Bessy's ship would have departed Albany in June 1867. That journey from Albany to Port Adelaide in South Australia and then Melbourne in Victoria was recounted enthusiastically by Bessy in her letters to Anne Camfield.

In silence, and so as not to miss a word, Bessy's Bryant family and Russell Nelly listened to Ezzard map the path of Bessy's departure from Albany aboard a 'steamer' with Rhoda, Ada, Nora and Emily. He told the story of this event as he imagined it to have taken place. He spoke animatedly about the harbour and its visible surroundings to his attentive audience. 'Back this way, up here,' he began, as a way of directing everyone's attention from the water's edge and to the higher ground of York Street, and then when all had changed their focus, continuing the story:

> Looking back up northwest is where the Camfield house is, where Nan used to stay. So, just reflecting back to the time and the moment that she would have had to leave and go on that boat like that one over there, they probably all would have walked with her down York Street there and then across along Princess Avenue, I think.
>
> And through there, see, there was a doorway that led all the way to here, which had a wooden bridge. So that's where they would have walked, and Anne and Henry would have escorted her and the other four girls onto the boat. And they would've sailed out here through King George Sound past the bins here and through the sound and out to sea.
>
> It wasn't mentioned if it was daytime or nighttime or if the sea was choppy like this here, or if there were big swells.[105]

All who were present listened to Ezzard's imagining of Bessy's departure, including a fictional description of her in the past walking from Annesfield to the awaiting steamship in the harbour. He added dramatic effect to the details that in this instance depended very little on the accuracy of historical events. He made it

CHAPTER 6: THE CERTAINTY OF LOVE

comfortable for the archive to be imagined as a flexible experience in time, which was a contrast to the restrictive nature of historical records generally not granted such creative licence.

Ezzard offered a story to his Bryant kin strongly rooted within individual and community knowledge and wisdom. It made the telling of Bessy's history one that was revealing of Ezzard's lived experiences, the source from which personal memories were made. This was the first time that Ezzard or any member of Bessy's living family had taken on the lead role of retelling the events of their ancestor's past on their own terms.

In the lead-up to the gathering at the pier, there had been no prior discussion about Ezzard taking on the role as the primary storyteller. It became apparent that the act of taking back historical records to the Bryant and Flowers families had developed meaning beyond the return of historical photos, missionary documents and both personal and official letters. The process of *being in* and attentive to place had become an energetic space for detailing a different story. It was one in which authorship was granted through lineages that recognised the powerful associations between ancestral connections to country, kinship and the life force of living generations of Bryant and Flowers family and kin.

The years of researching archives and the face-to-face meetings with the families all culminated at the pier through the experience of honouring and reviving a dignified presence for their shared ancestor. Bessy's letters vividly expressed her journey away from Albany and this provided admission for her descendants and kin to glean something about her life. They were understandings that permitted each person to respond with tools befitting of personal remembrance. Questions started to emerge and time was given to reflecting and feeling into the past at the pier, 'Why did the five women get removed?' and 'Where did she go teaching?'[106] Bessy's great-granddaughter Regina asked of Ezzard.

Ezzard answered confidently to his audience. Through his performance as the storyteller he reaffirmed how powerful the social charge of memory making can be when galvanised within the inclusive sphere of family:

NO LONGER A WANDERING SPIRIT

She never did her teaching here. She went and had her training in Sydney. She would have gone out on one of those boats there [finger pointing to a boat anchored in the water] prior to going to Ramahyuck to teach. Because when she came back from Sydney, she was an educated and a professional teacher in her own right.

The reason why she went with the other four girls was because there weren't enough Aboriginal women over there [at Ramahyuck] and there were some of the men from down there, and around Sale and from that area, wanting to marry an Aboriginal woman. So they sent four from here and Old Girl…She went over there to teach.

It was only supposed to be for two years, but she ended up meeting Old Boy [Donald Cameron] and marrying and settling down and having a family and she wasn't worried about anything else.

Even though her heart was longing and yearning for Albany, like most of her letters indicated by saying, 'Dear old Albany', 'Dear Mrs Camfield' – because the Camfields more or less reared her up from this high, yeah [holding his hand at the height of a toddler child] – so she leaves a strong spiritual legacy, not only over there in Victoria in regards to what she's done, but also what's going to be disclosed by us over the next couple of days, in regards to her history.

It's a powerful story of a powerful woman, you know, and a Minang woman at that, so you're not only coming back making contact with your country for the first time, but each of you brings a piece of her with you.[107]

In this portrayal of events, Ezzard's primary concern was not historical accuracy, but rather with sincere purpose, the injection of contextualising emotion.

CHAPTER 6: THE CERTAINTY OF LOVE

In Bessy's story he wanted the feelings created by their presence together at the pier, and at other locations they visited, to be the family version of events that would be remembered and retold. For instance, the act of Bessy looking back in her mind to Minang country when in the eastern colonies as detailed in a letter to Anne was an important trigger for Ezzard when consolidating values of belonging and of identity. He believed wholeheartedly that throughout her life Bessy maintained an interest in, and concern for, her traditional country of birth.

The seagulls on the pier added to the process of memory making with their lively squawks and wired commotion. During a brief interlude of silence, Phyllis reflected, 'This is special and significant…to be here where she last walked, never to return, her last footsteps [in her own country]'.[108] Phyllis's observation generated other images: 'Her last footprints',[109] said Amy, and Phyllis again, 'Out of town, out of her country, so sad'.[110] Inspired by the new score of imaginings, Ezzard took his turn to set the scene some more:

> Well, just imagine if we were back in the 19th century and you had your long white dresses on and your little caps, and we come here to send you off and wave goodbye to you. What would you be thinking about? Leaving your homeland, your home country, your people and everything that you're used to…and who knows how long you would've been on the boat for?[111]
>
> Have you seen that photo of her sitting on the chair? What did you notice about that?

Referring to Bessy's photo as a child at Annesfield had everyone in deep thought. Amy was the first to respond: 'Sadness. Far away eyes',[112] followed by Phyllis's perceiving agreement, 'Yes, sadness'.[113] The photo elicited more from Ezzard, who shared with his gathered family:

She was mindful that she was going to go away and leave family, and country, and people. But she had four other girls with her who she had to look after.

What's significant about the photo is that even though she's being photographed, she's not making full contact with the lens…she's looking down. She's being respectful, especially about what's happening, even though she doesn't want to depart.

It's because of the trust and the respect that she had for Mrs Camfield. Whatever Mrs Camfield would've asked her to do, she would have done and she did.

So going over there for the first time would have been daunting.[114]

Phyllis continued with her additions to the process of culturally taking back the photo:

I can imagine what the lady was saying to her. 'You are now the educated one here, and you now have to look after these girls who haven't left home before', a big responsibility that she carried at such a young age…She didn't have that choice of saying no.

There's always a penalisation at the end of disobedience. We all get penalised and I think that was her thing. She didn't want to be penalised for stubbornness or disobeying and, you know, I suppose in a white man's law that was a strong way of punishing people – being removed, being taken away from family or even locked up in jail. We couldn't refuse. She had no choice. There is sadness for me. She was such a young woman, a child.[115]

CHAPTER 6: THE CERTAINTY OF LOVE

Ezzard:

> One thing about that 1905 Act that was implemented on us kids and children, there were no emotional feelings shown to us. Even when she would have come here and everyone was greeting her to board the ship and saying goodbye, nobody would have come up to her and given her this here [a hug].[116]

As the final word was said, Ezzard had already walked forward on the pier to hug the five women: Phyllis then Regina, Flo, Amy and finally Betty. The next destination would be the St John's Anglican Church on York Street situated in the town's centre.

Figure 107 Left to right: Amy Hood, Flo (Marion) Hood, Russell Nelly, Phyllis Andy, Betty Hood, Regina Wilkinson and Ezzard Flowers, Albany, Western Australia, 2013

Figure 108 Russell Nelly and Phyllis Andy, Albany, Western Australia, 2013

Figure 109 Regina Wilkinson, Albany, Western Australia, 2013

CHAPTER 6: THE CERTAINTY OF LOVE

The St John's Anglican Church features in records that map the progressive years of Annesfield. Anne was a devoted Anglican who attended church each Sunday with Henry, together with selected Annesfield children. Bessy was an accomplished pianist and played on many occasions to congregations of mostly colonial settlers. She captured the ardent audience with her professional musicality and fondness for the instrument, which was described by Anne in the report that she presented to the Western Australian Parliament in 1871.

We entered the church grounds from the rear car park and followed a footpath through well-kept gardens that were abloom with roses and other fragrant flowers. While we walked along, Ezzard identified birds making their song overhead in a tree. Rain birds, he called them. Near the entrance, Father Edward Argyle and Robert Reynolds from the Department of Indigenous Affairs greeted the five Bryant women, who were accompanied by Russell Nelly and Ezzard. As introductions were being made, the sound of an organ coming from inside the church playing music from the 1800s floated outside to the garden.

To Father Argyle and Robert, each of Bessy's descendants identified themselves by name and provided their kin relationship to each other and to Bessy. Father Argyle respectfully recognised the Bryants' connection to Bessy by acknowledging in words their ancestral ties to Minang country. He welcomed the opportunity, in his words, to celebrate the lives of Bessy, Rhoda, Emily, Ada and Nora within what he described as a shared sacred space.

Inside the church Father Argyle and Robert communicated to everyone some of the church's history, including details about the original interior. They described whereabouts they believed the harmonium would have been positioned in the 1860s, which was a dedicated section of the church elevated above the congregation. This was where Bessy would have played hymns each Sunday. 'You've probably heard the story of people seeing the red ribbon on Bessy's hat bobbing around, particularly when [they] would turn and face the harmonium', Robert told everyone enthusiastically, then adding, 'They appointed her a paid organist and teacher. For an Aboriginal woman to be playing in a church in 1867 was remarkable.'[117] Listening nearby, Father Argyle contributed more detail to the story, while the present-day organist continued playing music of a bygone era, making for a sombre mood.

Bessy had earned a reputation as an accomplished musician and as a skilled teacher, all of which she took with her to East Gippsland. As Father Argyle gently observed and shared, 'her presence is very much here, and that's why it's lovely to welcome you as her family here…completing the circle'.[118] The Bryant women were deeply engaged in the emotion of retracing the historical paths made by their ancestor.

A letter to Anne dated 17 June 1867 has Bessy writing excitedly about the harmonium, which had been purchased from donations for church services at the Ramahyuck Aboriginal Mission: 'The harmonium is bought, dear Missie, and going up tomorrow. Mr Hagenauer says it is a beautifully toned one, it has six stops.' Walking with the women down the aisle at the St John's Church, with organ music and historical information resounding, Flo stopped to place a hand on her chest. The intense emotion was clearly visible on her face, as was the case for the other women.

Their sombre and single-file procession through the church was reminiscent of a funeral service. Regina broke the silence asking, 'Where's the organ? What did she play?'[119] Her question arose from Robert's history of the organ. He explained that they were now hearing a modern organ and not the original instrument from the 1860s. It was a harmonium she had played, he explained, a pedal organ. Amy joined the conversation and added her piece to Regina's question and to the organ discussion, 'Like our one at Tyers [Lake Tyers Aboriginal Mission]'.[120] she responded fervently.

The talk of Lake Tyers united the past that they were being called to participate within on imaginary terms with what the women knew to be real and true in the present. With eyes tightly shut, Regina said, 'I just want to let go of her spirit, can I do that? I just want to let go of her spirit.' Behind her, Amy, Flo and Betty had taken hold of each other in a fond and sincere embrace that moved them to lower

CHAPTER 6: THE CERTAINTY OF LOVE

their heads and sorrowfully look to the ground. The flow-on effect was Phyllis and Russell placing arms around each other and enfolding Regina's shoulders, calling her closer into the circle being formed. 'I love you. I brought you back home', Regina called out into the church. 'I brought you back home, here where you belong. Please, I ask for my spirit to stay with you, Granny, Granny.'[121]

Such words of devotion and longing for an ancestor continued on as Bessy's Bryant descendants physically united with recently found kin in a large and tearful embrace. The tears flowed with final words of belonging expressed by Regina: '[Bessy] is home. She's home tidda [sister]. Nan, you're home. We're proud of you… tears of joy…we all brought her back home and I feel happy now she's here and she's laid to rest',[122] and from Amy, 'We're not going to forget her now.'[123]

The intimate reunion between living family and an ancestor in the spirit world was aptly expressed by Regina, who declared, 'Wiping it on my clothes… snot and tears on my clothes. I thought I was going to be stronger than this, but I brought her home, I brought her home.'[124] The heightened state of emotion inside the church was also given expression by Betty, who moved among the tight circle of her Bryant family and kissed the cheek of each of her family. She then embraced her kin Ezzard followed closely by Russell and then Lester Coyne. Lester, a Minang spokesperson, had arrived at the church to meet the Bryant women and to welcome them to Albany. There existed a genuine tenderness in the actuality of retracing the tracks of their ancestor. All stood together in unison, arms knitted and heads bowed toward the centre of their shared embrace.

When the hug of recently acquainted relations was completed and space was created for the event to continue, Melva Flowers walked into the group. Melva, a senior member of the Flowers family, had been sitting in a prayer room at the side of the church as the five Bryant women entered and was waiting patiently for the right time to meet them. Melva's niece and carer, Helen Bellfield, had helped with the logistics of travel from the nursing home and made the introductions. 'This is Pa Cliffy's daughter',[125] Helen said to Phyllis, Betty, Amy, Flo and Regina, explaining proudly that Melva's father was Clifford Flowers and her mother was

Bonnie Woods. Ezzard shared with the women how his connection to this family was through his father, Seymour Flowers, who was Melva's brother.

For the Flowers family, the births and deaths records in the archives only go as far back as Henry and Trenan (Traynan) Flowers. There have been no records discovered so far that detail other extended family members or children of John (Bunger) and Mary (Kuibbalan) Flowers besides Matilda, Bessy, Ada and Harry. In terms of western genealogies, the Flowers family links are not all traceable. However, the presence of the Flowers family name in the Great Southern of Western Australia signifies a resilient connection that endures between the generations and in relationship to ancestral homelands to which Bessy culturally belonged.

In meeting Melva Flowers for the first time, Phyllis remarked on a physical resemblance that she perceived between Melva and Phyllis's father, Keith (Pop) Bryant. It stimulated stories of the Bryant family, which were shared with the robust purpose of identifying everyone by name so as to place them and Elders no longer living within the Flowers and Bryant lineages that connected them all to Bessy.

In the background to this family interaction, Father Argyle prepared an altar on a table that was lined with green felt and where candles had been ceremoniously placed to respect the spiritual presence of Bessy. He told the group, 'One of the things we would like to do is to light a candle, which is a symbol obviously of Jesus and the resurrection, but also of the spirits of those who we don't see anymore, but who are still amongst us'.[126]

Taking Melva by the arm, Phyllis walked with her to the altar to light a candle. Following in single file were Regina, Amy, Betty and Flo, along with Ezzard and Russell. Together they each passed by the candles that were alight and warmly glowing with a small flame, participating with silence or prayer in a memorialising act. The practice of prayer resonated with experiences of Christianity that had been imparted to them throughout their lives living on missions in Victoria and Western Australia. It was a faith that Bessy had also adopted as part of her life growing up within Annesfield.

The unified relations demonstrated the expansive reach of Bessy's life stretched between Minang country and Gunai-Kurnai country. The senior members of

CHAPTER 6: THE CERTAINTY OF LOVE

Bessy's Bryant and Flowers family sat with one another in the church, both in silence and as part of an intimate conversation about networks of family and relatedness. A position within this activity was even established for Bessy by the considered placement of her portrait as a girl on one of the chairs. A second act of remembrance while seated was the gifting of an unpublished family book that curated Bessy's past through photos as well as colonial correspondence, letters and oral history recordings by Ezzard, Phyllis and other family members.

The book provided family access to Bessy's life as it appeared in Anne's report to the Western Australian Parliament, and through the letters that Bessy wrote to Anne and those to missionary and government authorities. Sourced from the archives, this material had never before been returned to members of Bessy's family by historians or academics. This was the case also for the historical photos portraying their ancestor and her family, and the historical photos representing other Aboriginal families who had made a life at places such as the Ramahyuck mission. The gifted book also included life stories narrated by Ezzard, Phyllis and Betty. These personal explorations of identity and belonging were illustrated with the contemporary portraits taken of Bessy's descendants and kin, and photos of the events on country that reinstated a social place for being remembered by present-day family.

Upon leaving the St John's Church, the family and kin efforts of remembrance were moved to the former site of the Annesfield Native Institution, located not far from Albany's town centre. The residence required a short drive up the hill from the church. This was the place in which Bessy spent her childhood before leaving for Ramahyuck. She was part of institutional life and kept company with the other Aboriginal children in Anne and Henry Camfield's care. Being taken inside this residence generated a great deal of emotion for the Bryant women and for Ezzard and Russell. They walked through what were mostly empty rooms of an older part of the building and, as they did so, personal childhood and family memories began to surface. Some memories were expressed through stories for all to hear, and other memories were shared through the physical discomfort arising from the sensation of irreconcilable trauma and grief.

Figure 110 St John's Church, Albany, Western Australia, 2013

Figure 111 Left to right: Regina Wilkinson, Phyllis Andy, Betty Hood, Amy Hood, Flo (Marion) Hood, Father Edward Argyle and Ezzard Flowers, Albany, Western Australia, 2013

CHAPTER 6: THE CERTAINTY OF LOVE

Figure 112 St John's Church, Albany, Western Australia, 2013

Figure 113 St John's Church, Albany, Western Australia, 2013

Figure 114 Flo (Marion) Hood, Amy Hood and Regina Wilkinson, Albany, Western Australia, 2013

Figure 115 Left to right: Flo (Marion) Hood, Amy Hood, Regina Wilkinson, Phyllis Andy and Russell Nelly, Albany, Western Australia, 2013

Figure 116 Left to right: Regina Wilkinson, Phyllis Andy, Lester Coyne and Ezzard Flowers, Albany, Western Australia, 2013

CHAPTER 6: THE CERTAINTY OF LOVE

Figure 117 Left to right (front): Flo (Marion) Hood, Betty Hood, Amy Hood, Regina Wilkinson, Phyllis Andy, Melva Flowers, Helen Bellfield, Father Edward Argyle, Albany, Western Australia, 2013

Figure 118 Left to right: Flo (Marion) Hood, Betty Hood, Amy Hood and Father Edward Argyle, Albany, Western Australia, 2013

The Bryant women all stayed close to each other while they moved through the rooms that were emptied of historical props, yet still evocative of the colonial characters who had played a role in Bessy's past. Each room was inspired by personal interpretations of Bessy's history, which effectually created a pathway between her remotely situated past and the group's real-time presence in Annesfield. Personal histories were the conduit for their entry into the past of their ancestor in a place that once operated as an institution for Aboriginal children.

In the main room, once the dormitory for the children at Annesfield, the senior women examined the cast iron pots layered in dust and sitting in the old fireplace, which was painted in rusted red. They also inspected the bricks exposed by peeling wallpaper, as Ezzard had done when walking for the first time through Annesfield back in 2010. Ezzard explained they were within a place where memories of their ancestor had been left behind, saying: 'So this here would have been where all the memories, laughter and the happy times, and the sad times were left.'[127]

Annesfield was the domestic centre of Bessy's childhood and, though markedly different from a traditional cultural site such as the fish traps made and used by Minang people, it was treated by the Bryant women as a meaningful site for exploring memories and performing rites of remembrance, much of which in this situation relied upon the imaginary. Upstairs in a small room and looking out of one of the small windows to the township and waters of King George Sound below, Ezzard described what could be seen and what of the past was being imagined:

> If you look out of the window – and those trees wouldn't have been there – she would've been looking at that hill over there and that one over there and building up all of these recollections…and she would have left through King George Sound out there…and that sight of Albany would have been the last sight she's seen – and all depends, like I said, if it was day or night.[128]

CHAPTER 6: THE CERTAINTY OF LOVE

Phyllis who was standing nearby and listening responded:

> She might have stood there like you and collected a memory she could take with her and that no one could take from her. We do that, don't we…store memories. We look silently through the window and collect all those memories…we all just want to put our emotions into place. I just wish she had have lived in a time for us to have met her. That's my only regret…to sit and talk and have a conversation…to know her. There're plenty of stories I know I need to still hear.[129]

Speaking about Bessy creating memories of her Minang country for herself as a child and as a young woman was demonstrated through personal recollections of childhood experiences. Each Bryant woman held a different idea of how Bessy would have felt growing up in an institution. They shared feelings that arose when reflecting on her past and life's impactful qualities:

> Flo: I feel sad because she wasn't with her parents, she was brought here…she never grew up at home with her mum and dad.
>
> Regina: To be back in this place where she taught, I feel proud. I'm proud of my granny Bessy.
>
> Betty: I feel sad with all the work she had to do. It's really sad, and that she never had a decent rest.
>
> Amy: She didn't enjoy a teenage life and that's sad.
>
> Phyllis: I think what she was taught by living here made her stronger, a strong black woman. I feel sad she didn't have a childhood [a childhood with her Minang family], but I feel proud and very honoured to have

her as my great-grandmother and maybe tonight I'll get emotional, but standing here, I have a good energy and feeling about it.

Flo: I feel like she didn't have a choice, that she had to come here and be brought up here and have an education. She had no choice.[130]

When it was time for Bessy's family and kin to leave the building that had once been her home, Russell powerfully acknowledged the presence of Bessy's Bryant descendants, telling them, 'You're not exactly coming home to a strange country, you're coming home to your country'.[131] He recognised that the Bryant women needed to be given cultural connection to Minang country. This experience took place the following day back at St John's Anglican Church.

In the church gardens an event was held that was open to all Minang families as well as other residents of Albany. The public gathering was to acknowledge, on Minang country, the presence of the five Bryant women. It was an opportunity to respect their lineage and to culturally welcome them home to ancestral country. Phyllis described the immediacy of the event, saying as they prepared to be culturally witnessed, 'I'm walking in the footsteps of my ancestor and coming back to her home. We may not be born in Gunai-Kurnai country, but this is home.'[132]

***

Figure 119 Left to right (front): Amy Hood, Betty Hood, Flo (Marion) Hood and Phyllis Andy, Albany, Western Australia, 2013

CHAPTER 6: THE CERTAINTY OF LOVE

Figure 120 Russell Nelly, Albany, Western Australia, 2013

Figure 121 Betty Hood, Phyllis Andy and Flo (Marion) Hood, Albany, Western Australia, 2013

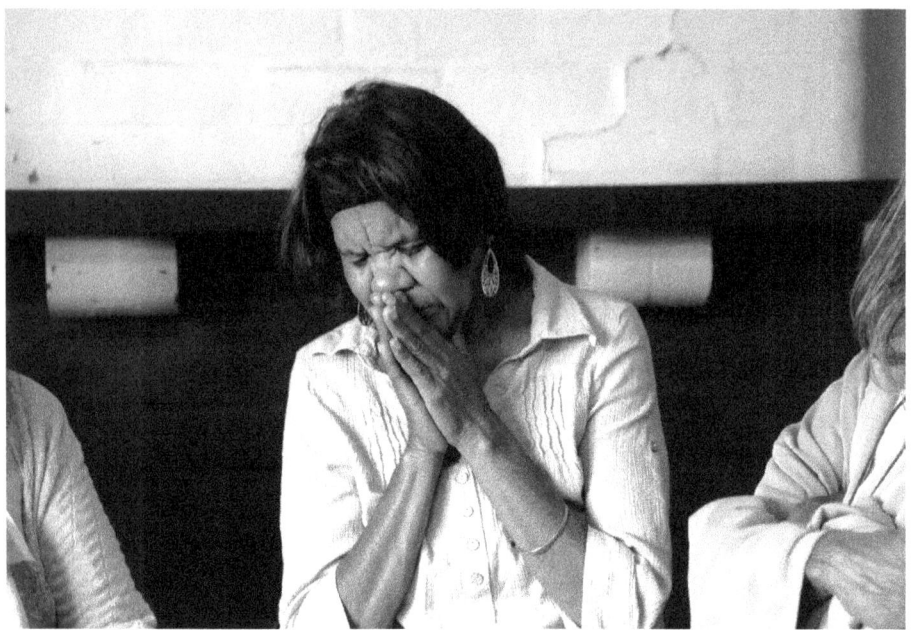

Figure 122 Flo (Marion) Hood, Albany, Western Australia, 2013

Figure 123 Left to right: Phyllis Andy, Flo (Marion) Hood, Betty Hood (front), Russell Nelly (back), Amy Hood, Regina Wilkinson and Ezzard Flowers, Albany, Western Australia, 2013

CHAPTER 6: THE CERTAINTY OF LOVE

The Welcome Home ceremony took place on the grassed area next to the St John's Church. The cultural preparations for the event were coordinated by the joint efforts of Russell and Ezzard. It was Ezzard's idea to hold a ceremony designed to respectfully acknowledge the descendants of Bessy's eldest daughter, Annie Magdalene (Maggie), as women kin belonging to Minang country.

The reclamation of broken kinship connections is usually cultural business kept safe within secured networks of kinship. For this particular event, Ezzard wanted the experience to be inclusive and part of shared intercommunity practices of healing. The invitation to attend the public ceremony was therefore extended to Minang families and also to residents of Albany and nearby regions.

Since meeting the Bryants, Ezzard had been inspired by the shifting elements of Bessy's history, strongly characterised by her ability to exist between two different cultural realities. Bessy's interaction with the Camfields and, with their demanding guidance, the adoption of Christian beliefs and values determined her experience both in Albany and at Ramahyuck in East Gippsland. Part of the ceremony aimed to cleanse and in some way free Bessy from an identity influenced by government administration and Christian scriptures. The creation of a dedicated cultural space gave non-Aboriginal audience members the opportunity to actively engage with the survival of Minang people. They were invited to witness remembrance practices intended to preserve and protect the custodianship of culture for future generations.

In the hours before the ceremony, Ezzard walked with Russell through the different activities as they would unfold. He gestured to an empty space where the general audience would be standing, then indicated the positioning of two fire tins and the seating arrangement for Bessy's family. One seat, he insisted, would be kept empty to symbolise the presence of their ancestor. He pointed to the side door of the church, from where the five Bryant women would emerge, in the company of members of the Elder Flowers family who had travelled to Albany from their home in Moora, north of Perth, a drive of more than 500 kilometres.

The walk-through performance that mapped how the space would appear did not specify what was actually going to happen, nor was it the rehearsal of a speech or script reading of the story that was to be told. Instead, room was left for improvisation. Happy with what was to be, they left the church grounds at Russell's request to find red wool and white ochre that he needed for his role in the ceremony. The red wool, Russell explained, meant solidarity, strength and unity, and that – in his cultural view – was what was needed these days for his family and for the broader community. In the search for these items, Ezzard produced a strip of red cloth torn from an old t-shirt, which Russell would wear tied around his forehead.

Several hours later the Welcome Home ceremony began. The five Bryant women waited in nervous anticipation. Standing inside the small prayer room at the church, they gathered and embraced, mirroring the holding of one another as they did in the church where Bessy had played the harmonium. Kooramyee, who had come along on the trip with her aunties from Victoria, offered support to all present in a prayer that called out to their ancestors back home in the east, in the shared belief that the old people were keeping a close watch. Absent from the ceremony were any domestic community politics that might normally arise within family occasions. This ceremony, and the events of previous days, demanded that cultural respect for ancestors overrode any domestic quarrels or differing opinion.

An understanding of the tensions existing between family social dynamics and cultural obligations was important. To negotiate a space for transformation, as cultural reclamation demanded, was very real for the participating Bryant women exploring the emotional and social complexities of restoring their ancestor to family memory. They had never before set foot on Minang country and were soon to be at the centre of a ceremony witnessed by a large crowd of both Minang and non-Aboriginal peoples. This was a ceremony holding no precedent or set procedure. It was designed to be a cultural fusion arising from western event formalities conjoined with Minang performances of identity and of belonging.

Outside the church, orange plastic chairs had been arranged in a semicircle on the grass, following the arc left by a trail of beach sand. The seats were positioned facing the audience, many of whom had begun to gather on the lawn and were chatting as they waited for the ceremony to begin. Ezzard had explained during the

CHAPTER 6: THE CERTAINTY OF LOVE

earlier walk around that there were two fire tins sitting between the audience and the seating reserved for Bessy's Bryant and Flowers families. Ezzard busied himself at these tins, setting alight the paperbark inside. He then laid branches of green wattle leaves over the flame, producing a billowing smoke that swelled around the area. This smoke, Ezzard explained, was a way to cleanse one's spirit, to protect the human spirit and to give the five Bryant women safe passage through, and into, Minang country.

Throughout the space that had been created, there was an underscore of audience conversation. There was no grand music or song. The first person to emerge from the church was Dolores Flowers or, as she was affectionately named, Aunty La La. She walked out of the chapel with her husband, Donald Flowers, following close behind. Back inside the church, daughter Rhonda Flowers had scolded her mother Dolores for the enthusiastic pride she was taking in her adoption of Bessy's story as her own family story, when culturally it belonged to Donald, who carried the Flowers name.

Aunty La La was unashamed of revealing her pride and passion for an ancestor's history, and her courageous display before the crowd gave strength to Bessy's descendants, who walked barefoot and in single file from the church amid the heavy smoke flowing from the tin cans. Phyllis led the procession of Bryant women, followed by Betty, Amy, Flo and then Regina. They took their seats, whereupon Ezzard stepped confidently forward to place on the empty chair a framed photo of Bessy as a girl at Annesfield in the 1860s. Ezzard said that this ceremony was not just about connecting the five Bryant women to the country of their ancestor, it was also about reconnecting the spirit of Bessy to her ancestral country.

With bare feet resting on whitest beach sand, Phyllis, Betty, Amy, Flo and Regina were acknowledged by the spokesperson for the community of Minang families, Lester Coyne. He told the audience blanketed in smoke why the five women had journeyed from their homes in East Gippsland to be on ancestral country for the first time. He warmly welcomed them, on behalf of all Minang people, the traditional custodians of the land upon which the ceremony was taking place. Lester provided context to the gathering, introducing Bessy to the crowd. He described how Bessy was a Minang woman, who had been taken into the care of settlers Anne and Henry Camfield at Annesfield. The Camfields, Lester reflected, were influential in shaping the direction of Bessy's life. As detailed historically, they were part of the St John's church congregation and had faithfully guided Bessy to acquire musical skills for hymn playing at the church.

To be present at this cultural welcome, Lester had said aloud, presented a unique opportunity for the audience to witness an uplifting event dedicated to bringing back to life an important ancestral history. He welcomed home Bessy's great-granddaughters and her great-grandnieces and extended kin while also acknowledging all her Koori descendants, including family that were still to be discovered as part of the reclamation story. As Lester completed his welcome, Ezzard busied himself with collecting from one of the tins a branch of green eucalypt leaves. He then brushed the smoking leaves over and around the bodies of each of the five Koori women. From an old Vegemite jar he also sprinkled red ochre onto the sand upon which each of the women had placed their feet. The smoke from the two fire tins continued to circle densely around the gathered family. Ezzard would later share with all who were present how this was now a story that was no longer just written on paper.

After the ritual smoking, Russell appeared from near the church to ceremoniously connect the women to Minang country. Instead of traditional dress and white ochre painted on his skin (as had been discussed between Ezzard and Russell when making preparations), Russell had chosen to stay in his navy-blue pinstripe suit, decorated with a rose in the jacket pocket. He stood before the seated family and kin amid the elemental placement of ochre and sand. With a commanding voice he addressed everyone present, carved walking stick in hand, and hair and beard thickly laden with red ochre. Russell spoke emphatically about the mixed emotions that were attached to Bessy's family coming back to ancestral country. To the gathered crowd, and with a care and tenderness towards the Bryant women and Flowers kin, he said:

CHAPTER 6: THE CERTAINTY OF LOVE

> We're gathered here this afternoon for an important part of our life. We've come to say hello, and welcome our family back, to [pay] tribute [to] the journey of Bessy Flowers and her going away from here [traditional country]. Who'd have thought it?
>
> Now we're dealing here with reconciliation, we're dealing with it in our own way. For these ladies [the Bryant women] to come over here to pick up the pieces and the remnants of their life, their great-grandmother's life, and find a whole new culture over here, that's a big step.
>
> To be here today on behalf of Wirlomin, Minang and Noongar people, I just want to say a big welcome to you, as we grow to know you and set about the business of repairing broken bridges. We've got a lot of them to cross.
>
> On behalf of myself, and the families around here, I'd like to welcome you home. It's come at short notice, it wasn't planned, and so what you're seeing here is spontaneity at its best. I just want to do something now.[133]

The 'something' that Russell was to perform involved walking into the open lawn within the semicircle of descendant family and kin. His distance from the microphone and nearness to the Bryant women created a sense of privacy that served the cultural gestures that unfolded. Reaching up to the sky, Russell blew with all his breath the collected red ochre from his hand. As the red ochre dispelled throughout the air he spoke of cultural recognition and of spiritual encouragement and validation:

> This is your great-grandmother's country. A lot of things have happened, but by you being here today means a big lot to us, so right now we're going to bring her home. I just want to pacify you, give you assurance that your nanny is home.[134]

In language, Russell then called out to his country, and to his ancestors in the spirit world. He approached in turn Phyllis, Betty, Amy, Flo and Regina, and breathed fiercely into a single clenched fist. He placed his hand on the shoulder of each woman and shared wisest words with them not audible to the audience. It was clear from observing the women's faces that emotions were intensifying. The meaningful acts that were taking place to spiritually return their ancestor to Minang country had become all encompassing. It would be an experience that was restorative in ways that would take considered time to digest and comprehend.

It was at this point in time that Ezzard returned to the microphone. He explained to the onlookers the significance of Bessy's spiritual return home and the homecoming of her descendants. To complete the rite of unifying family with country, Ezzard approached his women kin and scooped from beside their feet a handful of sand and ochre. He rubbed them together in his hands, turning the sand red. He then placed the combination into the waiting open hands of the Bryants. While the women folded their fingers over the sand and ochre, Ezzard spoke a welcome in Noongar language, 'Kia Minang Boodja, Kia Mia Minang Boodja Wirrin Mia – Welcome home to Minang country and welcome home to your great-grandmother's country. This is your spiritual homeland.'[135]

The words of welcome coincided with another ritualised gesture that aimed to symbolise the unification of the Bryant and Flowers families. Returning to the jar of ochre, Ezzard went about making an imprint of red ochre with his thumb on each person's forehead. The ceremony neared its completion. Bending down to the ground and taking a handful of sand, Ezzard faced the family group and threw the sand up into the air as he spoke the words, 'Kia Mia, welcome home'.[136]

While the crowd dispersed, the women remained seated. They took hold of one another's hands and, when the time came to break this seal of kinship, they stood up to replace it with heartfelt hugs and the freefalling tears of welling emotion. Regina picked up the framed portrait of Bessy and held it tightly in her arms. She looked at her great-grandmother closely, sharing with everyone what she discovered in the photo: 'Oh look, she's got tears in her eyes', and then, speaking

CHAPTER 6: THE CERTAINTY OF LOVE

to Amy, 'Teardrops, like us'. Flo and Betty also joined in the conversation. They also acknowledged their ancestor's tears they believed were present in this photo prepared for the ceremony. 'I just found teardrops in her eyes, both eyes', Regina told them, adding, 'Look at her clothes, aren't they pretty?'[137] This scene of memory making was consolidated by a group photo representing Bessy's great-grandchildren and great-grandnieces, who posed together holding central their ancestor's framed photo covered in ochre handprints.

There was relief and joy expressed among the many reflections that took place after the Welcome Home concluded. One unexpected occurrence was the presentation of unknown relations. Approached by two women who had been part of the audience, Phyllis met another family group who were connected to Bessy. They were two sisters. One sister lived in New Zealand and the other sister lived in Perth. They introduced themselves to the Bryants as the great-great-grandchildren of Bessy and Donald Cameron. They identified a lineage through Louisa, who was the second daughter of Bessy and Donald. This news amid a ceremony reconnecting Bessy's spirit to country and acknowledging her descendants extended Bessy's story further and confirmed the importance of keeping ancestors anchored in the world of everyday family life. The presentation of new relations and their warm reception by Bessy's family and kin was another piece of evidence Russell would describe as being 'the certainty of family love'.[138]

At a later time, and sharing his reflections about the ceremony, Russell said the experience was moving and 'proof that there was love'. He felt that cultural availability to Phyllis, Betty, Amy, Flo and Regina was crucial because they were individuals in a 'strange country'. This concept of being away from one's home country was a feeling that Russell had relayed in regard to his own trip to East Gippsland with Ezzard when they met Bessy's great-grandchildren for the first time. 'After we got to know the lay of the land, we did alright', he said. For Russell, the act of finding relations and maintaining a strong sense of family meant that 'it will strengthen us, it will serve to strengthen us physically, because we know, and mentally, because we have that bond'. He added to this sentiment saying that, 'It's good to know that you can see something tangible, knowing that you are related to people'.[139] To be related, however, was also to accept the responsibility of such relationships, particularly when they were new or, as Russell pointed out in respect to the five Bryant women, when one had to move on from the experience that was the welcome home to country. He talked about the work that remained to be done by generations of family into the future:

> They're very fragile at this point in time and vulnerable. Just the fact they've gone on the plane and come over here and been involved… it's bewildering to them. But if they sat down and analysed it and take assurance from what happened this weekend, they'll be better for it. I reckon anyway.
>
> I hope they take something away. I know for certain what they've taken away from us: the certainty of love, family love.[140]

For both the Bryant and Flowers families, the ceremony outside the church was a powerful experience that strengthened family ties. For the broader audience in attendance, the shared cultural performance allowed them to experience firsthand the social, moral and spiritual expressiveness of the bonds between country and people and between networks of family. The community as a whole had been invited to witness cultural practices that identified the power of cultural reciprocity. They had become active participants in a process that worked to repair broken cultural identities. They witnessed the making of memories, which were conjured in many moments of vulnerability and with heartfelt openness. A willingness to listen and understand the courage intrinsic to cultural reclamation fortified the original mission of fostering a meeting place from which participatory reconciliation was enabled.

CHAPTER 6: THE CERTAINTY OF LOVE

From Russell's perspective, the courage to learn from a situation and to move forward into the world with humility was a tribute to the power of love. He said of the event that:

> Those that came here were touched…There are experiences in our own lives that arrange themselves indelibly on our life…we don't [refuse it]…or as much as we like to ignore it, it is still there in black and white and we cannot refuse it. But we can understand where we're going with it.
>
> That's the big difference…knowing they've got family and re-establishing the ties their great-grandmother forged.
>
> Admittedly there's a lot of water under the bridge. A lot of bridges have been burnt down and broken, but in the long term our family unit will pull us together, I believe that…we went over [to east Gippsland] and established contact [with the Bryants] and now they've re-established contact, so the love is rekindled. Never forgotten. But, rekindled for the next time.[141]

The value of united families, whether situated geographically afar, or close by, continued the following day with travel through country to the Stirling Range. Instructed through culturally symbolic practices of Noongar storytelling, the Bryant women were gently beckoned by their kin into the social and natural landscape given to innately caring for and communicating with ancestors in the living world.

Figure 125 Welcome Home ceremony, Albany, Western Australia, 2013

Figure 126 Betty Hood, Phyllis Andy, Dolores Flowers and Donald Flowers, Albany, Western Australia, 2013

CHAPTER 6: THE CERTAINTY OF LOVE

Figure 127 Russell Nelly, Regina Wilkinson and Flo (Marion) Hood, Albany, Western Australia, 2013

Figure 128 Betty Hood, Phyllis Andy, Dolores Flowers and Donald Flowers, Albany, Western Australia, 2013

Figure 129 Amy Hood, Albany, Western Australia, 2013

Figure 130 Betty Hood and Regina Wilkinson, Albany, Western Australia, 2013

CHAPTER 6: THE CERTAINTY OF LOVE

Figure 131 Regina Wilkinson, Betty Hood and Flo (Marion) Hood, Albany, Western Australia, 2013

Figure 132 Regina Wilkinson, Albany, Western Australia, 2013

Figure 133 Regina Wilkinson with photo of Bessy, Albany, Western Australia, 2013

Figure 134 Red ochre and beach sand, Albany, Western Australia, 2013

CHAPTER 6: THE CERTAINTY OF LOVE

Figure 135 Phyllis Andy, red ochre and beach sand, Albany, Western Australia, 2013

Figure 136 Betty Hood, red ochre and beach sand, Albany, Western Australia, 2013

Figure 137 Left to right (seated): Regina Wilkinson, Donald Flowers and Dolores Flowers. Left to right (standing middle): Ezzard Flowers, Flo (Marion) Hood, Amy Hood, Betty Hood, Cameron descendants (sisters) and Phyllis Andy. Left to right (standing): Russell Nelly, Flowers and Rhonda Flowers, Cameron descendant, (daughter) Lizzie Brown, Albany, Western Australia, 2013

Figure 138 Regina Wilkinson and Donald Flowers, Albany, Western Australia, 2013

CHAPTER 6: THE CERTAINTY OF LOVE

Figure 139 Left to right (seated): Donald Flowers, Dolores Flowers. Left to right (standing): Regina Wilkinson, Flo (Marion) Hood, Betty Hood, Rhonda Flowers, Amy Hood and Phyllis Andy, Albany, Western Australia, 2013

Figure 140 Donald Flowers, Albany, Western Australia, 2013

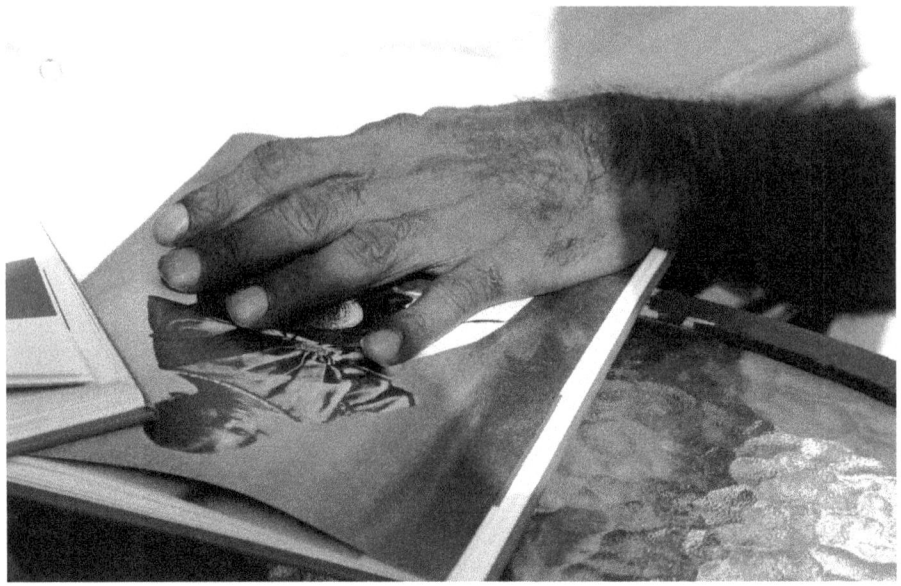

Figure 141 Donald Flowers, Albany, Western Australia, 2013

Figure 142 Russell Nelly, Albany, Western Australia, 2013

Chapter 7:
Where our spirits go

Ezzard often referred to a significant mountain range deeply imbued with the spirits of his old people when telling stories intrinsic to being a Wirlomin and Minang Noongar. He took inspiration from places on country evocative of childhood memories and from the instructive stories that had been handed down by Elders and knowledgeable members of his community. The teachings about seasonal cycles, healing plants, animals, language and kinship relations were often topical to an event or situation considered important for knowledge transmission, and to the passage of culture into the future. This was the case when Betty, Phyllis, Regina, Flo and Amy made a trip to the Stirling Range in the day following the Welcome Home ceremony, guided by Ezzard along with Harley Coyne from the Department of Indigenous Affairs in Albany.

The Stirling Range and part of the Porongurup Range make up the Stirling Range National Park, about 40 kilometres north of Albany. The national park, of more than 2,000 hectares, dates back more than one million years and is therefore among the oldest granite formations in the world. The landscape features hilly grasslands and thickly forested areas. For Wirlomin and Minang families in the Great Southern and for the Noongar community, this is an ancient homeland from which connections to ancestors are preserved and given meaning.

Over the roar of the minibus engine, Ezzard animated stories of this country for his kin listening with anticipation. From the front passenger seat he crafted a story that first told the history of settler occupation and the gradual transformation of traditional country into farmland. He explained how members of his family were part of the land clearing, mostly as unpaid labour, and lamented the continued desecration of the bushland in more recent years by corporate investors. To illustrate his point, Ezzard directed the Bryant women's attention to the plantations of Tasmanian blue gums endemic to southeastern Australia and visible through the bus windows. There in clear sight, he told them, was a species foreign to Western Australia that had been planted for profit. This had entailed further clearing of native vegetation and irreparable damage to a once rich and thriving land. Yet country was resilient:

> Trees here on the side of the road, with these white flowers, see them there? When they're in bloom that indicates there's going to be a good winter, but if they're not all in bloom and they're [blooming] just here and there, well that indicates it's going to be a dry winter.
>
> Not only does it indicate that, but the gum from those trees is also used for medicinal purposes. You can use the gum like a glue to make spears…to put the points in the spears and also axes. You mix it [the glue] with kangaroo droppings. So, even before European settlement, we had scientists within our community.
>
> It [the white flowers] means it's good overall regarding the land, the animals and the flowers. The land and the animals indicated to Aboriginal people exactly what's going to happen with the land, and the environment, and that's why every time they would go by the seasons. They did things by the seasons, and not [because of, or for]

CHAPTER 7: WHERE OUR SPIRITS GO

scientific research. Even at night, the moon tells them what's going to happen, and in the day, even the sun.[142]

The bus journey to the Stirling Range National Park continued as a story of country seen in passing from the windows and representing both an existing and bygone landscape. Along the way, there was sporadic sleep for some, which lasted until Ezzard called out urging everyone to look straight ahead into the distance. The long and narrow road led the onlookers to a mountain range not far away. It was the Porongurup Range or, as Ezzard named them, Borongurup, the Noongar identification for 'place of bush'. Asking that the Bryant women look intently at the mountain as it started to come into clear view, Ezzard presented a series of questions to them: 'Can you see in the distance? What does that look like? See there, the Noogiting Yorga…sleeping woman.'[143]

The sight of Noogiting Yorga generated sounds of curiosity. A great deal of discussion was stirred up among the Bryant women. What was the story of the sleeping woman? While they contemplated the significance of this place, Harley and Ezzard were occupied with where best to leave the main road in order to see the ranges. Getting out of the bus, the Bryant women looked out across the farming paddocks to the blue-hazed mountain rising up from the ground and taking the form of a woman in her sleep. Though it was summertime, there was a gentle breeze, which felt cool on bare skin.

As the nominated storyteller for his kin, Ezzard provided specialist knowledge about Noogiting Yorga. The throaty cawing of a crow flying overhead was the only sound imposing itself upon the rhythm of his narration. In fact, it was the appearance of the crow in the sky that drew Ezzard's attention to the darkening clouds. 'Hopefully these clouds will go away as we're going out there',[144] he said, gesturing with his hand to beyond the Noogiting Yorga to another important cultural place. This next site was Koikernerruph or Bulla Miel, which in the range could be identified by the ancient rock formation that appeared to be an old man lying on his back with his face skyward. If the weather continued to favour the current sunny skies and gentle breezes, Ezzard declared that it was going to be possible to see clearly an outline of the old man's features, including his forehead, nose, mouth, chin and even a beard.

On a map giving directions to the old man, the signpost read as Bluff Knoll. The Noongar community preferred its language names – Koikernerruph or Bulla Miel. Both these names are spelt in various ways by the different generations of family. In the years spent retracing his ancestor's history, Ezzard often talked about this place through stories about his ancestors and their strong spiritual presence at the range. One story detailed the sighting of clouds rolling in over the old man. It's a message to us, he would say, communicated a recent passing of one of our own people. To the Bryant women he said:

This here [pointing into the distance] is the Stirling Range.

It starts from the west over there from a town called Cranbrook, and it extends eastwards down to a town called Weststead, situated between Albany and Esperance. In between here are significant sites like this one out here. That looks like a lady sleeping. We call it Noogiting Yorga, which means sleeping woman. It's significant and the story is told in all the clan groups within the region, and extended regions, as far as the eye can see.

We're always talking about the sleeping woman.

Also, where we're going to over here [pointing into the distance again], is a significant tourist attraction, but also, it's important to who we are and where we come from as Minang people, and for other extended clans as well. It's known as Bulla Miel, which is 'the place of many eyes' and it's also a spiritual home and resting place for our spirits when we pass on. That place is a significant place there.

CHAPTER 7: WHERE OUR SPIRITS GO

> …As I was saying yesterday, when we were at Mount Clarence looking back this way, these two mountain ranges here, 'the Stirlings' we know as Koikernerruph, the place of mystical clouds. At this place [Koikernerruph], it could be blue skies one minute, and then the next minute there are clouds over the Stirling at Bluff Knoll, Bulla Miel.
>
> Once we see clouds rolling in on the northern side of the range it indicates that somebody from our country has passed on and that's usually followed by drizzling rain like snowflakes.
>
> We call that small drizzling death rain Chwril, and we know that somebody very close to us has passed on.[145]

Remembering kin no longer living produced reflections concerning the loss of community Elders and members of family. Each passing impacted upon the survival of culture for future generations. Ezzard explaining when telling his story that, true to his experience, 'A lot of people say, "Well our culture's gone" – the only time our culture will be gone, my culture will be gone, is when I'm gone'.[146] Anchoring self to place helped continue obligations to ancestors and secured a relationship to culture. The act of making his way, in his mind, and sometimes physically, to the sites of Koikernerruph or Bulla Miel instigated a process in which Ezzard felt inseparable from his Wirlomin and Minang identity. This was despite confronting in life hardship and multiple challenges.

Entry to the Stirling National Park was via a winding road leading to a car park and lookout that brought into close view the 'old man'. The view was breathtaking. This was to be the resting place of Bessy's spirit. The weather was overcast and reminiscent of a wintery day. The Bryant women watched with wonder as a pillow of white mist slowly crept across the grey rocky mountain face. They began to describe how they felt being in this place, while feeling the bodily impact of strong winds swirling around the mountains. Ezzard described the cultural meaning of the place:

> Bulla Miel means 'place of many eyes' and Koikernerruph is 'place of the mystical clouds', simply because when you get the clouds rolling in over that particular region, people in the region know that there's been a death for someone who comes from that place.
>
> But also, it's a resting place for where we go into the afterlife, where our spirits go. That's why Bulla Miel or Bluff Knoll is the place of many eyes.[147]

Bessy was never granted a chance to return to her Minang homeland and, after Henry Camfield's death in 1872 and the imminent closure of Annesfield, the bond of belonging that had been formed by the heartfelt exchange of letters between Anne and Bessy came to an end. It was documented that Anne moved from Albany to Perth and then finally to Adelaide after Henry's death. Meanwhile, Bessy remained in far-away Victoria, where she negotiated a life in the eastern colonies that was spent mostly at Ramahyuck.

Bessy's letter writing was a process that connected her over distance to those who were responsible for her care. The letters communicated the activities of domestic life or, in later years, mission politics. They were a tool used by Bessy to journey back to Annesfield in her mind, as a way of remembering where she had come from and where she had thought she was headed in life. This geographic dislocation pertinent to Bessy's story was not lost upon the five Bryant women as they retraced on country the youthful years of their ancestor.

Within sight of the cloud cover appearing as a white mist that drifted over the old man featured in the mountain they spoke aloud their private thoughts. 'This is where she's now resting, we've brought her here',[148] Regina proclaimed. It was a journey that held cultural and emotional importance for not only their individual wellbeing but also that of their children and grandchildren back home in Victoria. The desire to learn more about their ancestral roots had led the women to this large

CHAPTER 7: WHERE OUR SPIRITS GO

expanse of grey rock and to a landscape covered in the colourful wonder of wild summer flowers. Harley walked in close to the group to help forge greater knowledge of ancestral country through a Noongar story that explained the meaning of the moodjar tree, which was known in this area of Western Australia as the Christmas tree, or its botanical name *Nuytsia floribunda*.

Harley pointed out to the Bryant women the moodjar tree where it stood growing at the base of the mountain. He described some of its characteristics, firstly as a semi-parasitic plant that obtained water and minerals from a host tree species, and then its cultural significance as a burial tree. He told the women that traditionally the spectacular orange-flowered tree that grew in soft sandy soil was used to signify a place in which to bury the dead. Then, when the tree was in bloom during the summer months, the spirit of the dead would rise up through the roots of the tree and out through the flowers. Those flowers, Harley made very clear, were never to be picked: 'We were told to leave it alone',[149] he said. Harley continued to help the women conceptualise the meaning of country through the plants that they could see and in relationship to the stretch of land before them that held meaning for the living and was home to the memory of ancestral spirits. Talking more about the moodjar tree, he said it was often found in cemeteries throughout Noongar country.

The shared meaning of the moodjar tree inspired Ezzard to share his thoughts with the women about the meaning of home, particularly the experience of being away from country. He said, 'When I went to America, my focus was always on home, but not where I come from in a literal sense, but this place here, Bulla Miel and Koikernerruph was always in my mind.'[150] The act of keeping country present as part of an everyday sensibility combined remembering country with teaching others about country and expressing an emotional and physical concern for country. Speaking this sentiment to his Bryant kin, Ezzard said:

This is your country; this is your Dreaming story here.

> I'm handing knowledge of this place on to you and giving it to you as a gift, so that when you go home, you can tell this story of belonging to your families. This is your country, and so it becomes your story and also your connection to country.[151]

The return of Bessy's spirit to her cultural resting place turned out to be a tapestry of storied dreaming. Kinship networks, such as that of Bessy's descendants and kin, became a central part of weaving together the meaning of human and non-human connections that solidified both social and ecological binds inherent to respecting and caring for ancestral homelands.

Directing the Bryant women to look at another part of the mountains, Ezzard shared the story of two powerful spirits:

> Out that way, there were powerful spiritual Mumbura or Charnook who had power, back in the Dreaming. One was named the Kawar, which is a purple-crowned parrot that only sits up in tall trees, where all those blossoms is…that's where he lived. The other is the Waalitch, the wedge-tailed eagle. And that's where the eagle comes from, up here in this country.
>
> One day they both went hunting, and they crossed paths, and the Waalitch got jealous because the Kawar was coming into his territory. The Waalitch thought that, by throwing his magic – his Mumbura – at Kawar, he would get rid of him easily. But even though the little fellow Kawar was only a small bird, he too had the same mountain magic and power as the Waalitch.
>
> They got into a fight along here [pointing to a specific place in the landscape] and you can see how the formations in the hills is where their wings were touching the ground, and building up that land we

CHAPTER 7: WHERE OUR SPIRITS GO

> can now see. If you look up into the hills along here, you can see pigmentation, all the red ochre colour. That was the blood dripping from their wings and from their necks when they were fighting... especially that hill over there. That's called Mount Trio. You see that rock? At the base of that rock is where the eagle chased the parrot and couldn't get him.
>
> So the eagle rested on the rock, but the little bird Kawar went straight through. If you go there today at the bottom of Mount Trio, you'll see that rock. And at the base of that rock is where the Waalitch nest is, and in the middle of the rock is a little skinny, narrow passageway there. If you're skinny enough you can walk through there.
>
> Before the Waalitch died he went west, that way, and when he fell over, with his last bit of strength, his legs kicking and his wings flapping and with his last breath he created two lakes. His blood from his wings and blood from his body created a lake. The white sand he dug up there from under the earth, two ochre pits were created and that's out there today.[152]

The ancestral story of Kawar and the Waalitch deepened the emotions of Bessy's descendants at Bulla Miel, as they communed with their Minang kin for her culturally emplaced spiritual return. The five Elder Bryant women had left their homes in East Gippsland without knowing where this journey to the southwest would lead them. They trusted in the path shown to them by Ezzard and Harley, which allowed them a cultural passage into the early years of their ancestor and to her rightful place of belonging within country. It became evident that to powerfully seal in their hearts and minds an understanding of who they were in the world, they needed to develop a true sense of belonging to this country of the Great Southern that had been introduced to them by their kin.

This experience was significant to the women, not only for themselves, but also for their families at home, and for re-righting the divisive workings of Native

Title legislation, which had determined that the Bryant family did not belong to the lands of eastern Victoria where they were born and raised.

As the women sat on a tourist bench directly facing the old man in rock as he laid with his face to the sky, they listened attentively to Ezzard asking them to allow the gentle wind to pick up their prayers and in doing so carry the spirit of their ancestor back to her rightful resting place. As they made for this to happen in sombre silence, Ezzard stepped to the side and out of sight, giving space for the five Bryant women to find their own way into and through this experience of mourning, reflecting, respecting and celebrating. There were conflicting emotions. This was not a choreographed event. There was no script to map in any given moment how to feel or what to say. For this reason, silence came to dominate the significant occasion and caused the wind to feel stronger and sound wilder than perhaps it really was.

Breaking the silence, the women reflected on being at the St John's Church in Albany. In quiet conversation they shared how their emotional interaction within this space had given meaning to retracing Bessy's historical steps and bestowed the sensibility of being within her past. At the church, while candles were alighted, prayers had been said to God and also spoken to Bessy in the spiritual realm of the Dreaming. This time at the mountain, the prayers spoken aloud were proclamations about remembering where they had come from, and how far they had journeyed to get to this culturally significant place.

The women reflected upon Christian church funerals that had been performed since the missionary times for Koori people. They recalled those kin responsible for carrying the coffins of loved ones on country at the Lake Tyers Aboriginal Trust, and attending to their final resting place on country. Looking to the old man they gifted to the wind words that identified their Bryant heritage. They openly shed tears and held hands. They committed to keeping strong their unified quest of bringing Bessy home to her country. The cloudy mist was not yet ready to lift from the mountain, and in the stillness that followed their tributes honoured those they loved. Phyllis shared a prayer on behalf of her kin:

CHAPTER 7: WHERE OUR SPIRITS GO

> As always, we pay our respects to the Minang people, and to this land.
>
> We thank you that you could receive us back into country, and in coming here we bring our great-grandmother's spirit with us, to return her to this country so that she may now rest in peace among you all.
>
> We hope you will receive Bessy Flowers back to this country.
>
> She will remain with us in Victoria as her mortal body is still there [buried there], but we now know, not only hope, her spirit is back here, back home where she belongs and where we too belong.
>
> Thank you Elder ancestors for receiving her.[153]

Acknowledging the spiritual presence of Bessy, Phyllis continued aloud with her words of reverence: 'Your spirit can be free, back in your own country', and, to her Bryant family sitting with her in this experience, 'We know how hard she was asked to work; she was the obedient servant. Now she's not a servant any longer; we know her now to be free.'[154] Among the many moments of stillness, the only words were prayers and shared reflections. Symbolic was the cultural interaction between resting ancestors and the family present who had courageously named their ancestor's absence within their family story. By doing so they had collectively secured for themselves a self-determined way of resurrecting memories from the stronghold of colonial historicity.

The continuing release of emotion flowed out to the old man, Flo asking of Amy who sat beside her on the bench, 'Can you see it too?'[155] Looking up at the grey rock sculpted by time and weather into the shape of an old man lying down, Flo's attention was drawn to the place where his eyes appeared to be set in the mountain. She spoke of seeing a teardrop, which mirrored a sentiment made when the women were actively engaged with the framed photo of Bessy at the Welcome Home ceremony in Albany. The belief that the old man was shedding a tear deepened the connection that the women were feeling between themselves and this cultural place of mystical clouds and many eyes, reserved for Noongar ancestral spirits and stories of the Dreaming.

Now returned to the group and seated nearby on the ground, Ezzard began setting up their departure from this place. He did this by affirming for the Bryant women their bloodline connection to the mountains. He told them:

> These stories I've told you belong to Minang country. You are Minang women.
>
> You are spiritually home, connected to this land and to this country, and to her [Bessy's] Dreaming.
>
> I think it all feels good, with the strong breeze here, looking up there to the old man, and with the clouds rolling over – it's significant.[156]

Figure 143 Ezzard Flowers, Western Australia, 2013

CHAPTER 7: WHERE OUR SPIRITS GO

Figure 144 Left to right: Phyllis Andy, Regina Wilkinson, Betty Hood and Amy Hood, Western Australia, 2013

Figure 145 Left to right: Amy Hood, Regina Wilkinson, Ezzard Flowers, Phyllis Andy, Betty Hood and Flo (Marion) Hood, Western Australia, 2013

Figure 146 Bulla Miel, Stirling Range, Western Australia, 2013

Figure 147 Bulla Miel, Stirling Range, Western Australia, 2013

CHAPTER 7: WHERE OUR SPIRITS GO

Figure 148 Bulla Miel, Stirling Range, Western Australia, 2013

Figure 149 Regina Wilkinson, Western Australia, 2013

NO LONGER A WANDERING SPIRIT

CHAPTER 7: WHERE OUR SPIRITS GO

Figure 150 Left to right: Regina Wilkinson, Phyllis Andy, Flo (Marion) Hood, Amy Hood and Betty Hood, Western Australia, 2013

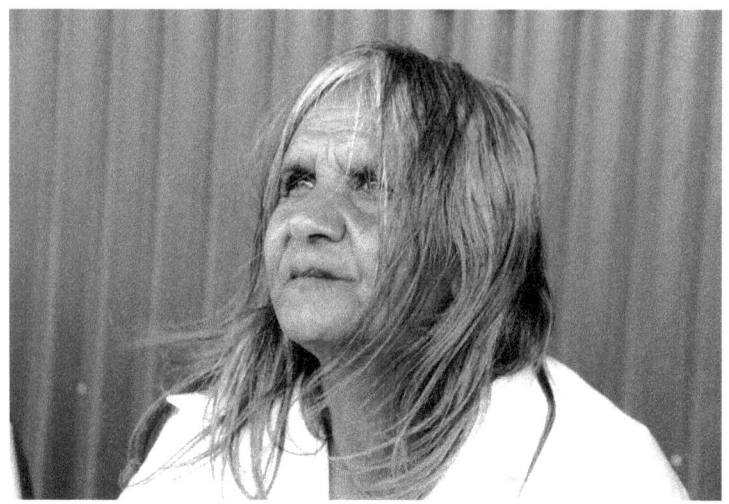

Figure 151 Amy Hood, Western Australia, 2013

Figure 152 Flo (Marion) Hood, Western Australia, 2013

CHAPTER 7: WHERE OUR SPIRITS GO

Figure 153 Regina Wilkinson, Phyllis Andy and Flo (Marion) Hood, Western Australia, 2013

Figure 154 Regina Wilkinson, Western Australia, 2013

Figure 155 Phyllis Andy, Western Australia, 2013

Figure 156 Flo (Marion) Hood, Western Australia, 2013

Figure 157 Amy Hood, Western Australia, 2013

Figure 158 Betty Hood, Western Australia, 2013

CHAPTER 7: WHERE OUR SPIRITS GO

From here, everyone returned to the minibus and journeyed to the Porongurup National Park for a picnic lunch and to visit one last site, which was the tree in the rock. They followed a walking trail that led to views of granite peaks, karri trees, the Stirling Range and the distant coastline. The women stopped with Ezzard at a large granite boulder. Within this mass of stone grew a large old-growth karri tree. The tree had made its home in the rock, its roots holding tight to the hard surface. Other roots remained deep in the earth, extending downwards through a series of rock crevices.

Inspecting the old karri tree up close, Amy and Flo sat themselves within a hollow in its tall trunk. They said aloud to the other women how they felt sitting in this place. It was as though they had brought a piece of Pop Bryant back to see this country, they said, adding also how strongly they felt a sense of belonging for Nan, their grandmother. Pop Bryant was always out in the bush, Flo said, sharing how she recalled him teaching her to hunt and to collect the honey from wild bush bees. 'When I go back home, I'm going to go and visit Pop Bryant', she remarked. 'We're going to let our grandfather know what we've done. I'll just let him know we brought Nanny [Bessy] Flowers home to country, and we hope we've done him proud.'[157]

Flo was referring to Keith Bryant's burial place at the Lakes Entrance Cemetery. The effect of sitting inside the old karri tree had evoked memories of home and of loved family who had passed away. Within the reverent experience that was granted to remembering Keith and Esther Bryant, the Bryant women spoke about what it would mean to take back to East Gippsland the sand and the red ochre that had been rubbed into their feet when outside the St John's Church and being welcomed home by their Minang kin, to place on the graves of Pop and Nan Bryant.

Amy and Flo also shared with everyone while they sat in the karri tree that they intended to make time to share this significant experience with their children and grandchildren. 'We can't say we don't have family here', Amy said. Reflecting on Pop Bryant, she added with concern, 'He might be lost without her now, but he's got us'.[158] The two women raised the concept of spirits back home in East Gippsland being lonely. They contemplated Pop Bryant resting in the Lakes

Entrance Cemetery, where they imagined him feeling the continued absence of his grandmother's spirit. With their efforts, they now hoped this ethereal bereavement had been transformed to that of respect for Bessy's spiritual return to her traditional homeland by his children and other representing family members.

There seemed to exist a moral weightiness attached to this journey for the five Bryant women and for that reason Amy and Flo took the time to distinguish this trip from many others they had taken before in their lives. 'I'm proud to say that I have brought his [Pop Bryant's] nanny home. I'm happy to say I was able to come here',[159] Flo said. While the sound of birds chattering dominated the gathering, a final group photo was taken with the old karri tree as a backdrop and as a way of remembering this time. 'I'm proud to be a descendant of the Flowers-Cameron family',[160] Amy said. She had found, after three days of walking in Bessy's tracks, a place for her voice that was usually concealed within private moments of journal writing and poetry compilations.

On the minibus and returning to Albany, Phyllis described in her own words the sensation of connecting with what she described to be a new culture and a new history. She clarified to all who were listening that by using the term 'new' she meant 'old stuff' that was already known but practised as part of a Minang experience of being in culture. She talked openly about respecting the differences, as well as recognising the similarities she believed existed between her lived experiences and that of her Minang and Wirlomin kin.

The next morning, all who had journeyed to Albany gathered at the local airport for the return trip to Melbourne, and then beyond to their homes in East Gippsland. Standing together for the emotional farewell, Ezzard instructed the five Bryant women to take in one hand a single gum leaf that he had collected from a nearby tree. He told them that the leaf he enclosed in their hand signified a lasting connection to their ancestral country. It represented a living piece of Minang country they could carry home with them on the return flight. The women responded to this cultural gesture with deep emotion. With Ezzard embracing each of his kin one at a time, tears flowed freely.

CHAPTER 7: WHERE OUR SPIRITS GO

For the five Bryant women – Phyllis, Betty, Amy, Flo and Regina – their birthplace was Gunai-Kurnai country and this they considered to be their cultural homeland. After the visit to the Great Southern and to their ancestor's country, they now possessed deeper knowledge about who they were as Bryant women. With family roots beholden of childhood memories and now imbued with the tenacity of the roots of the old karri tree, they had cared for and celebrated the memories of their ancestors, in particular Pop and Nan Bryant. They also recognised those ancestors who had lived before them in another era – Bessy and Donald Cameron and their children.

Time will tell if the Bryant family make ritual of the beach sand mixed with red ochre upon the graves of Pop and Nan Bryant, as Flo and Amy had suggested. Regardless of the decision made in the future, what is known is that, when at the Perth Airport, the responsibility for carrying the collection of ochre and sand through security was given to Phyllis. There was a strong consensus that her being an Anglican minister placed her in the best position for this job that they all jovially confessed would surely risk attention and reprimand by airline staff.

From a first meeting with Bessy through a historical photo to laying her spirit to rest on country, the Bryants navigated themselves through the history of their ancestor so that they might find for themselves, in their own way, a strong sense of who they are in the world. The path that they followed with their Flowers kin reflected the ways in which they chose to imagine, act and believe when seeking to return the spirit of Bessy to her home. Emplacing Bessy within personal and family memories that were strengthened through on-country practices of making history has ensured that she will always be remembered.

Figure 159 Flo (Marion) Hood, Porongurup National Park, Western Australia, 2013

Figure 160 Flo (Marion) Hood and Amy Hood, Porongurup National Park, Western Australia, 2013

CHAPTER 7: WHERE OUR SPIRITS GO

Figure 161 Flo (Marion) Hood, Phyllis Andy, Betty Hood, Ezzard Flowers and Regina Wilkinson, Porongurup National Park, Western Australia, 2013

Figure 162 Flo (Marion) Hood, Amy Hood, Betty Hood, Phyllis Andy, Regina Wilkinson and Ezzard Flowers, Porongurup National Park, Western Australia, 2013

Figure 163 Ezzard Flowers, Porongurup National Park, Western Australia, 2013

Figure 164 Ezzard Flowers, Flo (Marion) Hood and Betty Hood, Albany, Western Australia, 2013

CHAPTER 7: WHERE OUR SPIRITS GO

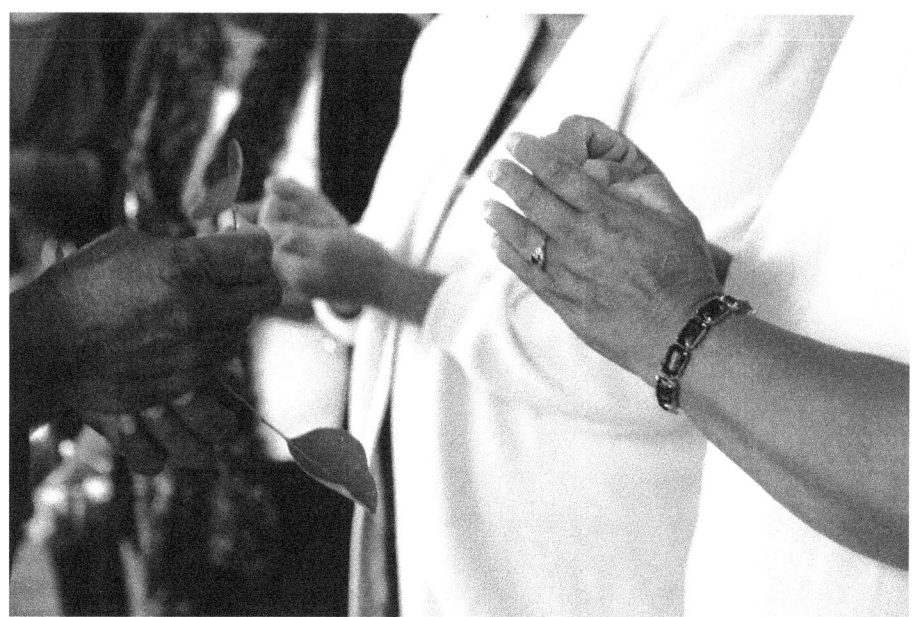

Figure 165 Ezzard Flowers and the Bryant women, Albany, Western Australia, 2013

Figure 166 Ezzard Flowers and the Bryant women, Albany, Western Australia, 2013

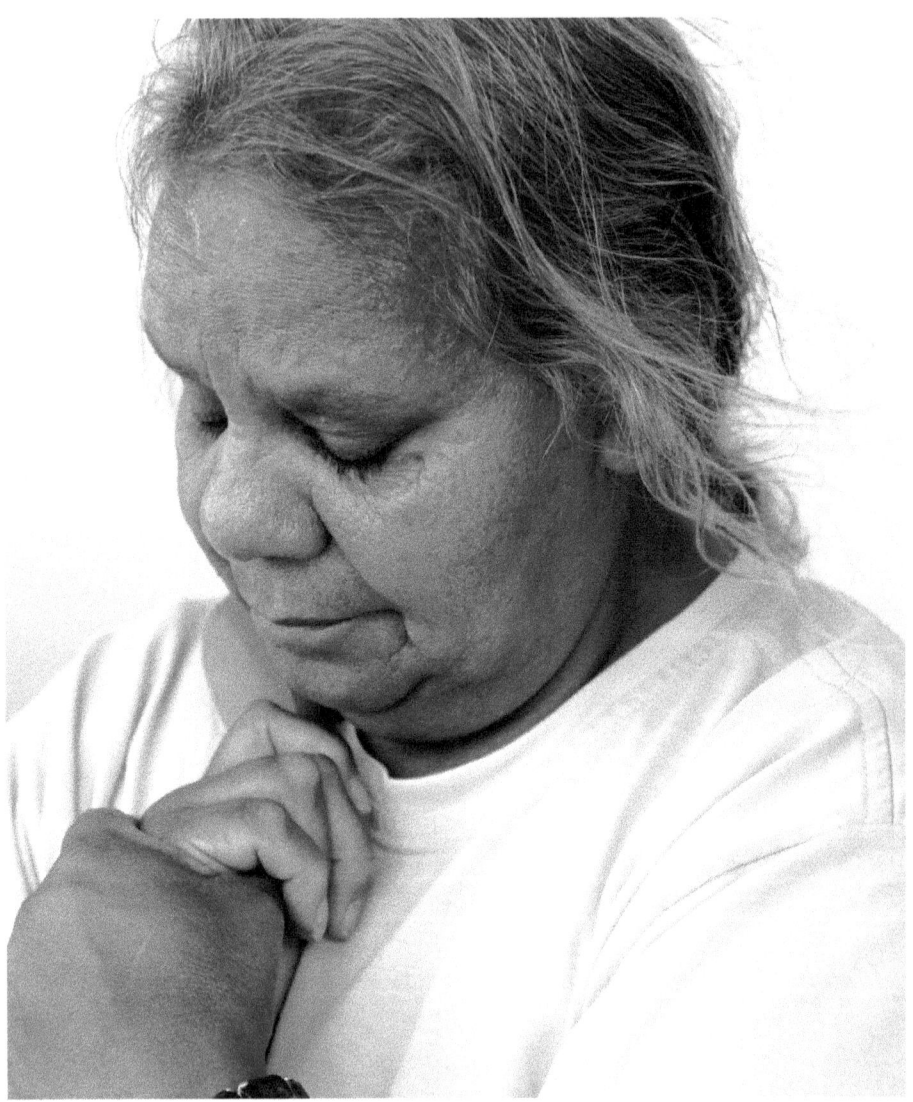

Figure 167 Regina Wilkinson, Albany, Western Australia, 2013

Chapter 8:
A lost grave and a pressed flower

One year after speaking with Betty Hood about the reunion of Bessy's descendants and kin, it became important to resolve the question of the authenticity of Bessy's grave. Niggling at the back of my mind were Betty's words, spoken in 2013 when we discussed the family reunion. Her initial reaction on hearing that Bessy's grave had been located was disbelief:

> We just said: 'You gotta be joking, no, we're not going to believe this…' When [they] found it, we said: 'How do you know it's the one?…We might be just talking to someone else's family.' And that's still going on in my mind.[161]

To confirm where Bessy was buried in Bairnsdale Cemetery, it was critical to carry out more conversations with experts and conduct further examination of the records. Finding what was thought to be Bessy's grave and bestowing upon it ardent prayer and cultural recognition was a display of family respect and love. The heartfelt words shared by Phyllis and the cultural acknowledgement spoken by Ezzard disclosed how the families respected, in their own way, the final resting place of their ancestor. What would it mean if Betty's doubts about the burial of her ancestor were correct? Would it alter in any way the reclamation of ancestral memories performed by the participating families?

The task of investigating the details of the actual grave's location proved to be a challenge. The initial information provided when the family reunion was planned through the Stolen Generations agency had been consistent with a first reading of the cemetery's online burial records. The records stated that Elizabeth Cameron (nee Flowers) was buried in 1895 at the Bairnsdale Cemetery in a plot numbered '1215'. Further study, however, led to a more complex reading of Bessy's burial records.

The East Gippsland Family History Group located in Bairnsdale helps the general public to carry out family history research. One of the researchers, Neil Cox, was able to locate a burial record for Bessy. The record detailed what was already known. Bessy was buried on 16 January 1895, two days after her death in Bairnsdale. He revealed from the records that Bessy's grave was also a 'reopen', which referred to an existing grave being opened for the burial of another person. As happened, Bessy and Donald had buried their nine-year-old daughter, Ada May Cameron, on 23 December 1889. Ada's burial was in the old Presbyterian section of the Bairnsdale Cemetery. Six years later, Donald had united mother and daughter, approving the reopen of Ada's grave for the burial of his wife, Bessy.

The location of Ada's grave was key to the search. The records confirmed that '1215' was the number given to Bessy's burial place. But the registration numbers of burials in the Bairnsdale Cemetery had been duplicated over the years. In the early 1900s, the register was begun again and this happened multiple times until there existed three different series of registrations with burials numbered '1215'. The cemetery records prior to the 1900s had been lost several decades earlier. The cemetery has a large number of unidentified plots, and the graves marked only with wooden crosses were bulldozed and destroyed some time in the 1940s or 1950s without the markers being replaced.

CHAPTER 8: A LOST GRAVE AND A PRESSED FLOWER

The Bairnsdale Cemetery Trust confirmed that Bessy was buried on 16 January 1895 in Section 23 of the old Presbyterian area. It also explained that the number '1215' was not an indicator of Bessy's grave. The Trust's secretary determined that: 'I have searched for this grave and have found it to be unidentifiable. The [Cemetery] Trust have mapped the cemetery, twice, over the past 10 years, and we have also employed professional cemetery mapping companies to do this in an effort to locate graves…there is nothing more we can do to find [the grave].'[162] In this situation of uncertainty, the placing of a memorial plaque in the Garden of Remembrance was the only way to acknowledge Bessy's final resting place.

Believing the Cemetery Trust, but also needing to validate in person that Bessy's grave was unidentified, the soundest solution was to perform another onsite inspection of the cemetery. Returning to Bairnsdale, I used a map of the cemetery as a guide. Following the narrow bitumen roads marking the boundaries of the varied religious denominations, I looked specifically for the old Presbyterian section. The layout of this part of the cemetery was an orderly arrangement of burials, but the effort to verify the existence of an unmarked grave proved ineffective, as I had been advised. None of the rusted iron crosses bore the markings of '1215'.

With the help of Neil Cox once again, the records were re-examined. Ada's burial registration was numbered '801', but there was no listing on the cemetery map of her grave. Coming from a different angle to locate Ada's grave, the search widened to include the names of people who had been buried during the same week and also in the old Presbyterian area. This led to the name and the grave of George McCallum. Inspection of the numbered iron crosses surrounding McCallum's grave revealed patches of dried earth and grass. Somewhere in Section 23 was the unmarked burial place of mother Bessy and daughter Ada.

***

Figure 168 George McCallum's grave in the old Presbyterian Section, Bairnsdale Cemetery, Victoria, 2014

Figure 169 Dried earth. The old Presbyterian section, Bairnsdale Cemetery, Victoria, 2014

CHAPTER 8: A LOST GRAVE AND A PRESSED FLOWER

Figure 170 A single cross. The old Presbyterian
section, Bairnsdale Cemetery, Victoria, 2014

On return to the State Library Victoria during the same year, I hoped to find any kind of clues in its collections that might contribute further to the family restoration of Bessy's memory. In partnership with her descendants and kin, the emotion of Bessy's story had been manifested over a period of more than five years through family social performances of kinship, identity and belonging. The recovery of memories was not achieved simply through the act of giving back copies of written records or photos, but in the unified social practices of culture. Entry to the different chapters representing Bessy's historical narrative occurred when the families bravely explored the St John's Church where Bessy had played church hymns and navigated the rooms inside the former residence of Annesfield where her formative years were spent. The archive was the kindling for a family experience of Bessy's distant past, but the palpable power ultimately resided in the decisions that were made to remember and memorialise her within a world full of life.

During the library revisit I discovered a tribute to Bessy in an article from the *Australian Weekly* newspaper dated 25 January 1895. It was written a short time after Bessy's death by a journalist by the name of Johannes Heyer. The article reported grieving Koori families at Ramahyuck Aboriginal Mission when they heard of Bessy's death. Heyer listed Bessy's achievements throughout her life by citing her accomplishments, which included reading and writing, and skilful performances on the harmonium. He also highlighted Bessy's aptitude for English literature. As an example of her education Heyer recounted the story of Sir William Stawell, who was a Victorian politician and judge. He had noted during a visit to Ramahyuck that a well-known book of essays by Lord Thomas Macaulay sat upon Bessy's bookshelf.

Lord Macaulay was an English historian and politician who was born in October 1800 and died in December 1859. He wrote extensively about British history and was also known for his role as the first Law Member of the Governor-General's Council in India. According to Heyer in his article, Stawell was impressed with Bessy's critical conversation with him about the content of Macaulay's essays. The tribute by Heyer reminded the reader that Bessy was an educated Minang woman, who held a self-determined place for herself and her family while living on Ramahyuck and other places within Victoria. This biographical observation was not typical of the conventional representations of Aboriginal people at that time.[163]

After reading Heyer's article I searched the library's catalogue for Macaulay's book. Surprisingly, a copy was available in the rare book collection. The book was notably weathered and worn with age. Its red cloth cover was loosened from the spine and the pages of small text were browned with age. In the volume of 28 essays, Macaulay had written about topics ranging from eighteenth-century English poet John Milton to war in Spain and the ancient ruins of Rome. In the essay titled

CHAPTER 8: A LOST GRAVE AND A PRESSED FLOWER

'Milton', a passage about the poet's work seemed to resonate with family efforts to reclaim ancestral memories:

> The most striking characteristic of the poetry of Milton is the extreme remoteness of the associations by means of which it acts on the reader. Its effect is produced, not so much by what it expresses, as by what it suggests; not so much by the ideas, which it directly conveys, as by other ideas which are connected with them…no sooner are [his words] pronounced than the past is present and the distant near. New forms of beauty start at once into existence, and all the burial places of the memory give up their dead.[164]

Macaulay's description about burial places of human memory giving up their dead was an unexpected echo of the reclamation of Bessy's memory by the Bryant and Flowers families. The contemporary Bryant and Flowers narratives of identity had been, in the first instance, activated by the desire to unearth buried memories. Bessy's portrait and letters produced profound effects. Of utmost value were the self-expressions galvanised from these materials. Bessy's descendants and kin had actively drawn on their imaginations and lived histories to bridge the gap between Bessy's past and their own present-day Gunai-Kurnai and Wirlomin and Minang everyday realities of being in the world.

While turning the pages of Macaulay's book, it was possible to imagine a time when Bessy had carried out this same action while reading the published essays. When she did so, how had she envisaged her future as a Minang woman living within the colony of Victoria? History demonstrates that she was highly literate and socially engaged. She was capable of making a place for herself within colonial settler society, which she disclosed in her letters. Perhaps her reading and imaginings of her future self had prompted the remarks she made to Anne Camfield, declaring on her arrival to the eastern colonies that: 'When I think of all the kindness we have received from people we have not seen I cannot tell you how I love you for taking us out of the bush and making us what we are.'[165]

The Macaulay essays put aside, I then searched once again for the letters and photos of Rev. Hagenauer, the missionary who held the most authority over Bessy when she lived at Ramahyuck. In one of the archival boxes there were two portraits. One pictured Rev. Hagenauer and the other his wife, Louisa (Christiana Louisa). Louisa wears a pair of wire-framed spectacles and a lace cap keeping her hair free from her face. She is elderly and modest in appearance. In contrast, Rev. Hagenauer is seated upright, stern and conforming. His beard is full and greying, his Germanic features filling the frame. Bessy was amused by Rev. Hagenauer on their first meeting in Melbourne, writing in a letter to Anne how she was forced to withhold her laughter while she observed what she regarded to be Hagenauer's 'strange' look.[166]

Rev. Hagenauer in the photo is a man who comes across with a defined sense of purpose. His sharp and piercing eyes command a second look of the photo. In his papers, Rev. Hagenauer detailed his commitment to missionary causes in Victoria. It was to be his life's work. He was well respected by the General Assembly of the Presbyterian Church of Victoria as evidenced in papers that were written to acknowledge his retirement.

The General Assembly thanked Rev. Hagenauer for: '[with the gospel] redeeming love to the degraded and neglected Aborigines of Australia, who had added to their own cruel and vile heathenism the worst vices of the lowest whites'. They congratulated Rev. Hagenauer for his pioneering work to 'turn many of these [Aboriginal] people from darkness to light and from the service of Satan to the service of the living God'.[167] This language was commonly used to describe Aboriginal people, as Henry Camfield demonstrated in a letter to his sister in 1850, writing: 'Anne is very much interested in the sable race…there is plenty to work upon if their [Noongar peoples] presently dark minds were duly cultivated.'[168]

Found in the collection was also a bible that had belonged to Rev. Hagenauer.

CHAPTER 8: A LOST GRAVE AND A PRESSED FLOWER

In his sermons, Rev. Hagenauer would have appeared tall and formidable at the pulpit, preaching to his mission congregation perhaps even from this same bible. The following extract taken from the Church of England 'Messenger' in November 1870 reveals Rev. Hagenauer's ideals about Christian converts and gospel instruction:

> Not many years ago they (the blacks) were all very wild and continually wandering about and practising all of the sins of the white and black people together. The simple approach of the blessed gospel has wrought a new creation among them. There is a settled and well-behaved Christian community now and almost all the old evils so usual them are passed away.
>
> At our last communion about three weeks ago there were fifteen native communicants all much impressed and in great earnest and

Figure 171 Rev. FA Hagenauer preaching at a church service with Bessy pictured in the congregation (standing near the wall, far right), Ramahyuck Aboriginal Mission, Victoria, c.1860s–70s © Charles (Carl) Walter. Collection: State Library Victoria.

NO LONGER A WANDERING SPIRIT

all growing in grace. There is a spirit of prayer among them, which is delightful to notice and at the same time every sign of true humility. In every family is the bible read and family worship performed, although we have daily service in Church, which is well attended…[169]

Upon closing the large bible so as to pack it away in its archival box, it happened to open to the middle pages. Revealed between these pages was a flower pressed paper-thin by the volume's weightiness. Why had this flower been preserved in Hagenauer's bible? The appearance of the dried pressed flower encouraged a second look at a historical photo by photographer Charles Walter. The photo depicts Rev. Hagenauer preaching from a wooden pulpit to residents at Ramahyuck. When enlarged for a closer inspection Bessy can be found in this photo. She is pictured standing among the church congregation and wearing a light-coloured dress. Nearby is a group of seated children.

Figure 174 A pressed flower in Rev. FA Hagenauer's bible, 2014

CHAPTER 8: A LOST GRAVE AND A PRESSED FLOWER

This family story of memory reclamation has revealed that no life can be completely told through archives of letters and photos. Many aspects of Bessy will always be memories secreted away by circumstance or personal choice. As such she has not given up all of herself to history. Though the meaning of Rev. Hagenauer's dried pressed flower may not be known, it justly symbolises for the purpose of this story a remarkable woman whose life experiences have, after more than 150 years, united two different families across the nation and provided a deepened sense of belonging and identity. Family unity is triumphant in this story of surviving and resilient culture and spirit.

NO LONGER A WANDERING SPIRIT

Afterword

I felt a sense of belonging and connection to my grandfather's family after hearing the story about Bessy, but also confusion and sadness. I'm proud because of what I now know about my ancestor, but confused because there wasn't any of this history spoken about within my community.

I remember looking at the photo of Bessy for the first time. I saw a girl who had humility, respect and strength, the three main traits that I believe sustained her throughout her life and times from Minang country to Gunai-Kurnai country. Straightaway there was no eye contact with the camera. In my mind she doesn't want to be there, but she's showing in her own way that she's respecting the person taking the photo. The photo along with the words made me think about her life experiences of loss, struggles and dispossession from culture, family and country.

Looking at that photo of the little girl on the stool I can proudly say that she's my matriarch and I believe this history needs to be acknowledged because it's a powerful human story.

Bessy was a humble and obedient girl learning how to survive in a world that was changing for Aboriginal people. Back in the colonial days, the Christian emphasis was on rehabilitating Aboriginal people; if they could change an Aboriginal's way of thinking and life, well they'd done their cause, which was changing our way of life. Her Christian faith and upbringing, along with her cultural values and beliefs, would have empowered her for whatever was to come. I think she definitely remained a true and obedient servant to the higher authorities at that time.

Bessy should be recognised because of her experience as an Aboriginal child who excelled during times of difficulties and as an Aboriginal woman who lived through tough times that were responsible for changing herself and her people, and their families both politically and culturally. I acknowledge my ancestor as one of the greatest Aboriginal pioneering women of her time, even though I think she struggled to fully adapt and to adjust to a world that was impacting upon Minang cultural sovereignty.

Looking at Bessy face to face in the photo helped me discover something from the past, which was important to my life as a Wirlomin and Minang Noongar. Seeing this young and shy-looking child sitting on a chair while getting her photo taken was my first visual encounter with a family history that would become clearer to me over the time of reclaiming her memory. I came to know my ancestor by reflecting on my personal story as a Stolen Generations survivor, including the experience as a boy of separating from my parents, family and culture.

I see loss in the photo but also survival when looking deep into her child's expression. Children are at the centre of my culture and are the reason why the security of our cultural values and beliefs are important for our survival and continuation into the future. Bessy lost her identity and her connection to the oldest living culture in the world because of interfering people who were not from here. The colonisers failed to understand our culture.

From both a cultural and spiritual perspective, reclaiming Bessy's story as part of my own story has been an empowering experience. I stepped back in time to understand more about the changing past for all Aboriginal people. I wasn't to know that this photo of a girl sitting on a stool and her letters would take me on a journey from one side of the country to the other. The journey took me into the story of my ancestor, but also on a journey to the country of Bessy's great-grandchildren and their families in East Gippsland, Victoria.

We – the Flowers and Bryant families – came together and embraced the history of our ancestor and we acknowledged how times for our people living under colonial law and rule were difficult and damaging to our culture and also to our hearts. We embraced not only the pain of these times on our people, but also the courage and resilience of Bessy and the other four young women who left Albany all those years ago.

On Bessy's journey eastwards, I imagined her being the mother figure for the other girls who were to be married. Perhaps their thoughts and feelings differed to those feelings of my ancestor. Bessy believed that she would be in the eastern colony for only two years, before her planned return to Albany. She was hopeful for this new experience and inspired by her travels to other places, such as Sydney. The other four young women knew they would be staying at the mission to be married to Koori men. Sending these girls out of their country to be married and without full cultural support and authority was taboo, and in opposition to our traditional ways.

I think that Bessy would have known what she had to do according to the agreement that she had with Anne from Annesfield. Her thoughts would have been on the girls' welfare and getting them settled into another Aboriginal settlement, a different culture norm. I imagine that she would have made sure she was by their side at all times.

The closeness and bond of these girls leaving country and moving to the eastern colonies for good would have been emotional. I wonder, did the girls say goodbye to their families, and to their country when leaving Albany? What were they feeling as they watched the waters of King George Sound disappear out of sight? Did leaving their Annesfield home and the other children evoke a feeling of sadness, or mixed feelings of joy and concern? Did Minang families mourn losing family from country?

These are some of the questions I asked myself when reflecting on the photo of my ancestor. I thought about time passing and what history might disclose to me if I accepted what can no longer be and instead embraced what's possible when bringing back the memory of Bessy to my family. I asked many questions when the past came back to me because of my Wirlomin and Minang roots, and because of how I felt about a story that was once culturally alien to me being returned home.

This book is a story told through the experience and emotions of my family. It's our journey of reconnecting and of discovering a stronger sense of who we are. Reflecting on my ancestor's past has united two families from both sides of this country and this connection is continuing to make right the past, in the present, by giving healing to all the families concerned. Connecting the Bryant families to Bessy's homeland and to other sites of her story reinforced the value of healing on country and as a family.

This journey has also connected two people from different cultural backgrounds. During Sharon's research and family engagement, we shared a vision to explore Bessy's loss of family, culture, country and language, as well as her resilience. The short film produced in 2016, *No longer a wandering spirit – imaginaries of Bessy Flowers*,[170] is proof of our collaboration and ongoing friendship, and evidence that life given to this story was important for bringing people together to celebrate and remember Bessy. This connection is still strong 11 years after it began and we still respectfully consult one another about what's to come next.

This story has made my spirit stronger. It has connected me to members of my family I didn't know I had and has also put me in touch with Bessy's history and what she achieved during her life. Her story has now connected me to family and all of us family finally know where she is resting. It's a great sense of relief that we found her and know where she is and since that day it has been a spiritual journey of remembering, reflecting and reconnecting from both sides of the country. This story now connects us and our conversations with one another and will continue as we walk forward along the path of Bessy, our Minang ancestor.

I'm sorry that we must keep up the fight to mend the broken stories of our ancestors and Aboriginal kin. I hope this book gives others the strength and the encouragement to reconnect with their bloodlines and to make stronger family legacies of cultural identity. Family and country is what culture is all about.

AFTERWORD

I hope that if your spirit has been wandering, your spirit will find its way home and will no longer have to wander.

The poem *Wandering Spirit* is about being separated from my family and being taken away from my country of birth. The poem expresses how time spent with family Elders, and listening to their stories, helped me to restore my broken heart, return my dignity, and heal my spiritual connection with the ancestors of our lands. *Wandering Spirit* is wholeheartedly dedicated to restoring my identity and that of my ancestor, Bessy.

Wandering Spirit

Wandering Spirit, Wandering Spirit
Where oh where can you be?
I need you back inside of me,
To help me through my destiny.

I'm lost, confused and all alone,
They have moved me far from home.
My culture, confidence and self-esteem
Is lost and destroyed, so it seems.

Wandering Spirit, Wandering Spirit
I've been searching far and wide.
I just cannot hide it any longer,
I need you back inside of me,
For only you will make me stronger.

NO LONGER A WANDERING SPIRIT

My journey almost destroyed me,
Their policies ignorance and pride,
The way they talked, the way they lied,
The way I've seen how my people cried.

Wandering Spirit, Wandering Spirit
Values and beliefs bring healing,
Culture and kinship embraces.
Empowerment,
Respect, recognition creates
Understanding.
But, with you in all of this,
You have given me DIGNITY
For now, I have IDENTITY.

Ezzard Flowers

Appendix A:
Children of Bessy and Donald Cameron

Elizabeth Bessy Flowers and Adolphus Donald Cameron had eight children over the years of their marriage, from 1868 to 1895: Annie Magdalene, known mostly in historical records as Magdalene and Maggie (born 1869; † 1925), Nellie Grace (born 1871; † 1872), Louisa Alice (born 1873; † 1896), Donald Boyd (born 1875; † 1877), Haines Adolphus (born c.1878; † 1949), Ada May (born c.1880; † 1889), Mena Blanche (born 1885; † 1922) and Keith Flowers (born 1892; † 1920). Sadly, several of Bessy and Donald's children passed away at birth or as infants. In correspondence to the Victorian Board for the Protection of Aborigines, Rev. Hagenauer provided details of births at Ramahyuck. He mentioned on one occasion how Bessy's health had suffered after childbirth.

Annie Magdalene, or Maggie, as she was affectionately known, was born at Ramahyuck Aboriginal Mission in 1869. On 25 December 1890 she married Thomas Bryant, a labouring settler from New South Wales. The couple had six children: Elizabeth (Bessy) (c. 1889–1922), Thomas Donald (c.1894–unknown), Roy (unknown), William Keith (c.1901–unknown), Muriel Winifred (c.1904–unknown) and Keith (c.1907; †1975). Maggie died on 2 January 1925 at 56 years of age. She was buried on 3 January 1925 in the Sale Cemetery in East Gippsland. Thomas Bryant died on 3 June 1918 at Maffra and was buried at the Heyfield Cemetery. Keith Bryant was only about 10 years of age when his father, Thomas, passed away, and a young man at the passing of his mother, Maggie.

Nellie Grace Cameron died in 1872. At this same time Bessy's younger sister, Ada, also suffered the loss of her daughter.

Louisa Cameron was 20 years of age when she married William Logan at the Primitive Methodist Parsonage in Sale. Bessy disapproved of this marriage, as detailed in letters between herself and Rev. Hagenauer. Louisa died on 28 July 1896 and was buried at the Ramahyuck Aboriginal Mission Cemetery on 29 July 1896. She was 22 years of age and had a son who was only nine months of age, William Pelham Logan. William Logan died on 22 April 1897 at 26 years of age and was also buried at the Ramahyuck Aboriginal Mission Station.

Donald Boyd Cameron was born on 18 November 1875 and died at one year and six months in 1877. Hagenauer reported to the Victorian Board for the Protection of Aborigines that Donald's death was caused by teething. Rev. Murdoch MacDonald visited Ramahyuck in 1877 and also wrote of Bessy's loss.

Haines Adolphus Cameron was born c.1878. Haines lived on the Lake Tyers Aboriginal Mission and married Isabella O'Rouke. His second marriage was to Elizabeth Alexandra Jennings on 30 April 1925, when Haines was 42 years of age. Witness to the marriage was Edward Foster and Charlie Green. Edward was the son of Charles and Nora Foster. Haines lived most of his life on the Lake Tyers Aboriginal Mission. He died on 9 October 1949 and was buried in the Orbost Cemetery in Victoria. He was 72 years of age.

Ada May Cameron was born in 1880 at the Ramahyuck Aboriginal Mission, and was the namesake of Bessy's younger sister. Ada died at nine years of age on 21 December 1889 and was buried in Section 23 of the old Presbyterian section of the Bairnsdale Cemetery.

Mena Blanche Cameron was born on 15 September 1885. She married William Rankin on 30 September 1911. Mena and William lived on the Lake

APPENDIX A: CHILDREN OF BESSY AND DONALD CAMERON

Tyers Aboriginal Mission and at Coranderrk Mission in Healesville. Mena died on 11 March 1922 at the Nhill Hospital in northwestern Victoria. She was 34 years of age. In the margin of Mena and William's marriage certificate it has been written, 'This couple are half-castes from no mission station'. Mena was buried at the Nhill Cemetery. At the time of her death, Mena had two surviving children, Samuel Richard who was 12 years of age and Gladys Isobelle aged six years. The third child, William, is listed as deceased on her death certificate.

Keith Flowers Cameron was born on 6 November 1892 in Bairnsdale, East Gippsland. At the time of Keith's birth, his siblings Nellie, Donald Boyd and Ada had passed away. Keith died on 2 August 1920 and was buried at the Lake Tyers Aboriginal Mission Cemetery. He was 27 years of age.

Historically, many of the Cameron family were buried at the Ramahyuck Aboriginal Mission Cemetery. However, there are no gravestones marking their place of burial. The Lake Tyers Aboriginal Trust has two cemeteries, the old cemetery and the new cemetery. There are no gravestones marking the graves of the Cameron family in the old cemetery.

Appendix B:
Parliamentary report by Anne Camfield, 1871

In 1868, Anne Camfield compiled the following report on the Annesfield Native Institution. The report was submitted to the Western Australian Parliament several years later in 1871.

The natives of Australia are capable of great improvement, but it will be in some generations hence that much good will be visible, and there must be great extension of the means now in operation.

We are too much inclined to look upon the civilization of this people as a hopeless work because so little good is apparent from the efforts that have already been made; but multiply the means, have institutions in each district, instead of having only one or two in the whole colony, and these left to the working (and hard-working) of a few individuals, and the results will be more encouraging.

To wean them from their wild habits and to give them a little insight into the comforts of civilization together with teaching them some of the simplest but most important Truths of the Gospel, is as much as can at first be done. 'Rome was not built in a day': Nor did Englishmen rise from the condition described in the early parts of English History to the high state of civilization to which they have now attained, in one generation. So, to expect that the Aborigines may be raised at once from their present wild state into that of perfect civilization is simply to expect what only a miracle could produce. Doubtless it is within the power of God to place them on an equality with the most refined and intellectual, at once.

The Creator of all, He could make equal, if he saw fit. But he works by means: and we whom His Providence has placed in this country are the means to effect the salvation of the Aborigines, in the same way as the Roman Christians were sent by and wrought so much for our Saxon Ancestors in early times. The overruling

APPENDIX B: PARLIAMENTARY REPORT BY ANNE CAMFIELD, 1871

hand of God directed us to the occupying of this land, where we 'live and get gain' and He places these objects of compassion before our eyes as trials of our faith in Him and if we are believers in Him and in the salvation which He has obtained for our race, surely we shall do what we can among this people, though what we individually do may be but as the offering of a widow's mite.

It was from an irresistible feeling that something ought to be attempted, though the result might be ever so small, that the Annesfield Native Institution was commenced. It was begun privately with one child for six months, when a favorable answer was received to an application to Government to support six children. It has now been in operation nearly sixteen years, the one child in question having been received into the House June 21st, 1852.

One thing is clearly proved – that the Aborigines have minds capable of comprehending their need of the Saviour Christ to die, and so procure for them the forgiveness of sin, and an eternal inheritance in heaven. That all who are taught believe this, I do not assert, but only that they can comprehend it, which is as much as can be said of hundreds and thousands of white people. There have been, however, several among the children who have died, in regard to whose death I am sure there has been good ground for hope that they savingly believed in the Gospel; and one soul saved is worth a life-time of labor.

The native children have all a great fondness for music and very quickly learn tunes. One little boy whom we adopted ourselves, so as to bring him up in a more refined way than is necessary or desirable for them generally (thereby to test his abilities as a native), gave evidence of a fine ear for music. He would listen untiringly to it and learnt to play on the Pianoforte with great facility; and there is no doubt that had he lived, he would, if properly taught, have become a good performer. He died at the age of ten years and two months. On one occasion the Piano had been tuned when he was absent and he was not aware of it: when he went to practice in the afternoon, a friend who was sitting by him will never forget the look of ecstasy which he turned upon her, when he struck the notes first, and he discovered the improvement.

Yet the instrument in the morning was not so much out of tune but that many children might have played without noticing it. He, as in the case with almost all of them, no application; they are naturally more or less idle. To encourage him at first with his notes and other music exercises, a little black girl was allowed to learn with him, simply as an encouragement to diligence, not at all with the idea of her becoming a performer. But she profited by the opportunity thus given her so far, that three years ago on her being taken by friends to the Eastern Colonies, she, on one occasion played the hymns for the afternoon service on the Organ at St. Phillip's Church, Sydney, when there was a full congregation, and she for some time, two years in all, played the Harmonium, an instrument with two key-boards, at Albany Church, because there was no one in the place who could play it better, and who was willing to do so.

Her knowledge and practice of music therefore has been made useful. She is now earning her living very creditably as a teacher in a native school in Gippsland. An extract from the German Missionary's letter of February 28th, 1868, will show that she is giving satisfaction. 'Bessy has been a very good girl ever since she came back from Lake Tyers. She is a great help already in our work, and puts her hands to every work, which we have to do either with the children (black, and also my own) or in the housework. I feel sure that in due time she will &c., &c.' but I forward the whole letter so that you will see what more he says of her, and also of the four others who are at the same station. This letter gives me a 'better account,' which implies that the last was not good.

If anyone undertakes to do anything with the natives and expects it all to be followed by unvarying good, nothing is more certain than that they will be disappointed. It is impossible for them not to go astray, and that not frequently. The badness of behavior here referred to by Mr Hagenauer was the running away of two married girls who enticed their husbands to accompany them, because they could earn more money at harvest time at other stations than they did at their own; but they returned, as you will see, the wiser for their loss of home comforts. Bessy had been on a visit to Lake Tyers.

APPENDIX B: PARLIAMENTARY REPORT BY ANNE CAMFIELD, 1871

Another Black girl is married to a native convert [Nathaniel Pepper] at the Moravian Wimmera station, and I constantly hear good reports of her and her husband, who does much real good among his fellow-blacks. They have been married five years. The missionary writes that he will be very glad when I can again send one or more girls; which proves that this young woman gives satisfaction. There are some others married, who are doing well, or not well, just as there are differences in the conduct of white girls who are married, and very much depends upon their husbands, as they are easily led to good or evil. They are great copyists: the manners, the language, the habits of those around them soon become theirs; so that it is not difficult to see when their associates are bad.

Two or three Sundays ago a child of one of these schoolgirls was baptized at the Church. Two young ladies, out of respect to the mother, were the sponsors, together with the husband, a white man; and a nicer more neatly dressed babe I was told could not be brought to the front. The clothes were made by the mother, and they were white, and plain as could be, but so beautifully got up and there was such a wholesome healthy cleanliness about the child, that they could not but admire it. The mother was admitted into the school when about seven or eight years old, and there are a few things in a house that she is now not able to do. She is a very good plain cook: she washes and gets up linen very well, makes bread and jams, cures pork when they kill their pigs, &c., &c. And her cottage is the picture of neatness. I often go in, and whether I go unexpectedly or not it is all the same. She also reads and writes very well.

You may perhaps accuse me of picking out one or two instances, and enlarging upon their well doing, leaving the less favorable cases untouched. I do not wish to mislead by bringing the good forward as if they were all equally satisfactory, or even to pretend that the conduct of the best has been without drawbacks; but it is certainly pleasanter to look on the bright side of any picture, and these instances prove that these poor children of the wilderness will repay efforts made for their welfare in as great a proportion as similar efforts made on behalf of a neglected white population. I could relate distressing circumstances, which have caused many sorrowful hours and anxious nights to those who have had the chief care of the school, and many a weary disappointment, and these circumstances have generally arisen from the wicked example and seduction of those who are of a superior race, working upon the untutored passions of these poor children, and thereby producing deceit and every other evil.

Several of the boys have gone out to service and are doing well; others have not been so satisfactory, but only two have asserted their independence and left the masters under whom we placed them. They are still, however, in the service of white men. Last week I was told that his master had not had to reprove one of these boys since he had been with him, now nearly two years, and that he could be thoroughly trusted.

A little girl who was the object of His Excellency's kindness, and who was sent by his direction, together with her little brother, from Guildford, about four years ago, has just brought me her copybook to look at. I have torn a leaf out of it and enclose it. She reads well, much better than she writes, and works with her needle nicely, besides doing her share of sweeping and cleaning. She has not strength yet to scrub; she has a tiny girl to take care of, and whose pinafores and frocks, &c., she has to patch. This little girl who we have had baptized Charlotte Owen, is a smart, intelligent, and very loveable child, and will make a useful woman if she lives; and she is just the character that would have been very troublesome, if she had not been taught, and led to act right.

The children are very observant of dress, and great admirers of it. Little Charlotte was raised up on a bench, so as to be heard, to read for a gentleman one day (they have all the fault of speaking very low in school). She is very shy, and almost turned her back, and hung her head down, so that it surprised me that she saw him at all; but it was evident that her whole attention was not on her book, for as soon as the gentleman had left the room, she ran up to her little school friend, and burst out with a laugh, 'Oh! Louisa, that gentleman has got a lady's part.' This was that his hair was parted down the middle instead of at the side, which she thought it was the orthodox method.

APPENDIX B: PARLIAMENTARY REPORT BY ANNE CAMFIELD, 1871

New shoes, new collars, or gloves, or ribbons, even the minutest change in the dress of any one in the house, is observed immediately by one of them, and very shrewd are the remarks on the new fashion when visitors from the steamers come to see the school. A strange footprint never escapes their notice. Some gardens were robbed lately of apples and onions, and from the stables saddlegirths and sacks were taken. Several of the school boys gave considerable help in tracking the party of delinquents six miles and more, so that their usefulness in this work is in no way diminished by their being civilized.

If a tradesman is required in carpentering or building, nothing delights the boys more than help; and they show great aptness in learning many useful works. They are not quick, as a rule, at their books, and especially not so at ciphering and the value of money; but they soon learn as much of the latter as is necessary; and many of them read and spell and write very well. Some are really fond of reading. A girl of about eleven or twelve years old, who came into the school much too late (her father had just been hanged, poor fellow! as an accomplice in the murder of another native) is constantly secreting books to read out of school; and at church, besides diligently plodding to follow the prayers, she keeps her prayer book open throughout the sermon, and almost during the whole time it occupies reads without any signs of weariness; and this is really more profitable to her than listening to the sermon would be, as she does not understand English sufficiently well to comprehend rapid or fluent speaking.

The difficulties are great to the children when they first come to school. The language and habits of their new friends are foreign to them and they have much to unlearn as well as to learn and acquire. Bessy who is now a teacher in Gippsland, was never without a book in her pocket by day or under her pillow by night. Her love of reading often brought her into scrapes, from reading at inconvenient times, but not withstanding, it was very improving to her, as (though she liked as well as any girl to read stories, yet) she is much interested by history, travels and more serious works, and she was often referred to if such books were under discussion. Her memory is so very good that she retains what she reads.

This girl alone is sufficient proof of the intelligence of the Aborigines, for she was not chosen by us to receive greater advantages of education than the rest from anything superior in her. She was selected simply because she was the sister of the first child we took, and who died after being in the school three years, and also because she was the daughter of a very faithful old native servant, who died believing in Jesus Christ (as far, I cannot but think, as an untutored mind could comprehend) as his Saviour. We have had many equal, and one or two decidedly superior to Bessy, and the question is: 'is it right to let such intelligence be wasted, or worse, be turned to evil without some effort to prevent it?'

I recollect well the kindness of a late Governor, who, when he honored us with a farewell visit, to wish us success with the school, asked if he could do anything for us in England; the only reply made was, laughingly, that what would give us most pleasure would be, if he could influence the lawgivers there to make a law to compel the aborigines and half-caste children to be brought into civilized training, so as to make them useful members of society (if there were no higher motives for raising them), in a country where population is needed and where as they now are—in their degraded state—they are a pest to society. He good-naturedly answered that such a plan would trench upon the liberty of the British subject, that compulsory education would not be tolerated. Prussia was the only country where it existed. He agreed with us, that the poor natives could not understand what would be for their children's good; but yet thought the plan impracticable, though it would be a happy thing if it could be accomplished.

Only a few years have passed since this conversation, and now the late English papers tell us that the subject of obliging all classes to have their children educated is under discussion in Parliament. If the lower, or lowest, class of people in England need coercion to act for the good of their children's good! The objection many people make, that it is cruel to take their children from them, is not a solid one; because the children left to the parent's management, or non-management, soon cast off all submission, and all care or love for the parents, so that when the latter become old and helpless, they are almost wholly neglected. When, on the contrary,

APPENDIX B: PARLIAMENTARY REPORT BY ANNE CAMFIELD, 1871

the children are brought to school, the parents see them whenever they like, and their children are taught to treat them with kindness and consideration.

Since this Institution was commenced there have been fifty-five children, black and half-caste, admitted. Seventeen of these have died; but eleven were ill, almost hopelessly ill, when they came. Of the six who were healthy when they were admitted, but who died afterwards, were: Matilda, our first native; she died from inflammation of the lungs consequent on a cold. Andrew died at Fremantle; his parents both died of consumption. Caroline and Emma died in the Melbourne hospital. They were proceeding to Gippsland, where they were to be married, but took typhus fever soon after their arrival in Melbourne and sank under it. Sarah died from scarlatina at the same time with a baby who was ill when he came. There were sixteen ill in bed at this time, together with the young lady who was my chief help, besides another poor lady in the house who was mentally affected. Under more favourable circumstances, humanly speaking, I think Sarah would not have died, as she was a strong girl.

The sixth death of a healthy girl was Ellen. She left four or five years ago, and went as a servant to a lady who was going to South Australia; I had arranged with friends at Melbourne to look after her, if her mistress should go on to Sydney or Queensland: but unfortunately for the poor girl, she was taken on too. Here, she was soon dismissed by her mistress, for alleged bad conduct and she was thrown upon her resources. Her own evil passions were seconded by those of wicked people around her, and her life therefore was such as might be expected.

But God raised up friends for this poor fallen orphan girl, confirming His word that He is the Father of the Fatherless; and to the last hours of her life she was watched over by a Miss W… a Wesleyan, whom I do not know; but who constantly gave me information of her, and made the best of any trifle I could send for poor Ellen's benefit. She died in a hopeful, though not much enlightened state, October 2, 1866. Her illness led her to think of the future. The Bishop of Brisbane interested himself much for this poor girl, and kindly proposed to me to raise funds to send her back: but the evils would have been greater in her return than in her remaining, and especially as she was not allowed to suffer want there. A long voyage home, without protection, was very undesirable, and her presence among the school children would not have been good for them.

Six out of the eleven children who were sick when they entered the school and who afterwards died, were babies, without mothers. One of these was only three weeks old. Their sufferings were alleviated by being here if no other good was done by admission. It may be asked why the girls, after they grow up to be of a useful age, are sent away to other colonies. Simply for this reason that they have Institutions for adult natives and half-castes, where they have farms on which these people can find profitable employment.

In the Moravian Missionary Stations, they wanted wives for the converts, and a teacher for their school. We had girls here who were too old to remain in the school, and to send them to service was to send them to almost certain ruin, as we found in more than one instance to our cost: therefore it was much better, we thought, to send them where they would be appreciated and comfortably married, than to keep them here. The expense to us, personally, is very considerable, in fitting them out and sending them under the care of a matron, though the Government gave aid in the last five of going, and the Missions there also assist.

Bessy was very useful here in the school; but we thought it would be good for her to go, as there was the favorable opportunity, because she would supply an urgent need of theirs and at the same time she would learn much herself from the noted industry and usefulness of the Moravian Missionaries' wives. Her engagement is only for two years. Three of these five girls have been married, and they each have comfortable little cottages and they bake (beautiful bread as I have been told), and wash, and cook, and do all that is necessary in a little household.

What I have always urged is more than ever essential, an Institution in the Australian Colony to receive the boys and girls as they become old enough to work profitably, and where they can marry and live happily and usefully. Until such an Institution is established the amount of good done will be very small. Institutions of this kind, under judicious management, would in a few years be self-supporting.

APPENDIX B: PARLIAMENTARY REPORT BY ANNE CAMFIELD, 1871

There are at present in the school nineteen Aboriginal and half-caste children, besides three white children, orphan or deserted by the mother. These, of course, are not on the Government list, for maintenance.

Appendix C:
Letters (1867–1894)

1867

Bessy Flowers, Port Adelaide, to Anne Camfield, Annesfield, Albany.

12 June 1867

My dearest Missie,

I know you will be glad to hear that we arrived quite safely & had such a nice voyage.

The Captain kindly allowed us to go on deck by the funnel. We went to Church on Sunday morning, at first we could not find one but a lady shewed us where to go & spoke to the clerk to give us some prayer books & hymn books. The service was beautiful. Oh! the music & singing was delicious, they sang the Amen after everything.

In the afternoon we went for a walk & we met the clergyman, he said that he would see us tomorrow (Monday); his name is Mr […]; oh he was so kind & another gentleman his name is Mr […]. They came yesterday & took us up to Adelaide, fancy dear Missie was it not kind of them? We went into the Legislative House & into the Assembly room, & then we went into the museum. There were such a lot of birds & all sorts of things, it was so pretty.

Afterwards we went to the gardens, a baker drove past us in a cart, & dropped a double loaf in the mud, we could not help laughing. Mr […] called out to him but he did not hear. Emily went to pick it up & she told me to tell you, it was so hot & smelt so nice, she was going to pick a piece out of it (we have so much fun with her). After we had gone to the gardens, we saw a tiger, a bear, all sorts of peacocks; there was a white one, a lama & ostrich the place is laid out beautifully, I only wish that you were with us.

APPENDIX C: LETTERS (1867–1894)

The gentlemen shewed us four guns that the English took from the Russians at the Crimea. There was the prickly fur in the garden. Mr […] knows Mr […], he said that he would like some of those pink everlastings, I wish you could send some to him, he lives at the Port. When Mr […] mentioned your name, the clergyman said "Oh! she is a great friend of Bishop Halle's is she not?" I know you will like to know that there were such kind people. I have brought a mug for Louisa to drink her water at the table. Mrs […] says she will bring it. I have only spent 3/6. I am going to leave the rest for Melbourne. I hope you are all quite well, Ada was not seasick, but we were – Rhoda & Emily were the worst. How did the singing get on? On Sunday I thought of it several times, & on Sunday I fancied I could hear Martie asking me if I had all my music ready.

On Thursday I wished I was going to the Church instead of rocking about in the steamer. One day when we were on deck the second officer came to us & was talking about Albany, he said they considered it a great banishment to be sent there, that nothing grew but rocks & stones & I said that that added to the beauty of the place, he laughed so, & said a good deal more, but when I could not say anymore, I spoke about the climate being the best & he said "Oh, you are right there, it is the best". I did not answer rudely though, dear Missie.

I hope you will be able to read this, I shall write from Melbourne too. Please give my best to Miss […] and […] (if she will accept it) & my love to poor dear Mother & tell her that Ada & I are quite well. I am sorry that I am come to the bottom of my paper, I was going to cross it but I heard you say it was rude & so I have divided another sheet. I have written to poor Bobby; will you please send it to him? We will think of dear Martie's & Miss _'s birthday. I wish them many happy returns of the day.

Whenever I talk of coming home again, Rhoda says she feels so jealous. Mr […] says will you tell Miss […] that her baby is coming to tease her again bye and bye. I forgot I have said nothing about Nora's baby [Charles Foster], he has been so screaming & crying in the night, I often wish I could pitch him overboard, he is asleep now. Please will you give my best love to Phoebe. I will try & write to her soon. I hope to hear from you soon. Will you please give my grateful love to Martie & accept the same.

From your grateful & loving B

I am very sorry I did not see Mr […]. Mrs […] was so kind to us all the way down. I am so glad she came with us and all the girls send their best love to you all.

Bessy Flowers, Victoria Street, South Yarra, to Anne Camfield, Annesfield, Albany.

17 June 1867

My own dearest Missie,

Oh, how I wish you were here with us. I received your dear letter on Saturday morning on board the steamer. We had a very quick passage from Adelaide.

On Saturday morning as [we] were coming to the pier I was looking out for Mr H [Hagenauer]. After some time we saw a gentleman with a dark beard, when he saw us he smiled & shook his hand. I could not help laughing he looked so funny.

There was another clergyman (who is going to Sydney) came with him. I must finish about Adelaide first. Mr […] met us the next day & took us to see the Town Hall & treated us with lollies & oranges. When I think of all the kindness we have received from people we have not seen I cannot tell you how I love you for taking us out of the bush & making us what we are. I hope you are all quite well. We are going to Gipps Land on Friday. So when this reaches you I hope we shall be settled in our new home. Emily is going with us; Mr H thinks it will be better than separating from us.

We went to the Scotch Church yesterday, we did not kneel down at all, we stood up while Mr […] prayed, & sat down whilst they sang; once when they were going to pray, I was going to kneel down & I felt very funny. I shall now tell you about Mr Menzies & his family, he is something like Mr [...] of Adelaide, only he has a black beard & Mr [...] had red. His wife is a kind lady & very much like Mrs [...]; there are two young ladies only, & they are children of the first Mrs Menzies. After church as we came out there were 3 or 4 gentlemen & ladies, who shook hands with us & asked us how we were.

There was a lady dressed in black, her name is Mrs [...] & she said she knew Mr [...] & told me to tell him when I wrote, to say that she was asking about him, she had a kind face. In the afternoon we went to the Sunday School & Mr H spoke to the teachers & scholars about his mission station, when he had done speaking, Mr Menzies told them that they wanted a harmonium at Gippsland. I asked the children to save up their pence & shillings to buy one.

As we were going up the street to a lady's house to tea (dear Missie they are not ashamed to ask us to tea). I am sure we have reason to be thankful. When I read your letter I could not help crying to think of you lying awake half the night. I did not hear the steamer either. I wish I had not come in so soon but I dare say it is all for the best.

Will you please tell Mrs [...] I am very sorry I did not see her before I came away, & would have been very glad to have spent a day with her, & will you please to give her my love too – and – I suppose she will be married soon. As we came from the Railway Station we drove up to Mr Chase's; he came out, he has altered oh so much, looking so old, he shook hands with all of us & said he would be very glad to see us. When I asked him how Miss Chase was, he asked me twice (I think he thought I said Mrs Chase); his son Charles came out too.

We are staying a little way out of the city, at an old Lady's house. Mr Menzies took lodgings for us before we came. The old lady's name is Mrs [...]; she is so kind to us, her husband is in Adelaide, he could not get any employment here so he had to go away, she has 3 girls. I did not finish about the harmonium, as we were going to the lady's house to tea, a young man touched Mr H's shoulder and gave him ½ a sovereign towards it.

We are going to the Manse on Wednesday afternoon to tea; & on Thursday we are going to the Cemetery to see poor Anna's and Carry's graves, & then to drink tea at Mr Chases's, & on Friday we are going away to Gippsland. After I had written the above, Mr H has been here & we are to pack our boxes tonight to go tomorrow or Wednesday morning. We are going tomorrow to see Anna's & Carry's graves & then we are going to tea at Mr Chase's.

Prehaps I am going to stay in Melbourne with Mr H because he won't be able to go with us, as he has to go to Ballarat to a meeting, & he cannot get out of it; if the girls go they will be in charge of the Captain (who is a great friend of his) & he will put them at the garden of the station so that will be better than going in the coach (we were to go in that first).

Again, I hope you are quite well. Please tell Miss […] that we thought of her on her birthday, & I hope she will have many more, & we will think of dear Martie too, I hope he will have many more. I wish I had a likeness of you both it would be so nice. All the girls are quite well & so are the babies, Nora is getting so fat, Emily says with her seasickness & she tells me to tell you that she calls it Monkey-Jack, she says with love, & she sends many kisses to you & many shake hands to Martie and the same to […]. This afternoon we went to see the Governor lay the foundation of the Masonic Arms Hall: the band played beautifully afterwards; they sang 'God Save the Queen'.

I hope you will be able to make out my letter dear Missie. The harmonium is bought, dear Missie, & going up tomorrow. Mr H says it's a beautifully toned one, it has 6 stops. Mrs […] will have such a lot to tell you, she says she thinks she will have to come up every day to tell you something new.

Now I must conclude, my dear Missie, but will you please give my love to my poor dear mother & Ada's too, & tell her we are all quite well and I hope her arm is getting better, I must not forget her. Give my love to dear […] & […]

and all the children, tell them I hope they are all trying to be good to you, I do not forget Harry with the children. Accept my grateful love too dear Missie and Martie, & God bless you both is the prayer of your loving girl.

Bessy

Bessy Flowers, Port Adelaide, to Anne Camfield, Annesfield, Albany.

24 July 1867

My dearest Missie,

We are not at home yet as you will see, but I thought you would like to know how we are, so I have written two or three lines. The steamer that we are in started from Melbourne on Tuesday evening at 9 o'clock in the evening.

We drank tea at Mr […]'s and went away from there at ½ past six, but I shall leave all of the particulars for next month. Mrs […] will return today. Oh, how I wish I was coming too, but never mind I won't have very long to stay. Mr […] is so kind to us all. I wish you were here with us, but I must tell you we have been a week coming so far as we have; we stayed two days in Queenscliff & the Captain took me on shore. I went up to the lighthouse, it was beautiful.

How are they all at home? Quite well, I hope? We were at Queenscliff on […]'s birthday. We thought of you all & wondered how you passed the day. Give my best love to dear Miss […] & Susan, dear mother (and Ada too), all the children, and tell Harry I hope he is a good boy.

Goodbye dearest more than Mother, for the steamer goes now.

My love to […]

Your loving Bessy

Bessy Flowers, Ramahyuck, Gippsland, to Anne Camfield, Annesfield, Albany.

August 1867

My own dearest Missie,

I received your kind and welcome letter yesterday. Mr Hagenauer went to Stratford (a small township eight miles away) to get the letters, but on to Sale, so he was three days away. I was looking out so anxiously all the time. I had written and closed a letter before I received yours, so have sent one by Miss […] to tell you that I have got yours.

I forgot to tell you a lot of things; first I have had my plaid frock washed; only the skirt, for I wore it all the way from Melbourne & I am trying to sew it on again. I have begun school in great earnest, we sing, say a Catechism. Joseph, Harry and Albert write in copybooks and Theo (Mr Hagenauer's little boy) Alfred, Bert, Rosanna, and Emily read and say the A.B.C; all in that class are as big as Harriet; they are as quick in learning & mind me quickly. All of them call me Miss Flower[s] because Mr Hagenauer says they will show me more respect. And I hope dearest Missie I shall be able to keep it up & I will try. I have sent you dear Mr Hagenauer's likeness & Captain's too, they were both very kind to us. Don't you think that Mr Hagenauer's like Mr […] of Adelaide.

Emily washes our clothes on Tuesdays. I am sure you must have been very glad to have the Bishop at home, I wish I were at home. Never mind, I must work hard & then it will be all the sweeter when I come home to help you & be your right hand always. All the girls send their best love to you and a kiss. Charles and James are such good fellows and Rhoda and Nora love them very much. All the girls have new boots for Sunday. Mr Hagenauer bought them in Stratford. Ada's ankles are so weak, so Mrs Hagenauer thought cloth boots would be better for her.

When the Steamer was coming up the river this morning we were thinking if you and Martie were in it what would you do. Emily said she would jump in & swim to it, I said I would give the girls a good thumping & Rhoda and Ada would get into the boat & row to meet you. Oh, if you did come Mr & Mrs Hagenauer they would be so delighted.

I have begun to knit this afternoon, we are going to have sewing class every afternoon.

I must not forget to tell you I am making gruel for Mrs Hagenauer every night, she says it is very nice. Emily is so wild here, will you dear Missie write and tell her she must not be so. I am sorry about the […] and hope he will soon be better. God bless you dear Missie and Martie. I hope you are quite well.

I am your affectionate & loving Bessy

P.S. Please give a kiss to dear little Louisa and Jela

Bessy Flowers, Ramahyuck, Gippsland, to Anne Camfield, Annesfield, Albany.
August 1867

My dearest Missie,

I am so glad you had a little taste of the wedding cake. Mr Hagenauer was determined you should have some, if it was ever so little.

The other day (Tuesday the 23rd) Mrs Hagenauer & Miss Login went to Mr Bolden's (a station at Lake Wellington) & stayed until Wednesday; they went in the boat & left it at Mr Bolden's. After they had gone sometime two gentlemen came from Sale to cross the river, of course the boat was not there, so they had to walk to Greenwood, about 4 miles, & get a boat to come down; the funny part was they had come in a buggy & had sent it off before they had known that there was not [a] boat; well they came up about 8 o'clock & had tea (I poured it out).

One of the gentlemen knew me directly, he had seen me at Mr Hagenauer's & had come when the young ladies were playing & singing, he said; and I remember directly, we had a game of chess & I beat him, I had to fight so hard though & was very glad you may be sure, dear Missie; his name is Mr […].

Mr Hagenauer is a very good player, he had never been beaten once in this Colony; in Geelong he had a game with a Mr […], & there was such a lot of people that came to see it & he was beat. I forgot to ask how is dear Miss …? I hope she is well, I mean not in pain.

Bessy Flowers, Ramahyuck, Gippsland, to Anne Camfield, Annesfield, Albany.

9 August 1867

I have been looking out for the mail so anxiously these two or three days, but I was thinking that as it came in so early last month it will come in late.

Bessy Flowers, Ramahyuck, Gippsland, to Anne Camfield, Albany.

16 August 1867

As I was teaching Theo and Cissie this afternoon Mrs Hagenauer came in & said they might go; they gazed at her in astonishment because we had been in only ½ an hour instead of an hour, then she threw me a letter & how I screamed with delight.

I did not know what had happened at home that I did not get a letter, for the steamer has been in for some time.

Oh what do you think dear Missie, I thought you were coming here, & I worked myself into such a state that I was continually looking out for you across the river & at the gate to see if I could see a carriage & I looked into the newspapers to see the names of the passengers. I hope you won't laugh too much dear Missie, for I hope you will soon come & dear Martie too.

Will you please tell him that I am very thankful to him for writing, & will think & do, as you would like me to do. Often & often my thoughts fly to dear Albany. I had a letter from dear […] I did not expect one at all. I was sorry you did not write but will look forward for a long one next time.

I thank you dear Missie for the magazine. I was so glad to get it too. I hope you like Mr M[…]'s likeness. Mr Hagenauer has put up two or more cottages, since we have been here, he works so hard & so does Mrs Hagenauer, but in a different way. She is going visiting at the end of the week & will be away for 3 or 4 weeks so I will be left in charge of Theo & Cissie as they do not go only Ede & the baby. I shall try & have everything in nice order when she goes & comes back again home.

Nobody spoke of my mother. I hope she is well. I was very pleased to get Harry's letter.

Nora & Rhoda are very happy. Last Sunday (I mean the 9th) Mrs Hagenauer, James, Charles & I, took the Sacrament in the evening at Church. On Friday we had a prayer meeting & they both of them prayed such beautiful prayers.

I am trying to be a comfort to Mrs Hagenauer. I dress the children & make their beds, then its breakfast time, we have prayers at the church & then its school time. In the afternoon I have Theo and Cissie.

I have not begun regular school but tomorrow I think we will. Mr Hagenauer says when Mr B […] comes it will be better. The children's names are Theophilius, but I have told you this before, I forgot.

Mr Hagenauer says he is going to teach me to speak German and French; I am so glad.

While Mr […] was here I used to play chess, & I beat him on Wednesday & Thursday he beat me every game; but I was so excited I did not know what I was doing: after he had done he asked me if my temper was all right because I told him I used to cry when I was beaten, & he laughed so.

In the morning he asked me how I was; but I am running on & forgetting that you have many more letters to write than me.

I hope this won't tire you, & I divided this sheet that I could not go on any further. Will you please give my love to Mrs […] and […], I think I will write to Mrs […] this time.

Mrs Hagenauer is such a dear lady; I sleep in the nursery with the little children. There has been a young lady staying with us, her name is Miss Login, a very nice lady. We dressed the Church with green leaves, we got four round hoops & put wreaths round them, & put them in the middle of each side of the Church & leaves in the windows. It looked very pretty.

I am going to bed now, dear Missie, it is quarter past nine, Mr & Mrs Hagenauer are going to bed, so I must not sit up any longer.

Goodbye (dearest Missie and Martie) for the present; I hope you are quite well.

All the girls are going to write.

I am your affectionate, grateful and loving Bessy.

1871

Bessy Flowers, Ramahyuck, Gippsland, to Captain Darby, Victoria

11 October 1871

My dear Captain Darby,

It is a long time since any of us wrote to you.

This morning the "Avon" steamer passed down & stopped for a short while to take Mr Bulmer away who has been paying us a visit for a fortnight.

Captain Clarke showed us your letter & asked why we had not written to you.

My brother Harry is so glad to write to you, whenever we speak of you his eyes fill with tears, he is getting on nicely in school, and is very tall.

My little daughters are quite well. Annie Magdalene will be two years old on Sunday the 22nd. Nellie Grace the baby is about 4 months old. Annie is a pet she tries to help me. I wish you could see her make a curtsey, she calls Harry "Anky" for Uncle, he is so fond of both of them. Willie Ada's boy is a clever little fellow, I think after the inspection has been here, he will go to school. Charlie Nora's boy is clever too. Rhoda and Nora are going to Lake Tyers for a change, poor Rhoda has never been well since her baby died. She suffers so much from headaches. Mrs Kramer has a dear little girl her name is "Clara".

APPENDIX C: LETTERS (1867–1894)

There is to be another schoolroom. I am so glad as it will leave the present one more free for dining and cooking.

When do you think you shall come to see us?

I forgot to tell you that Mr & Mrs A'Beckett were here they slept one night, we liked them so much, they were so amused to see little Annie trying to play on the harmonium as she was on my lap during prayer. Mrs A'Beckett gave her a little present to keep…her thimble needles pins and cotton…

We have a lot of arrowroot this time growing in [?] when Donald made some we had about 25 pounds, we will have more.

I must conclude now, all the girls send their love to you. Donald joins to with me in kindest regards from

Your grateful

Bessy Cameron

P.S. Please when you write will you kindly let me know the price of a hand sewing machine, but don't buy one til I send the money.

BC.

1872

Bessy Flowers, Ramahyuck, Gippsland, to Captain Darby, Victoria.

22 April 1872

My dear Captain Darby,

I have sent you my brother's likeness with Joseph & Albert, they were taken together & I know that you would be happy to get one. I heard that you were coming up the lakes in the Murray. I hope it is true we shall be very happy indeed to see you.

I was hoping to get a letter from you but it has never come. I hope you & Mrs Darby are well.

Emily had her likeness taken with her husband and two children. Rhoda is always ailing & never free from pain. I am so thankful that I have good health. Ada is well & Nora is well too. Harry has good health, he is getting to be a good cricketer & he likes it very much. It is getting very cold now in the mornings & evenings.

It will be soon 5 years since we came to Gippsland, it seems much longer to me, it is our home now for good, but I never thought it was to be my home. Donald is making our new bedroom, at least making it longer. I must stop now as they are going to Stratford & I do not wish to keep this letter any longer.

All send their love to & accept Donald & mine.

Our best respects to Mrs Darby,

I am yours truly

Bessy Cameron

1873

Bessy Flowers, Ramahyuck, Gippsland, to Captain Darby, Victoria

16 April 1873

My dear Captain Darby,

I am not sure if I had answered your kind letter, which I got about six months ago. If I have not [?] I beg your pardon over & over again. My naughty brother began a letter in Feb but has not finished yet, he will write this week, I believe. How is dear Mrs Darby? I hope she has got over the whooping cough & also your nieces and nephew, could you send some of their likeness to us to see. We should like to see some of your relations as you have been so kind to us. On Easter Monday all the children from Stratford with some grown who came, we had a very happy day. You know I suppose, Mr Chase of Melbourne his son is here staying for a few months, he cut out the letters for "Christ is risen", we sewed ivy leaves on the wall together & he pinned it over the harmonium, also "Hallelujah" over the side door & on the wall over the reading door was a large wreath of evergreen leaves & some daleahs [dahlias], it was very pretty. Over the door was a diamond shape with flowers on it. On the reading desk was a white cloth and the text "Behold the lamb of God" & rose leaves. Mrs Kramer did that one. Rhoda and Jimmy are living in the boarding house with the children. Did you know Captain I lost one of my children, it was the youngest Nellie Grace so have only the one Annie Magdalene, who goes to school. She is a spoilt little rouge I am afraid. I am very happy when I think of dear wee Nellie for I know she is safe with the Lord Jesus. Also dear Theo Hagenauer I suppose you heard of his death in Germany, poor boy he was only ill three days and must have suffered fearful agony …

1874

Rev. Hagenauer, Ramahyuck, to Robert Brough Smyth, Secretary, BPA.

4 May 1874

Sir,

We the aborigines residing at this station have heard and read in the Argus and the Gippsland Times, that our kind friend and protector, the Revd. F.A. Hagenauer has been accused of unkindness and cruelty to the blind man Bobby, & also that he prevented us from giving food and shelter to him, which we beg to assure you, is an intolerable lie.

We cannot suffer such accusation to pass, without stating to the Board of Protection, that we feel sorry such an unfounded complaint should have gone abroad, especially by such a man who did already everything to injure us, and tried to burn our fences and grass in the paddocks.

I have the honour to be Sir

Your most humble servant

B. Cameron

in the name of the aborigines of Ramahyuck

1879

Rev. Hagenauer, Ramahyuck, to Captain Page, Secretary, BPA.

20 August 1879

…I beg also to mention to you that the black woman Bessy Cameron has left Ramahyuck yesterday, as she does not want to live with her husband anymore. Before she left, she burnt his best clothes and abstracted his bankbook, no doubt with the intention to get his money from the savings bank. She said she was going to you to ask if you would forward her to Condah [Lake Condah Mission]. I do not know what to say, because she was quite friendly to us, yet I fear she will make some story. Besides I am afraid she [is] either losing part of reason and common sense or is awful wicked, as she had made known she would stab her husband. Please let me know when she comes.

Rev. Hagenauer, Ramahyuck, to Captain Page, Secretary, BPA.

24 August 1879

Sir

I have the honour to acknowledge the receipt of Donald Cameron's bank book and to report that Mrs Cameron has returned, but states that she is going to live at Condah [Lake Condah Mission] and likewise that she will take the two girls with her as well as the boy. Her husband is sending enclosed a petition to you that the girls may be left here in the boarding house for the season as he says Mrs Cameron is not a good housekeeper, which is quite correct…

Mrs Cameron did agree to neither and will go to Condah, to which proposal I can say nothing, she must please herself, but as regards the two girls, I think like Cameron, they are here as well cared for as elsewhere and will not improve under Mrs Cameron's direction, but will certainly be a conflict to the deserted husband.

Donald Cameron, Ramahyuck, to Captain Page Secretary, BPA.

27 August 1879

Dear Sir

My wife just returned from Melbourne, & tells me that you had given her a place at Lake Condah; well perhaps I can do nothing if she goes she may, but I humbly beg you and the Board not to remove my children from Ramahyuck, I have put them in the boarding house, & they are happy & cheerful, & well cared for, if they should be taken away, it will be for misery, for my wife is very careless of house-keeping, I must now conclude Dear Sir.

   I remain yours truly
       Donald Cameron

Rev. Hagenauer, Ramahyuck, to Captain Page Secretary, BPA.

30 August 1879

I received your letter in reference to Mrs Cameron and thank you for the steps you took in the matter. From all I can observe I think she wishes to go to Condah [Lake Condah Mission] which may perhaps be the best for her at present as it will be easy to come back at any time. If you send her a pass from Sale to Melbourne, I think she would be glad. As for myself, I told her from the first she may please herself and will not make any difficulties. I only hope she speaks the truth in regards to her story.

1883

Rev. Hagenauer, Ramahyuck, to Bessy Cameron, Briagolong.

27 February 1883

My Dear Mrs Cameron,

After I had spoken to you and Donald last week I got your letter in reference to your wishes to go to Lake Tyers and live with Emily Brindle [Peters]. Since then you wrote to Mrs Hagenauer in the same manner expressing your desire to live with Emily Brindle and thus separating from your husband.

We have been so busy with picking hops, otherwise I should have written to you sooner, but you know how much I have to do at this time of season. In regard to your wishes to go and live at Lake Tyers with Emily, both Mrs Hagenauer and myself are of the same mind that we cannot recommend that course, for we could never be a party of recommending that you should separate from your husband. Of course for the sake of the children you ought to go to one station, as otherwise the children would have to suffer for it. I just heard that the Brindles are coming to live at Ramahyuck for some months, to arrive sometime in April, so that you're going for that reason to Lake Tyers, would be in vain, I wish to say to you at the same time, that I shall make no opposition to whatever place you all like to go, and it will be best to write to Capt Page and arrange matters for you & you should have a home soon. I will be glad if you write to me again.

Kindest remembrance to Donald and the children.

    Yours truly F.A. Hagenauer.

Bessy Cameron, Briagolong, to Captain Page, Secretary, BPA.

6 March 1883

Dear Sir

I send you Mr Hagenauers letter, which I received on Saturday evening, so I hope you will let us all live at Lake Tyers station now. I dread the Wimmera climate, it is enough punishment to Donald that he has to live on a mission station. I pray that you will have mercy on me and not send us out of the district; the children and I are picking hops at Mr Blundy's Briagolong; it will take a fortnight more before we will finish, then I hope we will be ready.

I remain Dear Sir

your obedient Servant

Bessy Cameron

Captain Page, Secretary, BPA, to Bessy Cameron, Briagolong.

12 March 1883

Dear Mrs Cameron

I have received your letter of the 6th instance & should have answered it before but wished to hear further on the subject from Mr Hagenauer before replying – You ask to be allowed to go to Lake Tyers as you dread the Wimmera climate. In the summertime it certainly is not an agreeable climate but during the winter it is preferable to that of Gippsland. I do not imagine that there will be any necessity for you to be at Lake Hindmarsh more than a few months…It is only for your good, as you know that Mr Hagenauer & myself recommend for a time the Wimmera to Lake Tyers so I hope you will assist us to get Donald off as soon as possible. Do not pass through town without calling at the office – I will send passes as soon as you are ready.

Bessy Cameron, Briagolong, to Captain Page, Secretary, BPA.

14 March 1883

Dear Sir

I received your kind letter last night & I thank you for your patience to me. It will take another week to finish the hops but I will leave off on Saturday as I have to make some clothes for the children & myself, we will be ready I hope the first week in April, but I will send you a letter when we are ready. Again, I thank you for your kindness.

I remain Dear Sir your obedient Servant

  Bessy Cameron

Bessy Cameron, Briagolong to Captain Page, Secretary, BPA.

9 April 1883

Dear Sir

I was looking out very anxiously for a letter last week, and when Donald came home on Saturday evening, I knew the reason why you had not written as Mr MacFaintosh [?] had given Donald your letter & also mine to read. Dear Sir we will still go as it was first arranged so if you will grant my request which I asked in my letter last week, and also send the passes this week, we will start on Monday next.

Dear Sir I remain your obedient Servant

  Bessy Cameron

Bessy Cameron, Ebenezer, to Captain Page, Secretary, BPA.

29 August 1883

Dear Sir

This is the last of the winter months, and I hope you will send us the pass, according to your promise.

 Your obedient Servant

  Bessy Cameron

Bessy Cameron, Ebenezer, to Captain Page, Secretary, BPA.

24 September 1883

Sir

I am very sorry you did not answer my letter, which I wrote last month.

Please sir let me know if you will send a pass or not. If you are willing to send one, will you send one at the end of next month? You promised that we should only be here at Ebenezer for the winter months, or else I would never have come. Donald wishes to get a home of our own; we don't want to be dependent on Government supplys. We both promise too that we never set our feet at Ramahyuck.

Your obedient servant

    Bessy Cameron

Rev. Hagenauer, Ramahyuck, memorandum to BPA.

1 October 1883

That the Camerons should live in the Wimmera District is no hardship, for Cameron has only returned to his home and his relatives, and Mrs Cameron is neither a Gippsland native. Mrs Cameron states in her note to Captain Page that they will not take Government supply, if they are allowed to go to Gippsland. This was not the case, when away from here, as I supplied them with a great deal besides which they sold about £30 worth of furnitures and other things during the short time they were away. At Ebenezer the children can go to school, and Cameron is at home. No promise of theirs has ever been kept and if they return to Gippsland it would become a public scandal. Captain Page would do well to refer the question with my former letters to the consideration of the Board, or, if desirable I shall be quite willing to address a memorial to the Honourable Chief Secretary, not to allow their return here to Gippsland.

Bessy Cameron, Ebenezer, to Captain Page, Secretary, BPA.

10 October 1883

Sir,

I thank you very much for your kind letter, & I have thought much over it, &

I have come to the conclusion, that I can never be happy on a mission station. Donald has told me to ask you if you would be so kind as to let us stay here till Xmas, Mr Kramer has given him a little work to do for the 2 months coming, only we were afraid you might not be willing to send a pass then. Hoping dear Sir that you will kindly send us word again

I remain Dear Sir your obedient Servant

        Bessy Cameron

Rev. Hagenauer, Ramahyuck, to Captain Page Secretary, BPA.

13 October 1883

My Dear Captain Page

I was very glad to hear from you, that Mrs Cameron will stay at Lake Hindmarsh [Ebenezer] and it would be better in every way if she remains there. I heard that Bessy Cameron had written to people in Gippsland to get employment for Donald, but she was not successful, which may be the reason of their not coming just now. I have no doubt that she will do her best to keep away from the control of the stations, but they cannot maintain themselves alone far less their children. You should appoint the children to some station where they should go to school, for they have not well attended whilst at Stratford and had to be brought before the Police Court. Whilst personally I feel very sorry for them all, I can only say that they should not be allowed to walk straight away into temptation. If the Board, however, sends them here, of course, I shall make the best of the difficulty, feeling sure at the same time that it will give endless trouble. Do your best to persuade them to remain where they are.

Bessy Cameron, Ebenezer, to Captain Page, Secretary, BPA.

19 December 1883

Dear Sir

Will you be so kind as to send our pass for home, my little girl cannot stand the climate, the few months we have been here, she has had two attacks of fits, the last one she had was a fortnight ago, & was very severe, so I hope you will send the pass by the end of this week.

Hoping you are quite well, Dear Sir

I remain your obedient Servant

    Bessy Cameron

Bessy Cameron, Ebenezer, to Captain Page, Secretary, BPA.

31 December 1883

Dear Sir

I received you letter on the 29th inst. You wish to know how many there are of us. There are four children & Donald & myself. Please send it by Friday's mail; then we will get it on Saturday & please give us time to get our luggage with us in Melbourne, as we had some trouble when we got there, had to wait a month before we got our bedding & there were no spare blankets.

Thanking you so much for your kindness to me.

  I remain Dear Sir

    Your obedient Servant

      Bessy Cameron

1884

John Bulmer, Lake Tyers, to Captain Page Secretary, BPA.

11 January 1884

Sir

I have the honor to acknowledge the receipt of your telegram of yesterday re

Donald and Bessie Cameron…Mr Hagenauer has explained his objections to their living here. I dare say you are aware that he is an official visitor to the Station so of course some notice should be taken to his objection, besides which we have worked amicably together for over 20 years and it would hardly do to sow seeds of discord, which I fear this would do.

Rev. Bulmer, Lake Tyers, to Captain Page Secretary, BPA.

16 January 1884

Sir

I have the honour to inform you that Bessie Cameron and her family arrived here on Monday the 14th…conveyed from Cunninghame by Mr Laughton's buggy. She was on Tuesday delivered of a stillborn child. As the journey is rather rough between Cunninghame & Lake Tyers, and she being much nearer her confinement that she thought, perhaps this was the cause of her mishap, however she is doing very well. Donald did not arrive with her as he was detained by Mr Howitt in Sale. He is to be here on Saturday.

Rev. Hagenauer, Ramahyuck, to Captain Page Secretary, BPA.

20 January 1884

…Mr Kramer wrote to me that Donald and children could have gladly remained at Ebenezer, but that Bessy was continually talking to get them to go to Lake Tyers. The reason no doubt, of her going there is well known to you and it is a great pity that through her the happiness and peace of another family (the Thorpe's) should be destroyed. I am afraid that the trouble is now only beginning. They should never have been allowed to go back to Gippsland.

Rev. Bulmer, Lake Tyers, to Captain Page Secretary, BPA.

22 January 1884

APPENDIX C: LETTERS (1867–1894)

My Dear Captain Page

Please do not trouble yourself about the Camerons; the difficulty will soon be settled, as I believe Donald has got a job with Mr Howitt and will take his wife & family with him. I think with you it is a pity to punish the wife and the little ones for the husband's misdeeds. I am very glad I got Bessy over to Lake Tyers at once as there could have been some scandal had the poor woman been confined at the Entrance.

Donald came here but only remained a day or two; he went away yesterday to arrange with Mr Howitt as to residence for his family. He says he never intended to live on a Mission Station & for this I highly recommend him.

Bessy Cameron, Lake Tyers, to Captain Page, Secretary, BPA.

25 January 1884

Dear Sir

We did not meet Mr Hagenauer in Sale, & we did not know what to do, so Donald went to Mrs Howitt the police magistrate's wife, & she gave us an order to go to a boarding house where we stayed till Saturday dinner time, then she gave us another order for the steamer which brought us down to the entrance that same evening, (Donald & the old man stayed in Sale at Mr Howitts).

Sunday morning the two girls & Bob walked out to Lake Tyers. Mr Bulmer got a trap for the 2 little ones & myself for Monday. I got out at dinner that day; the following day Tuesday I was laid up & my baby was born dead. I have just got up today. Donald was down this day week, & he told me that he has work from Mr Howitt, who has a hop garden in Bairnsdale. Donald will get 30/shillings a week & a house rent free, I am very thankful for that.

I believe Mr Hagenauer was in Stratford waiting to give us a welcome to Ramahyuck, but both Donald & I never hope to go there again. When we wished to come back to Gippsland, it was not to go back to Ramahyuck.

Please Sir I want to ask you if you could let us have 2 iron bed steads & a sofa & 4 chairs, also a camp oven & boiler, would you please let Mr Howitt get it for us, we need them so much, we are going to stay here until the hop picking commences.

Robert Harrison likes this place very much, he goes out to work every day.

Hopeing you are quite well

    Dear Sir

        Your Obedient Servant

        Bessy Cameron

Bessy Cameron, Lake Tyers, to Captain Page, Secretary, BPA.

15 May 1884

Dear Sir

I hope you will be so kind as to listen to my petition & allow us to live on the station. I have tried living on our own earnings & it won't do. Donald has not been earning regular wages, & it takes all he earns to pay for our food, he said when we had paid what we owed he would go to Ramahyuck, but I won't go there, perhaps you might say why did we not stay at Ebenezer, but dear sir, I would rather have seen my little child in her coffin than in another fit, & if you were a father you would feel the same, I hope you will allow us to stay on this station it comes hard on the children and myself wandering about without a home, & I feel it more as I had a good home when I was young & then to be tossed about in old age. Please listen to my prayer for it is a prayer for a home.

Hoping you are quite well

    Dear Sir, I remain

        Your obedient servant

        Bessy Cameron

APPENDIX C: LETTERS (1867–1894)

Rev. Bulmer, Lake Tyers, to Captain Page Secretary, BPA.

17 May 1884

Sir

Mrs Cameron & her children have just come to the station; she says that her husband Donald Cameron cannot support her, as his earnings are not very much. Before she came, I wrote to her telling her that she would not be allowed to live here while her husband was in Bairnsdale, however she has come and now I think it best to inform the Board of the circumstance. She tells me that she wishes to live here until Donald can save enough to purchase a bag of flour as they cannot make his earnings meet their wants while they have to purchase bread ready-made, but I fear Donald has acquired habits of extravagance which may make the purchase a remote matter.

Bessy Cameron, Bairnsdale, to Captain Page, Secretary, BPA.

1 July 1884

Dear Sir

Having heard the Board is going to allow rations to be given to those people who are away from the stations, I am writing these few lines hopeing we may be allowed rations too, if it is to be given to us can we get it at Mr Bulmer's as the steamers are running up and down the lakes 3 times a week.

    I remain Dear Sir
        Your obedient Servant
            Bessy Cameron

Bessy Cameron, Bairnsdale, to Captain Page, Secretary, BPA.

4 August 1884

Dear Sir

I received your letter & would have written before only my hands were sore, I am very sorry to see that we cannot get any rations, it would have been such a help to us, as we are such a large family, you ask how we are getting on, well pretty well considering, I go out for a day's work & get 5/ a day but it is slack time as there are no visitors now, but it will be better in the summer I hope. I saw Mr Hagenauer at Lake Tyers.

Dear Sir, if, I only say if we asked for a pass to Dimboola could we get it; please let me know, I don't care to go but Donald was talking of it. Please Sir, Mr Bulmer lent me 10/ could you pay him please.

Mrs Brindle is coming to live in Bairnsdale. There will be work for Jimmy now in the hop garden; her little girl can go to school with my girls, my children have not yet been to school as they have had the hitch dreadful; we are just getting rid of it. If it is not asking too much, please sir will you send me a few lines.

    I remain Sir

        Your obedient Servant

            Bessy Cameron

Bessy Cameron, Bairnsdale, to Captain Page, Secretary, BPA.

14 October 1884

Dear Sir

Donald & I have been talking matters over, & find it so difficult to make ends meet, he was laid up with a bad hand all last week & I have been day after day seeking for work & can find nothing to do, & now we have made up our minds to live on a mission station & find Lake Tyers the best, if you will kindly give your consent. You could give the contract to put up a cottage for us to live in to Donald. Donald wants to go out to work on some station. I am of some use to Mrs Bulmer & else where I am not.

Accept my gratefulness for past favours. We would like to go after the training of the hops are over.

    Hoping to hear a favourable answer

        I remain Dear Sir Your Obedient Servant

            Bessy Cameron

Robert Harrison, the young man who came with us from Ebenezer was married at Lake Tyers by Mr Hagenauer last month.

Rev. Bulmer, Lake Tyers, to Captain Page Secretary, BPA.

22 October 1884

Sir

Before anything is decided about the Camerons it would be well to write to Donald himself as unless I very much mistake his wife's idea is to come to Lake Tyers and leave him to work outside. This of course would never do. Personally, I have no objections to their living here. Though possibly Mr Hagenauer would rather they lived at Ramahyuck. In case it is decided that they come here, accommodation would have to be provided for them as all the houses are occupied. There is an ill feeling that I am aware of between the Camerons & Thorpes.

1891

Rev. Hagenauer, Secretary, BPA, to Bessy Cameron, Ramahyuck.

6 May 1891

My dear Mrs Cameron

I duly received your letter of the 4th. instant, asking me to allow your daughter Maggie to come and live at Ramahyuck for a few months etc. I am really very sorry that it is not at all in [my] power to comply with your wish, which I would gladly do if I could. The same applications come constantly from other stations and have to be refused, as the Law is quite stringent on this point. I am sorry for Maggie also, but of course, as she has married, she has to be with her husband, and he has to support her under all circumstances. I think it was a pity that you did not let them go to Maneroo when he wanted to go there. Again, I assure you that I would gladly say yes to your wishes, but it cannot be done. I think you should tell Maggie to go with her husband to Orbost, so that she may assist him in his work.

With best wishes

    Yours faithfully

        F.A. Hagenauer

1892

Rev. Hagenauer, Secretary, BPA, to Bessy Cameron, Ramahyuck.

9 August 1892

My dear Mrs Cameron

When I stated to Donald that I had got a railway pass for yourselves and Haines, he replied that under no circumstances would he ever consent to let Haines go on board ship. I asked him again if he would consent, but he clearly declared that he would never consent. I had to therefore…go to Melbourne alone and now let you know this result [?]. If I was in your place, I would return home and live with my husband.

With very kind regards

    Faithfully yours F.A Hagenauer

BPA Minutes, 1892.

7 September 1892

Bessie Cameron at Bairnsdale applied for 3 months ration to be granted to her at her present residence. As this application would open a new depot & would soon be followed by other Blacks, the request could not be granted.

APPENDIX C: LETTERS (1867–1894)

1893

Rev. Hagenauer, Secretary, BPA, to Bessy Cameron, Bairnsdale.

26 April 1893

My dear Bessie

You will have been surprised and perhaps pleased you saw Donald bringing Haynes [Haines] to you, but it was absolutely needed for him to leave Ramahyuck. Now in order that you may have time to find employment for him I have arranged that he shall get rations to the 31st June, so that he will not be a burden to you, and I only hope that he will do well.

When I come to Bairnsdale, I will call on you. Hoping that you all are doing well, I remain Yours Faithfully, F.A. Hagenauer

Rev. Hagenauer, Secretary, BPA, to Bessy Cameron.

29 June 1893

My dear Mrs Cameron

Donald wished me to send you 15/. by post, which I herewith do. As you have not got a place for Haynes [Haines] yet, I brought the matter before the Board and am happy to be able to enclose you another Order for 4 weeks longer but after that it will cease altogether. Please bring the order at once to Mr Patterson for he has to make up the amount on the 30th or on [the] day you get the order.

   Best wishes
         yours faithfully
                F.A. Hagenauer

Rev. Hagenauer, Secretary, BPA, to Bessy Cameron, Bairnsdale.

12 July 1893

My dear Mrs Cameron,

I duly received your letter of the 10th instant and forward pass for you and Haynes [Haines].

I will leave the orders here for Haynes clothes, so that when you come to Melbourne Mr Ditchburn will get the outfit. I think if you could come on Friday morning it would be best, as I shall be back from Warrnambool by that time and go to get the things myself.

There will also be here at the office your return pass to Gippsland

  Kindest wishes to you & Haynes

    F.A Hagenauer

Rev. Hagenauer, Secretary, BPA, to Bessy Cameron, Bairnsdale.

8 August 1893

My dear Mrs Cameron,

I was glad to observe from the papers that the steamer had safely passed Thursday Island – all well – so that Haynes [Haines] may be all right.

The object of my writing is by direction of the Board on the following subjects.

Mr Dreversmann of Bairnsdale has sent an account for rent due to him, which the Board cannot recognise, but states, that you must pay it yourselves or live at one of the stations.

J. Brodribb Esqr. Secretary of Education has written to me in regard to 10/- which you borrowed from him with the promise that you would send weapons for the amount. The weapons should be sent at once, as otherwise you will certainly come into difficulties.

Dr Duncun of Bairnsdale has also written and forwarded an account for £3.3.0 for attending your daughter during confinement. The Board could not pay that account and you will have to look to the white father of the child to pay it at once.

I feel exceedingly sorry that you have yourself into such difficulties and I am afraid that if these complaints come up next time before the Board matters will be more serious than you expect.

You know how much interest I take at all times in you and would like to see you as an old friend happy but when matters come so much wrong it is really time that you should consider your own and your children's happiness, which you really have not done hitherto. I hope to hear from you or see you soon.

With kindest regards

Yours F.A Hagenauer

1894

Rev. Hagenauer, Secretary, BPA, to Bessy Cameron, Bairnsdale.

30 July 1894

My dear Mrs Cameron

I wish to send you a few lines in account of the proposed marriage between your daughter Louise and Willy Login. They have made up their minds to get soon married and, of course lawfully they can do so at any time. Now considering the whole matter, I think it would be very nice if you would not only give your written consent, but that you should, if it is possible, come to the Ramahyuck marriage on the day…I do not wish to marry them myself against your will, but I understand that in that case they will go to Sale and get married there. This would cost a great deal of money, which they could use better in their new household, and if you would give your consent and come yourself it would make matters very pleasant and I am sure will be the best for Louise, as otherwise her child could not be on any [?] station. Donald desires ere long to get some building employment elsewhere, but says that he will not do so before Louise is married – I have carried out my promise and sent her material for a nice and useful wedding dress and only expect your letter to Ramahyuck in reply to this.

I hope your Maggies trouble will be [over?] by this, so that you may be able to return home. I suppose Louise will have written to you herself on the subject.

    With kindest wishes

        yours faithfully

            F.A Hagenauer

Rev. Hagenauer, Secretary, BPA, to Bessy Cameron, Bairnsdale.

8 August 1894

Dear Mrs Cameron

Your letter of the 2nd instant has duly come to my hands, but I fairly must say that it was a very bitter reply to my kind note to you. Well, of course, the [?] of your daughter was carried out for they got married at Sale, but not by me. This money could have been saved if you had not been so selfish in the matter. I hope the young married will live happily and rightly together at all times.

I understand that your old household is now broken up for Donald will have left Ramahyuck with young Macredie to work elsewhere. Of course I feel sorry for so doing, but I am sure I felt long ago it would come to that.

I have now [?] you to inform [?] your daughter Mrs Bryant to be prepared to receive her little boy Roy to her own home or to send her written consent to have him transferred to the Industrial Schools at an early date, because his certificate to live at Ramahyuck cannot be renewed in the future.

I am really glad to observe that your daughter has safely come through her trouble and wish her much blessing for the little one – I hope I hear here at the Office about Maggie's decision about Roy by return of post, for he now must leave Ramahyuck.

Your son Haines has returned to Melbourne and is discharged; as he has already cost so much to the Board he cannot get any more and must earn his living. I have asked him to go by steamer or any boat to join you at Bairnsdale, and I hope you will find work for him or go perhaps with Mr [?] to dig for gold.

With best wishes

Yours Faithfully

F.A Hagenauer

Rev. Hagenauer, Secretary, BPA, to Maggie Bryant, Bairnsdale.

31 January 1894

My dear friend,

The letter you sent to Mrs Hagenauer asking permission to live for sometime at Ramahyuck has been handed to me, and this morning I referred it to the Board and after consideration of the letter, I am sorry to inform you that the petition cannot be granted. It is not lawful to do so, and it would also be quite unfair to the others not to be allowed to go to the stations. There is already one of your children there under a certificate but no more can come. You are young and must do your best to earn your living in case your husband does not or will not care for you. I wish only in conclusion to say, that you must not try and go to Ramahyuck as you really would come into great trouble.

With kindest wishes

Yours faithfully

F. A. Hagenauer

Secretary

1895

On 14 January 1895 Bessy passed away in Bairnsdale, Victoria.

Notes

1. The spelling of Bessy's first name and surname changes throughout the historical record. Refer to the explanation made in the notes on Bessy's name at the beginning of the book.
2. Penelope Van Toorn, *Writing Never Arrives Naked: Early Aboriginal Cultures of Writing In Australia*, Aboriginal Studies Press, Canberra, 2006, p. 194.
3. Aboriginal writing unsettles the stronghold of colonial society perspectives and principles that are often considered to be dominant histories. In Van Toorn's *Writing Never Arrives Naked*, the ways in which Aboriginal people used reading and writing to negotiate a changing world is examined and justly positioned in opposition to oppressor perspectives about country and kin.
4. Rosendo Salvado, *The Salvado Memoirs: Historical Memoirs of Australia and Particularly of the Benedictine Mission of New Norcia and of the Habits and Customs of the Australian Natives*, trans. and ed. by Edward James Stormon, University of Western Australia Press, Perth, 1977, p. 121.
5. Flowers to Anne Camfield, 12 June 1867. Reproduced in Neville Green, *Aborigines of the Albany Region 1821–1898: The Bicentennial Dictionary of Western Australian Volume VI*, University of Western Australia Press, Perth, 1989, pp. 121–126.
6. The character Bobby, Wabalanginy, at sea in Kim Scott's *That Deadman Dance*, Picador, Sydney, 2010, p. 32.
7. Kim Scott's Miles Franklin Literary Award Oration was held on 1 May 2012 at Curtin University in Perth.
8. Green, *Aborigines of the Albany Region 1821–1898*, pp. 121–126.
9. Flowers to Captain Page, Board for the Protection of Aborigines (BPA), 15 May 1884. Reproduced in Green, *Aborigines of the Albany Region 1821–1898*, pp. 121–126.
10. Henry Lawson, 'The golden nineties', in D.G. Sellick (eds.), *First Impressions of Albany 1791–1871: Travellers' Tales*, Western Australian Museum, Perth, 1997, p. 191. (Article originally published in *Australian Star*, Sydney, 1899).

Preface

11. Nora (Eleanor) was born in c.1846 in Western Australia. She married Charles Foster on 10 July 1867 at the Ramahyuck Aboriginal Mission in Victoria. Nora had a child from a previous relationship travelling with her from Annesfield to Ramahyuck who was also named Charles (c.1866–1929). Other children included: Ellen (c.1867–1920), Florence (c.1869–1924), Edward (c.1872–1944), Annie (c.1873–1885) and David (c.1881–1881). In a letter from Rev. Hagenauer to Captain Page he states that, 'Nora(h) Foster, aged 34 years, full black, died of consumption at Ramahyuck, 29 November 1880' – National Archives of Australia (NAA), B313, Box 10, Item 175. In an earlier letter dated 20 July 1878, Rev. Hagenauer commented that: 'the other is Charley Foster, who is of no account but is led astray by his wife Nora(h) one of the worst women here. These few ought to make feel that there is such a thing as law and order.' NAA, B313, Box 10, Item 172, p. 17A.

NOTES

12. Ada Flowers married James (Jimmy) Henry Clark on 7 September 1868 at the Ramahyuck Aboriginal Mission, Lake Wellington, with permission given by Anne Camfield, who was Ada's legal guardian. Ada and Henry had one son, William. He was born in October 1870 and died at 19 years of age on 23 December 1889. He was buried at the Ramahyuck Cemetery. In 1886 William travelled to England to assist at the Victorian Court of the Indian and Colonial Exhibition: 'It may be of interest to state here that two full black youths, William Clark and Willie King, had been selected by the Commissioners of the India and Colonial Exhibition as attendants in the Victorian Court of that exhibition in London, and that they gave, as far is known, general satisfaction. Their return to the colony is very near, and we hope to see them safely again in our midst in a short time', BPA, 22nd Report, 1886, pp. 5–6.

13. In 1853 Rev. John Ramsden Wollaston compiled a list of students attending the Annesfield Native Institution. The admission year for Rhoda Tanaton is listed as 1852 at eight years of age. Wollaston uses the surname Tanaton rather than Toby, as it sometimes appeared in historical missionary correspondence. Rhoda Tanaton married James Fitchet(t) on 10 July 1867 at the Ramahyuck Aboriginal Mission in Victoria. She was about 15 years old. On the marriage certificate Rhoda's parents are father Toby and mother Mary. Rhoda and James had one child, Fred Fitchet(t), born on 10 August 1874. He died in 1879 and was buried at the Ramahyuck Cemetery. Rhoda died on 16 November 1878 and was also buried at the Ramahyuck Cemetery. In a letter to Capt. Page on 26 November 1878 Rev. Hagenauer wrote: 'Rhoda Fitchett aged 28 died Nov 16, 1878 of consumption. Tommy Clark aged 37 died Nov 18, 1878 of consumption. Both had long and painful illnesses. The doctor had attended to them but could give no hope of recovery', NAA, B313, Box 10, Item 172.

14. Emily Peters from the Annesfield Native Institution married John Ellis on 28 January 1868 at the Ramahyuck Aboriginal Mission. She was about 15 years old. At age 24 she married James Brindle on 21 August 1879 at the Ramahyuck Aboriginal Mission. Witnesses to the marriage were Bessy Cameron and Harry Flower(s). Emily was born in c.1854 and died on 3 July 1905 at the Gippsland Hospital in Sale. She was about 50 years old and was buried at the Sale Cemetery on 4 July 1905. Her children were Mary (c.1878–1892), James Alexander (5 November 1880 – 19 February 1893), John (21 March 1883 – unknown), Henry (October 1888 – 5 April 1892). Mary died at 13 years of age in Bairnsdale and was buried at the Bairnsdale Cemetery on 15 April 1892. Henry was buried on 6 April 1892 and James Alexander on 21 February 1893 at the Bairnsdale Cemetery.

15. The land title of the Lake Tyers Aboriginal Trust was officially handed over to local resident Charlie Carter on 24 July 1972. Charlie represented Koori families connected to this place that was once the Lake Tyers Aboriginal Mission.

16. The Central Board for the Protection of Aborigines was established in 1859 and was succeeded by the Board for the Protection of

Aborigines (1869–1957) and the Aborigines Welfare Board (1957–1967). The *Aborigines Protection Act 1869* granted statutory powers for authorities to govern the lives of Aboriginal peoples in the state of Victoria. The Act prescribed where people lived and set out restrictions on care, custody and education of children. Other provisions of the Act included the authority to inspect homes on a regular basis, the need for people to seek written permission to leave the mission, station or reserve, the payment of low or no wages, and the possible expulsion from the mission for behaviour considered to be misconduct or the breach of lengthy and prohibitive mission rules.

17. The Koorie Family History Service (KFHS) began in October 2001 as a result of the Human Rights and Equal Opportunity Commission's 1997 *Bringing Them Home* report. The commission reported on the separation of Aboriginal and Torres Strait Islander children from their families. Recommendation 27 of this report (in total there were 54 recommendations) was that each state and territory government, in consultation with relevant Indigenous services and its Records Taskforce, establish an Indigenous Family Information Service to operate as a 'first stop shop' for people seeking information about and referral to records held by the government and by churches. One year later, in 2002, the Stolen Generations Taskforce was also set up in response to the *Bringing Them Home* report. The Stolen Generations Taskforce with Aboriginal representation only (on the taskforce) was established to advise the Victorian Government on how to address the social, cultural and health-related issues faced by members of the Stolen Generations.

18. The Koorie Heritage Trust Inc. was created in 1985 from partnerships between both Koori and non-Koori political and legal activists and supporters of Koori affairs. Gunditjmara Elder Jim Berg, the late Ron Castan AM QC and Ron Merkel QC established The Trust after a landmark legal case against the University of Melbourne for the return of Aboriginal skeletal remains, held within the Anatomy Department's Murray Black Collection. George Murray Black collected Aboriginal skeletal remains of approximately 1800 individuals. The collection was divided between the Australian Institute of Anatomy in Canberra and the Anatomy Department of the University of Melbourne. At this time, Jim Berg was the Victorian Aboriginal Legal Service Chief Executive Officer and an Inspector under the 1972 *Archaeological and Aboriginal Relics Preservation Act*. The Victorian Government created the Archaeological and Aboriginal Relics Office under the Chief Secretary's Department. One of the aims of the Relics Office was to curate a list of archaeological sites throughout Victoria as part of the Victorian Aboriginal Heritage Register. Further information about The Trust is available at <https://koorieheritagetrust.com.au>.

19. Human Rights and Equal Opportunity Commission, *Bringing Them Home: Report of the National Inquiry into the Separation of Aboriginal and Torres Strait Islander Children from their Families*, Human Rights and Equal Opportunity Commission, Sydney, 1997.

20. Green, *Aborigines of the Albany Region*

NOTES

1821–1898, p. 79.

21. Phillip Pepper and Tess De Araugo, *What Did Happen to the Aborigines of Victoria? The Kurnai of Gippsland*, Hyland House, Melbourne, 1985; Bain Attwood, '"In the name of all my coloured brethren and sisters": a biography of Bessy Cameron', *Hecate: An Interdisciplinary Journal of Women's Liberation*, vol. 12, nos 1–2, 1986, pp. 9–53; Green, *Aborigines of the Albany Region 1821–1898*.

22. Biographical information about Alfred Hawes Stone was shared by his great-granddaughter, Dorothy Croft.

23. JS Battye Library of West Australian History, State Library of Western Australia, collection of photos taken by Alfred Hawes Stone (1801–1873). The collection includes photos from the 1860s and 1870s housed within the Hampton Album, which was named after Fanny Annette Hampton (née Stone) (1839–1925). The second digital album (6923B) has been donated by Stone's great-granddaughter, Dorothy Croft, and includes photos of people, buildings and scenes in Perth. During the research for this book this particular album was in the private care of Mrs Dorothy Croft in Perth, Western Australia. Photos by Alfred Hawes Stone have also been published in Jacqueline O'Brien and Pamela Statham-Drew, *Court and Camera: The Life and Times of A. H. Stone*, Fremantle Press, Fremantle, 2012.

Chapter 1

24. The Wergaia Jaardawa Wotjobaluk Djupabaluk group of ancestors comment that Pelham Cameron (1854–1932) and Adolphus Donald Cameron (born c.1849) were the sons of Kitty Tullum (c.1825–1875) and Tullum. Accessed from Victorian Traditional Owner Land Justice Group, *Clan Based Treaties and Treaty Commissions are the Treaty Negotiator and Representative Body*, submission to Clans and our Elders belong to Country and Treaty, 2017, p. 109, <https://www.referendumcouncil.org.au/sites/default/files/submission/2017-07/PMC%2026.%20Victorian%20Traditional%20Owner%20Land%20Justice%20Group.pdf>.

25. *Perth Inquirer and Commercial News*, 'Natives' Institution, King George's Sound, Western Australia', 18 August 1858, p. 3.

26. ibid.

27. Bonnie Hicks, *Henry and Anne Camfield*, Department of Anthropology, University of Western Australia, 27 January 1965 (self-published).

28. ibid.

29. John Ramsden Wollaston, Diary entry, 21 February 1853, *The Wollaston Journals 1845–1856* (Volume 3), eds H. Walker Mann & G. Bolton, University of Western Australia, Perth, 2006, p. 303.

30. ibid.

31. Anne Camfield, 'Report to the Western Australia Parliament', in *Information Respecting the Habits and Customs of the Aboriginal Inhabitants of Western Australia*, presented to the Legislative Council by His Excellency's Command, Perth, 1871, pp. 23–26.

32. Wollaston, Letter to the Colonial Secretary, 16 August 1852, *The Wollaston Journals 1845–1856* (Volume 3), p. 283.

33. Henry Camfield, letter to sister Bessie in England, in Bonnie Hicks (1965), Battye

Library, State Library of Western Australia, Q B/CAM; Henry Camfield to Elizabeth (Bessie) Camfield, 15 November 1850, Camfield and Windeyer Letters, D30, CY494, Mitchell Library, Sydney.
34. Wollaston, Letter to Rev. Ernest Hawkins, Secretary of the Society for the Propagation of the Gospel in Foreign Parts, London, 21 February, *The Wollaston Journals 1845–1856* (Volume 3), p. 343.
35. Anne Camfield, 'Report to the Western Australia Parliament', 1871 (see Appendix B of this book).
36. ibid.
37. ibid.
38. ibid.
39. ibid.
40. Flowers to Anne Camfield, 12 June 1867. Duplicate copies of letters from Bessy to Anne are held at the State Library of Victoria, MS 12117.
41. Moravian Missions in Australia, Annual meeting of the Victorian Association in and of Moravian Missions to the Aborigines of Australia. Aboriginal Mission Station, Ramahyuck, Gippsland, 30 September 1872, p. 6.
42. Flowers to Anne Camfield, 17 June 1867.
43. Pepper and De Araugo, *What Did Happen to the Aborigines of Victoria?* p. 133.
44. Moravian Missions in Australia, Annual meeting of the Victorian Association in and of Moravian Missions to the Aborigines of Australia, Aboriginal Mission Station, Ramahyuck, Gippsland, 30 September 1872, pp. 5–6.
45. ibid., p. 6.
46. Jane Millet, *An Australian Parsonage; or Settler and the Savage in Western Australia*, Edward Stanford, London, 1872, p. 131. Quoted in John Harris, *One Blood: 200 Years of Aboriginal Encounter with Christianity: A Story of Hope*, Albatross Books, Sutherland, New South Wales, 1990, p. 268. Jane Millet (1821–1904) and her husband, Edward Millet, arrived in Fremantle on 13 December 1863. Jane wrote several books and articles about Aboriginal people from Western Australia.
47. Rev. Hagenauer to Anne Camfield, March 1867.
48. Flowers to Anne Camfield, August 1867.
49. ibid.
50. Rev. Hagenauer to Anne Camfield, August 1867.
51. Rev. Hagenauer to Anne Camfield, November 1867.
52. Board for the Protection of Aborigines (BPA) report 1869. The BPA was given statutory authority by the Victorian *Aborigines Protection Act 1869*. The reports detail the Victorian Government's involvement in Aboriginal affairs between 1869 and 1957.
53. Bessy also had several children who were stillborn, which was noted in correspondence by Rev. Hagenauer to the BPA. Limited detail is provided in this correspondence except that Bessy's health had suffered at the time. For information about Bessy and Donald's children, refer to Appendix A.
54. Harry Flowers to Captain Alfred Darby, 6 October 1873. The letters from Bessy to Captain Darby appear in Pepper and De Araugo, *What Did Happen to the Aborigines of Victoria?* p. 167.
55. Flowers to Anne Camfield, August 1867.
56. Flowers to Captain Alfred Darby, 22 April 1872, in Pepper and De Araugo, *What Did*

NOTES

Happen to the Aborigines of Victoria? p. 162.
57. Bessy to Captain Alfred Darby, 16 April 1873, in Pepper and De Araugo, *What Did Happen to the Aborigines of Victoria?* p. 164.
58. Bessy to Captain Alfred Darby, 31 July 1874, in Pepper and De Araugo, *What Did Happen to the Aborigines of Victoria?* p. 168.
59. Bessy to Captain Alfred Darby, 4 July 1874, in Pepper and De Araugo, *What Did Happen to the Aborigines of Victoria?* p. 168.
60. Hagenauer to Page, Secretary BPA, 20 August 1879.
61. Hagenauer to Page, Secretary BPA, 24 August 1879.
62. Cameron to Page, Secretary BPA, 27 August 1879.
63. Bessy Cameron to Page, Secretary BPA, 15 May 1884.
64. Bessy Cameron to Page, Secretary BPA, 4 August 1884.
65. BPA to Bessy Cameron, August 1894.
66. *Gippsland Times*, 11 February 1895.
67. *Australian Weekly*, 25 January 1895.
68. Clerk BPA to Donald Cameron, 18 January 1895.

Chapter 2

69. 'In order to have their rights in this country recognised under Australian law, the descendants of the Aboriginal people who were in Gippsland at the time of white settlement filed applications for a determination of native title under the *Native Title Act 1993* (Cth) (the Act). The first application for a determination for native title (VID 6007 of 1998) was filed on 7 April 1998 and a further application (VID 482 of 2009) was filed on 29 June 2009. The applications sought a determination in relation to over 8,000 specific parcels of land within the general area of Gippsland. The second application was filed to include a number of parcels, which had not been included in the first application. The outer boundary of the application area extended in very approximate terms from a short distance east of Warragul on the western side, to the waters off the southern coast of Victoria on the southern side, to the Snowy River on the eastern side, and to the Great Dividing Range on the northern side. The claim group comprise the Gunai/Kurnai people being the descendants from 25 named apical ancestors. The State of Victoria (the State) and the Commonwealth of Australia are respondents as well as a large number of parties who are grouped for the purpose of representation by reference to their interests in local government, mining, farming, commercial fishing, forestry, water, petroleum, telecommunications, public access, fishing, and recreational land use', sourced from *Mullett on behalf of the Gunai/Kurnai People v State of Victoria* [2010] FCA 1144 (22 October 2010) (North J).
70. For more information refer to: *Rose on behalf of the Kurnai Clans v State of Victoria* [2010] FCA 460 (14 May 2010) (North J); 268 ALR 47; *Mullett on behalf of the Gunai/Kurnai People v State of Victoria* [2010] FCA 1144 (22 October 2010) (North J); *Gunaikurnai People Native Title Claim Group v State of Victoria* [2018] FCA 23 (30 January 2018) (Mortimer J).
71. Betty Hood, interview conducted by Sharon Huebner in Bairnsdale, Victoria, 15 January 2013.

72. Bessy Cameron to Captain Page, Secretary BPA, 15 May 1884. NAA, B357, Item 10, p. 8.
73. Phyllis Andy (Bryant), interview conducted by Sharon Huebner in Tyers, Victoria, 10 December 2011.
74. Phyllis Andy (Bryant), interview conducted by Sharon Huebner in Melbourne, Victoria, 16 January 2013.
75. Phyllis Andy (Bryant), interview conducted by Sharon Huebner in Melbourne, Victoria, 16 January 2013.
76. The process for the Bryant family making decisions about history interventions based on cultural terms also appears in Sharon Huebner and Ezzard Flowers, '"It's a resting place, where our spirits go": bringing back lost ancestor memories to Western Australia's Great Southern – Noongar boodja', *Journal of Arts & Communities*, vol. 8, nos 1 & 2, 2016, pp. 75–92.

Chapter 3

77. John Dowson, *Old Albany: Photographs 1850–1950*, National Trust of Western Australia, Fremantle, 2008.
78. Ezzard Flowers, field recording conducted by Sharon Huebner in Albany, Western Australia, 26 September 2010.

Chapter 4

79. Attwood, *Hecate*, p. 44. Historian Bain Attwood briefly describes the journey of Bessy from Ramahyuck Aboriginal Mission to Bairnsdale on 12 January 1895, which was two days before she died. This trip was also reported in the local *Gippsland Times* on Monday 11 February 1895 and in the *Australian Weekly* on Friday 25 January 1895.
80. Kooramyee Cooper, field recording conducted by Sharon Huebner in Melbourne, Victoria, 5 September 2011.
81. Aldo Massola, *Journey to Aboriginal Victoria*, Rigby, Melbourne, 1969, p. 183.
82. Pepper and Araugo, *What Did Happen to the Aborigines of Victoria?* pp. 234–235.
83. Kooramyee Cooper, field recording conducted by Sharon Huebner in Melbourne, Victoria, 5 September 2011.
84. Kooramyee Cooper, field recording conducted by Sharon Huebner in Melbourne, Victoria, 5 September 2011.
85. The logistics for this event were supported by Larry Levi, a regional Bringing Them Home worker, whose role it was at the time to assist Stolen Generations and local community family members to take part in reunions and return to country events for Stolen Generations going home for the first time.
86. Betty Hood, interview conducted by Sharon Huebner in Bairnsdale, Victoria, 15 January 2013.
87. Field recording conducted by Sharon Huebner in Bairnsdale, Victoria, 28 September 2011.
88. Phyllis Andy (Bryant), interview conducted by Sharon Huebner in Tyers, Victoria, 10 December 2011.
89. Ezzard Flowers, field recording conducted by Sharon Huebner in Bairnsdale, Victoria, 28 September 2011.
90. Phyllis Andy (Bryant), field recording conducted by Sharon Huebner in Bairnsdale, Victoria, 28 September 2011.
91. Russell Nelly, interview conducted by Sharon Huebner in Katanning, Western Australia, 1 December 2011.

NOTES

92. Phyllis Andy (Bryant), interview conducted by Sharon Huebner in Tyers, Victoria, 10 December 2011.
93. Russell Nelly, interview conducted by Sharon Huebner in Katanning, Western Australia, 1 December 2011.
94. Russell Nelly, interview conducted by Sharon Huebner in Katanning, Western Australia, 1 December 2011.
95. The pages in the box detailed a Bryant and Hood family tree. In years gone by, Betty had received paper copies of the family trees, which had been compiled by Native Title Services Victoria. She found these pages of information difficult to understand if read without verbal explanation by family members or others with knowledge of the family connections.
96. Betty Hood, interview conducted by Sharon Huebner in Bairnsdale, Victoria, 15 January 2013.

Chapter 5

97. Clara Flowers, field recording conducted by Sharon Huebner in Katanning, Western Australia, 1 December 2011.
98. Hazel Brown, field recording conducted by Sharon Huebner in Albany, Western Australia, 1 December 2011.
99. Hazel Brown, field recording conducted by Sharon Huebner in Albany, Western Australia, 1 December 2011.
100. Tracie Pushman and Robyn Smith Walley, *Koorah Coolingah – Children Long Ago*, Berndt Museum of Anthropology, The University of Western Australia, Perth, 2006. In 1956 a New York art collector, Herbert A. Mayer, purchased 119 paintings by children from the Carrolup Native Settlement. The art had been created with the encouragement of mission teacher Noel White and were collected by Englishwoman Florence Rutter in 1949. In 1966 Mayer donated the paintings to Colgate University, New York, and in 2004 Australian academic Howard Morphy discovered the works by chance during research he was undertaking at the university. In 2013 the paintings were returned by Colgate University to Curtin University in Western Australia and displayed as part of a welcoming home exhibition for the Noongar and wider community.
101. Ezzard Flowers, interview conducted by Sharon Huebner in Albany, Western Australia, 2 December 2011.
102. The authors have communicated Aboriginal principles and conceptions of belonging and identity in the twenty-first century as part of the script development and production of a short film, *No Longer a Wandering Spirit – Imaginaries of Bessy Flowers*, 2016. The film is available at <https://www.youtube.com/watch?v=l1dAynpp9R4&t=233s>. More information about the creative process involving intercultural collaboration processes is detailed in the co-authored publication by Sharon Huebner and Ezzard Flowers, 'The relational language of First Nations cultural sensibilities, principles and storytelling ethics as an intercultural approach to script development', in Stayci Taylor and Craig Batty (eds), *The Palgrave Handbook of Script Development*, Springer Nature, Cham, Switzerland, 2021.
103. Ezzard Flowers, interview conducted by Sharon Huebner in Riddles Creek, Victoria,

8 December 2012.

Chapter 6

104. Phyllis Andy (Bryant), interview conducted by Sharon Huebner in Tyers, Victoria, 10 December 2011.
105. Field recording conducted by Sharon Huebner in Albany, Western Australia, 23 February 2013.
106. Field recording conducted by Sharon Huebner in Albany, Western Australia, 24 February 2013.
107. Field recording conducted by Sharon Huebner in Albany, Western Australia, 26 February 2013.
108. Ezzard Flowers, interview conducted by Sharon Huebner in Albany, Western Australia, 2 December 2011.
109. Betty Hood, interview conducted by Sharon Huebner in Bairnsdale, Victoria, 15 January 2013.
110. Helen Kilpatrick, Bairnsdale Cemetery Trust, email correspondence, 14 March 2014.
111. Johannes Heyer, *Australian Weekly*, 25 January 1895.
112. Thomas Babington Macaulay, *Lord Macaulay's Essays and Lays of Ancient Rome*, Longmans, Green, London, 1886.
113. Flowers to Anne Camfield, 17 June 1867.
114. ibid.
115. Rev. Hagenauer (1829–1909) papers c.1870–1908, State Library Victoria, MS 9556.
116. Henry Camfield to Elizabeth (Bessie) Camfield, 15 November 1850, Camfield and Windeyer Letters, 1829–65, Mitchell Library, CY494.
117. Extract from the Church of England 'Messenger', 5 November 1870, Hagenauer (1829–1909) papers c.1870–1908, State Library Victoria, MS 9556.

Afterword

118. The short film *No Longer a Wandering Spirit – Imaginaries of Bessy Flowers* premiered at the State Library Victoria on 1 December 2016. Ezzard Flowers narrated the film. In representing the story of Bessy Flowers in the context of her Bryant and Flowers families, both past and present, the film promotes a family history that was not part of the historical record. Following cultural methods for developing the script, the film screening replicated and centralised family relatedness, kinship and the emotional and cultural capacity for these families to deal with the lost memories of their ancestor on their own terms and as part of contemporary practices of heritage reclamation. The 18-minute film is available online at <https://www.youtube.com/watch?v=l1dAynpp9R4&t=116s>. Recordings of the State Library Victoria event are available at <https://www.youtube.com/watch?v=A6UWQ3P_M2Y&t=2053s> (Part One) and <https://www.youtube.com/watch?v=dEVd-BZ2n5s&t=14s> (Part Two).

Bibliography

Primary sources

Appendix A

Genealogical information about Bessy and Donald Cameron's children has been compiled from archival sources and the kinship knowledge of Aboriginal people. Sources available were the papers of the Victorian Board for the Protection of Aborigines, missionary correspondence and letters from Aboriginal family members. Other sources were genealogical records by Australian ethnologist Norman Barnett Tindale at the South Australian Museum and those by Canadian-born anthropologist Diane Elizabeth Barwick at the State Library Victoria. Barwick's Aboriginal genealogies cover the period from 1800 to the 1966 census. Another contributor to Victorian Aboriginal genealogies has been Sandra Smith when a family history research officer at Museum Victoria. Sandra cross-referenced her comprehensive findings of genealogies against the works of Tindale and Barwick as well as Aboriginal community knowledge.

Appendix B

Anne Camfield, 'The Annesfield Native Institution, Albany, a sketch of its history and present condition, 1868', Western Australia Parliament, Votes and Proceedings 1871, Paper No. 2, pp. 23–26.

Appendix C and correspondence cited throughout

Battye Library, State Library of Western Australia, Q B/CAM.
Mitchell Library, Sydney, Camfield and Windeyer Letters, 1829–65, D30, CY494.

National Archives of Australia (NAA), B313, Box 10, Item 172, p. 17A.

NAA, B313, Box 10, Item 175.

NAA, B313/1, 99, 173, 177, 178.

NAA, B314, 4.

NAA, B329, 3, p. 606.

NAA, B329, 5, pp. 407, 929.

NAA, B329, 6, pp. 283, 377, 396, 415, 608, 855, 874.

NAA, B356, 10 and 10A.

NAA, B357, Item 10, p. 8.

Phillip Pepper and Tess De Araugo, *What Did Happen to the Aborigines of Victoria? The Kurnai of Gippsland*, Hyland House, Melbourne, 1985.

State Library Victoria, MS 12117.

State Library Victoria, MS 9556.

State Library Victoria, Bessie (Bessy) Flower[s] Letters.

Interviews and field recordings conducted by Sharon Huebner

Field recording, Albany, Western Australia, 26 September 2010.

Field recording, Bairnsdale, Victoria, 28 September 2011.

Russell Nelly, interview, Katanning, Western Australia, 1 December 2011.

Field recording, Katanning, Western Australia, 1 December 2011.

Field recording, Albany, Western Australia, 1 December 2011.

Ezzard Flowers, interview, Albany, Western Australia, 2 December 2011.

Phyllis Andy (Bryant), interview, Tyers, Victoria, 10 December 2011.

Ezzard Flowers, interview, Riddles Creek, Victoria, 8 December 2012.

Betty Hood, interview, Bairnsdale, Victoria, 15 January 2013.

Phyllis Andy (Bryant), interview, Melbourne, Victoria, 16 January 2013.

Field recording, Albany, Western Australia, 23 February 2013.

Field recording, Albany, Western Australia, 24 February 2013.

Field recording, Albany, Western Australia, 26 February 2013.

BIBLIOGRAPHY

Legal cases

268 ALR 47

Gunaikurnai People Native Title Claim Group v State of Victoria [2018] FCA 23 (30 January 2018) (Mortimer J).

Mullett on behalf of the Gunai/Kurnai People v State of Victoria [2010] FCA 1144 (22 October 2010) (North J)

Rose on behalf of the Kurnai Clans v State of Victoria [2010] FCA 460 (14 May 2010) (North J)

Newspapers

Perth Inquirer and Commercial News, 18 August 1858, p. 3

Gippsland Times, 11 February 1895

Australian Weekly, 25 January 1895

Secondary sources

Attwood, Bain, '"In the name of all my coloured brethren and sisters": a biography of Bessy Cameron', *Hecate: An Interdisciplinary Journal of Women's Liberation*, vol. 12, nos 1–2, 1986, pp. 9–53.

Dowson, John, *Old Albany: Photographs 1850–1950*, National Trust of Western Australia, Fremantle, 2008.

Green, Neville, *Aborigines of the Albany Region 1821–1898: The Bicentennial Dictionary of Western Australian Volume VI*, University of Western Australia Publishing, Perth, 1989.

Grimshaw, Patricia, Elizabeth Nelson and Sandra Smith (eds), *Letters from Aboriginal Women of Victoria, 1867–1926*, History Department, University of Melbourne, 2002.

Harris, John, *One Blood: 200 Years of Aboriginal Encounter with Christianity: A Story of Hope*, Albatross Books, Sutherland, New South Wales, 1990.

Hicks, Bonnie, *Henry and Anne Camfield*, Department of Anthropology, University of Western Australia, 27 January 1965 (self-published).

Huebner, Sharon, and Ezzard Flowers, '"It's a resting place, where our spirits go": bringing back lost ancestor memories to Western Australia's Great Southern – Noongar boodja', *Journal of Arts & Communities*, vol. 8, nos 1&2, 2016, pp. 75–92.

Huebner, Sharon, and Ezzard Flowers, 'The relational language of First Nations cultural sensibilities, principles and storytelling ethics as an intercultural approach to script development', in Stayci Taylor and Craig Batty (eds), *The Palgrave Handbook of Script Development*, Springer Nature, Cham, Switzerland, 2021.

Human Rights and Equal Opportunity Commission, *Bringing Them Home: Report of the National Inquiry into the Separation of Aboriginal and Torres Strait Islander Children from their Families*, Human Rights and Equal Opportunity Commission, Sydney, 1997.

Lawson, Henry, 'The golden nineties', in D.G. Sellick (ed.), *First Impressions of Albany 1791–1871: Travellers' Tales*, Western Australian Museum, Perth, 1997, p. 191. (Article originally published in *Australian Star*, Sydney, 1899.)

Macaulay, Thomas, *Lord Macaulay's Essays and Lays of Ancient Rome*, Longmans, Green, London, 1886.

Massola, Aldo, *Journey to Aboriginal Victoria*, Rigby, Melbourne, 1969.

Millet, Jane, *An Australian Parsonage; or Settler and the Savage in Western Australia*, Edward Stanford, London, 1872.

O'Brien, Jacqueline, and Pamela Statham-Drew, *Court and Camera: The Life and Times of A. H. Stone*, Fremantle Press, Fremantle, 2012.

Pepper, Phillip, and Tess De Araugo, *What Did Happen to the Aborigines of Victoria? The Kurnai of Gippsland*, Hyland House, Melbourne, 1985.

Pushman, Tracie, and Robyn Smith Walley, *Koorah Coolingah – Children Long Ago*, Berndt Museum of Anthropology, The University of Western Australia, Perth, 2006.

BIBLIOGRAPHY

Salvado, Rosendo, *The Salvado Memoirs: Historical Memoirs of Australia and Particularly of the Benedictine Mission of New Norcia and of the Habits and Customs of the Australian Natives*, trans. and ed. by Edward James Stormon, University of Western Australia Press, Perth, 1977.

Scott, Kim, *That Deadman Dance*, Picador, Sydney, 2010.

Scott, Kim, and Hazel Brown, *Kayang & Me*, Fremantle Arts Centre Press, Fremantle, 2005.

Wollaston, John Ramsden, *The Wollaston Journals 1845–1856* (Volume 3), eds H. Walker Mann & G. Bolton, University of Western Australia, Perth, 2006.

Van Toorn, Penelope, *Writing Never Arrives Naked: Early Aboriginal Cultures of Writing in Australia*, Aboriginal Studies Press, Canberra, 2006.

Victorian Traditional Owner Land Justice Group, *Clan Based Treaties and Treaty Commissions are the Treaty Negotiator and Representative Body*, submission to Clans and our Elders belong to Country and Treaty, 2017, <https://www.referendumcouncil.org.au/sites/default/files/submission/2017-07/PMC%2026.%20Victorian%20Traditional%20Owner%20Land%20Justice%20Group.pdf>.

Audiovisual material

No Longer a Wandering Spirit – Imaginaries of Bessy Flowers, 2016, produced by S. Huebner, <https://www.youtube.com/watch?v=l1dAynpp9R4&t=233s>.

State Library Victoria event, 1 December 2016, Part One, <https://www.youtube.com/watch?v=A6UWQ3P_M2Y&t=2053s> and *Part Two* <https://www.youtube.com/watch?v=dEVd-BZ2n5s&t=14s>.

 The Charles and Joy Staples South West Region Publications Fund was established in 1984 on the basis of a generous donation to The University of Western Australia by Charles and Joy Staples.

The purpose of the Fund is to highlight all aspects of the South West region of Western Australia, a geographical area much loved by Charles and Joy Staples, so as to assist the people of the South West region and those in government and private organisations concerned with South West projects to appreciate the needs and possibilities of the region in the widest possible historical perspective. The fund is administered by a committee whose aims are to make possible the publication by UWA Publishing of research and writing in any discipline relevant to the South West region.

Charles and Joy Staples South West Region Publications Fund titles

1987
A Tribute to the Group Settlers
Philip E. M. Blond

1992
For Their Own Good: Aborigines and Government in the Southwest of Western Australia, 1900–1940
Anna Haebich

1993
Portraits of the South West
B. K. de Garis
A Guide to Sources for the History of South Western Australia
Compiled by Ronald Richards

1994
Jardee: The Mill That Cheated Time
Doreen Owens

1995
Dearest Isabella: Life and Letters of Isabella Ferguson, 1819–1910
Prue Joske
Blacklegs: The Scottish Colliery Strike of 1911 Bill Latter

1997
Barefoot in the Creek: A Group Settlement Childhood in Margaret River L. C. Burton
Ritualist on a Tricycle: Frederick Goldsmith, Church, Nationalism and Society in Western Australia
Colin Holden
Western Australia as it is Today, 1906 Leopoldo Zunini, Royal Consul of Italy, edited and translated by Richard Bosworth and Margot Melia

2002
The South West from Dawn till Dusk Rob Olver

2003
Contested Country: A History of the Northcliffe Area, Western Australia
Patricia Crawford and Ian Crawford

2004
Orchard and Mill: The Story of Bill Lee, South-West Pioneer
Lyn Adams

2005
Richard Spencer: Napoleonic War Naval Hero and Australian Pioneer
Gwen Chessell

2006
A Story to Tell (reprinted 2012)
Laurel Nannup

2008
Alexander Collie: Colonial Surgeon, Naturalist and Explorer
Gwen Chessell
The Zealous Conservator: A Life of Charles Lane Poole
John Dargavel

2009
"It's Still in My Heart, This is My Country": The Single Noongar Claim History South West Aboriginal Land and Sea Council, John Host with Chris Owen
Shaking Hands on the Fringe: Negotiating the Aboriginal World at King George's Sound
Tiffany Shellam

2011
Noongar Mambara Bakitj and *Mamang*
Kim Scott and Wirlomin Noongar Language and Stories Project
Guy Grey-Smith: Life Force
Andrew Gaynor

2013
Dwoort Baal Kaat and *Yira Boornak Nyininy*
Kim Scott and Wirlomin Noongar Language and Stories Project

2014
A Boy's Short Life: The Story of Warren Braedon/Louis Johnson
Anna Haebich and Steve Mickler
Plant Life on the Sandplains: A Global Biodiversity Hotspot
Hans Lambers
Fire and Hearth (revised facsimile edition) Sylvia Hallam

2015
Running Out? Water in Western Australia Ruth Morgan
A Journey Travelled: Aboriginal–European Relations at Albany and Surrounding Regions from First Colonial Contact to 1926
Murray Arnold
The Southwest: Australia's Biodiversity Hotspot
Victoria Laurie
Invisible Country: South-West Australia: Understanding a Landscape Bill Bunbury

2016
Noongar Bush Medicine: Medicinal Plants of the South-West of Western Australia
Vivienne Hansen and John Horsfall

2017
Never Again: Reflections on Environmental Responsibility After Roe 8
Edited by Andrea Gaynor, Peter Newman and Philip Jennings
Ngaawily Nop and *Noorn*
Kim Scott and Wirlomin Noongar Language and Stories Project

2018
Dancing in Shadows: Histories of Nyungar Performance
Anna Haebich

2019
Refuge Richard Rossiter
That Was My Home: Voices from the Noongar Camps in Fremantle and the Western Suburbs
Denise Cook

2020
Many Maps: Charting Two Cultures First Nations and Europeans in Western Australia
Bill and Jenny Bunbury

2021
Naturalist on the Bibbulmun: A walking companion
Leigh W. Simmons

2022
The Alert Grey Twinkling Eyes of C.J. DeGaris
David Nichols

www.ingramcontent.com/pod-product-compliance
Lightning Source LLC
Chambersburg PA
CBHW061245230426
43662CB00021B/2436